CITY KIDS, CITY SCHOOLS

OTHER BOOKS BY WILLIAM AYERS
City Kids, City Teachers: Reports from the Front Row
Edited by William Ayers and Patricia Ford

To Teach: The Journey of a Teacher
A Kind and Just Parent: The Children of Juvenile Court
Teaching Toward Freedom: Moral Commitment and Ethical Action
in the Classroom
Race Course: Against White Supremacy
With Bernardine Dohrn

OTHER BOOKS BY GLORIA LADSON-BILLINGS
The Dreamkeepers: Successful Teachers of African American Children
Crossing Over to Canaan: The Journey of New Teachers
in Diverse Classrooms
Beyond the Big House: African American Educators on Teacher Education

OTHER BOOKS BY GREGORY MICHIE
Holler If You Hear Me: The Education of a Teacher and His Students
See You When We Get There: Teaching for Change in Urban Schools

OTHER BOOKS BY PEDRO A. NOGUERA
City Schools and the American Dream: Reclaiming the Promise
of Public Education
Unfinished Business: Closing the Racial Achievement Gap in Our Schools
Edited by Pedro A. Noguera and Jean Yonemura Wing

The Trouble with Black Boys . . . and Other Reflections on Race, Equity,
and the Future of Public Education

CITY KIDS, CITY SCHOOLS

MORE REPORTS FROM THE FRONT ROW

EDITED BY

William Ayers, Gloria Ladson-Billings, Gregory Michie, and Pedro A. Noguera

FOREWORD BY RUBY DEE

AFTERWORD BY JEFF CHANG

THE NEW PRESS

NEW YORK
LONDON

Requests for permission to reproduce selections from this book should be
mailed to: Permissions Department, The New Press, 120 Wall Street,
31st floor, New York, NY 10005.

Published in the United States by The New Press, New York, 2008
Distributed by Two Rivers Distribution

ISBN: 978-1-59558-560-8 (e-book)

LIBRARY OF CONGRESS CATALOGING-IN-PUBLICATION DATA

City kids, city schools : more reports from the front row / edited by William
Ayers . . . [et al.] ; foreword by Ruby Dee, afterword by Jeff Chang.
    p. cm.
  ISBN 978-1-59558-338-3 (pbk.)
  1. Education, Urban—United States. 2. Children with social disabilities—
Education—Social aspects—United States. 3. Cities and towns—United
States—Social conditions. I. Ayers, William, 1944–
LC5131.C525 2008
370.9173'2—dc22

                                                        2008000845

The New Press publishes books that promote and enrich public discussion and
understanding of the issues vital to our democracy and to a more equitable world.
These books are made possible by the enthusiasm of our readers; the support of
a committed group of donors, large and small; the collaboration of our many
partners in the independent media and the not-for-profit sector; booksellers,
who often hand-sell New Press books; librarians; and above all by our authors.

www.thenewpress.com

Book design by Kelly Too
Composition by Westchester Book Group
This book was set in Janson

Printed in the United States of America

BOY BREAKING GLASS

Whose broken window is a cry of art
(success, that winks aware
as elegance, as a treasonable faith)
is raw: is sonic: is old-eyed première.
Our beautiful flaw and terrible ornament.
Our barbarous and metal little man.

"I shall create! If not a note, a hole.
If not an overture, a desecration."

Full of pepper and light
and salt and night and cargoes.

"Don't go down the plank
if you see there's no extension.
Each to his grief, each to
his loneliness and fidgety revenge.
Nobody knew where I was and now I am no longer there."

The only sanity is a cup of tea.
The music is in minors.

Each one other
is having different weather.

"It was you, it was you who threw away my name!
And this is everything I have for me."

Who has not Congress, lobster, love, luau,
the Regency Room, the Statue of Liberty,
runs. A sloppy amalgamation.
A mistake.
A cliff.
A hymn, a snare, and an exceeding sun.

—Gwendolyn Brooks (1917–2000)

CONTENTS

FOREWORD

Ruby Dee

Ruby Dee is a legendary stage and screen actor whose work in such productions as A Raisin in the Sun, Do the Right Thing, *and* American Gangster *has spanned more than a half century. A longtime civil rights and political activist, she is the author, along with her late husband Ossie Davis, of the autobiography* With Ossie and Ruby: In This Life Together. *Dee has won numerous awards for her creative work, including an Emmy, two NAACP Image Awards, a Lifetime Achievement Award from the Screen Actors Guild, and the Kennedy Center Honor.*

I am a city kid. Whenever I am asked about the state of urban education in America, I cannot help but be informed and inspired by my own experiences in the public schools of New York City. I find among those memories the spirit that I believe has made a vital public educational system an absolute necessity and a promise well worth keeping. The spirit of those parents who, like my own, spoke of going to college not as an "if" but as a "when." The spirit of those teachers whose expectations stiffened our backs and pushed us toward a greater definition of ourselves. The spirit of nine girls whose story epitomizes the true meaning of "no child left behind":

> Most of the girls who graduated from junior high schools in neighborhoods like Harlem went to Julia Richmond, Wadleigh, or to industrial or commercial high schools. They were good schools, but they didn't . . . have Hunter High School's reputation. . . . It so happened, however, that Mrs. Madelyn Henderson, the mother of my friend, Carlotta, felt that the children of Harlem were being shortchanged. . . . The fact that inner-city children

were being shunted to less demanding schools impelled her to do something about it. She encouraged teachers and parents to insist on the right to compete for admission to the best schools available. Why not make it possible for students at P.S. 136 to take the entrance examination for Hunter High, a school known for its academic rigor, excellence, and concern? Surely those students on the rapid track . . . should automatically take the test.

. . . I was among those students in the rapid classes. Mother, therefore, was first among those parents fervently supporting Mrs. Henderson's position: Our children needed to be prepared to compete with students anywhere in this world.

With the involvement of the teachers, parents, community, and especially the church leaders, P.S. 136 voted to enter students in the Hunter High School competition. And so the teachers, some of whom were black, selected nine of us from the rapid track. . . . After a preliminary exam. . . . it was decided that we nine girls should stay after school three days per week during the ninth grade to be . . . drilled and grilled until finally it was time to go downtown for the real exam. . . . As I went from question to question, choice to choice, problem to problem, a peace came over me. I had been prepared well. . . .

There had been tension in the air at P.S. 136 beginning the week before the test, and it lasted until about a week later, when we received the results. Not only had all nine of us passed, but we were ranked in the top percentile in the whole of New York City! . . .

Teachers scurried out from their classrooms into the hallways to hug each other. They were ecstatic. . . . It was as if they were reliving a hard-fought battle. . . . [T]heir joy burst forth like firecrackers.[1]

I am never far from the memory of that skinny ninth-grade Ruby perched on the precipice of life. It is her voice that I raise in support of public education which, at its best, is valuable, intelligent, accountable, and visionary. To the extent we lose sight of that, we lose those who serve and are served by it. We devalue our past and our future.

City Kids, City Schools holds the banner high for a more rewarding quality of life, reminding us of our responsibility as citizens to work for,

[1] Excerpted from Ossie Davis and Ruby Dee, *With Ossie and Ruby: In This Life Together*, 1998.

to insist on, and to ensure a free, quality education to every child. It will not happen without our vigilance, our profoundest commitment—especially those of us whose voices, like mine, like those in this book—have been nourished by some of the great minds that steady and enlighten our lives. This book engages all our sensibilities toward the glorification of our remarkable species.

PROLOGUE: "A TALK TO TEACHERS"

James Baldwin

When City Kids, City Teachers *was published in 1996, the editors included the following piece by renowned novelist and essayist James Baldwin, originally delivered as a talk to New York City school teachers in 1963, for its prescient, fiery take on racism in U.S. society and the miseducation of African American children. We open this follow-up collection,* City Kids, City Schools, *with Baldwin's essay because his words remain, save a few dated references, as relevant as ever. They serve as a potent reminder that the educational challenges of today are intimately linked to longstanding inequities that continue to beleaguer so many among us.*

———————

Let's begin by saying that we are living through a very dangerous time. Everyone in this room is in one way or another aware of that. We are in a revolutionary situation, no matter how unpopular that word has become in this country. The society in which we live is desperately menaced, not by Khrushchev, but from within. So any citizen of this country who figures himself as responsible—and particularly those of you who deal with the minds and hearts of young people—must be prepared to "go for broke." Or to put it another way, you must understand that in the attempt to correct so many generations of bad faith and cruelty, when it is operating not only in the classroom but in society, you will meet the most fantastic, the most brutal, and the most determined resistance. There is no point in pretending that this won't happen.

Since I am talking to schoolteachers and I am not a teacher myself, and in some ways am fairly easily intimidated, I beg you to let me leave that and go back to what I think to be the entire purpose of education in the first place. It would seem to me that when a child is born, if I'm the child's parent, it is my obligation and my high duty to civilize that child. Man is a social animal. He cannot exist without a society. A society, in turn, depends on certain things which everyone within that society takes for granted. Now, the crucial paradox which confronts us here is that the whole process of education occurs within a social framework and is designed to perpetuate the aims of society. Thus, for example, the boys and girls who were born during the era of the Third Reich, when educated to the purposes of the Third Reich, became barbarians. The paradox of education is precisely this—that as one begins to become conscious one begins to examine the society in which he is being educated. The purpose of education, finally, is to create in a person the ability to look at the world for himself, to make his own decisions, to say to himself this is black or this is white, to decide for himself whether there is a God in heaven or not. To ask questions of the universe, and then learn to live with those questions, is the way he achieves his own identity. But no society is really anxious to have that kind of person around. What societies really, ideally, want is a citizenry which will simply obey the rules of society. If a society succeeds in this, that society is about to perish. The obligation of anyone who thinks of himself as responsible is to examine society and try to change it and to fight it—at no matter what risk. This is the only hope society has. This is the only way societies change.

Now, if what I have tried to sketch has any validity, it becomes thoroughly clear, at least to me, that any Negro who is born in this country and undergoes the American educational system runs the risk of becoming schizophrenic. On the one hand he is born in the shadow of the stars and stripes and he is assured it represents a nation which has never lost a war. He pledges allegiance to that flag which guarantees "liberty and justice for all." He is part of a country in which anyone can become president, and so forth. But on the other hand he is also assured by his country and his countrymen that he has never contributed anything to civilization—that his past is nothing more than a record of humiliations gladly endured. He is assured by the republic that he, his father, his mother, and his ancestors were happy, shiftless, watermelon-eating darkies who loved Mr. Charlie and Miss Ann, that the value he has as a black man is proven by one thing only—his devotion to white people. If you think I am exaggerating, examine the myths which proliferate in this country about Negroes.

All this enters the child's consciousness much sooner than we as adults would like to think it does. As adults, we are easily fooled because we are so anxious to be fooled. But children are very different. Children, not yet aware that it is dangerous to look too deeply at anything, look at everything, look at each other, and draw their own conclusions. They don't have the vocabulary to express what they see, and we, their elders, know how to intimidate them very easily and very soon. But a black child, looking at the world around him, though he cannot know quite what to make of it, is aware that there is a reason why his mother works so hard, why his father is always on edge. He is aware that there is some reason why, if he sits down in the front of the bus, his father or mother slaps him and drags him to the back of the bus. He is aware that there is some terrible weight on his parents' shoulders which menaces him. And it isn't long—in fact it begins when he is in school—before he discovers the shape of his oppression.

Let us say that the child is seven years old and I am his father, and I decide to take him to the zoo, or to Madison Square Garden, or to the U.N. Building or to any of the tremendous monuments we find all over New York. We get into a bus and we go from where I live on 131st Street and Seventh Avenue downtown through the park and we get into New York City, which is not Harlem. Now, where the boy lives—even if it is a housing project—is in an undesirable neighborhood. If he lives in one of those housing projects of which everyone in New York is so proud, he has at the front door, if not closer, the pimps, the whores, the junkies—in a word, the danger of life in the ghetto. And the child knows this, though he doesn't know why.

I still remember my first sight of New York. It was really another city when I was born—where I was born. We looked down over the Park Avenue streetcar tracks. It was Park Avenue, but I didn't know that Park Avenue meant *downtown*. The Park Avenue I grew up on, which is still standing, is dark and dirty. No one would dream of opening a Tiffany's on that Park Avenue, and when you go downtown you discover that you are literally in the white world. It is rich—or at least it looks rich. It is clean—because they collect garbage downtown. There are doormen. People walk about as though they owned where they are—and indeed they do. And it's a great shock. It's very hard to relate yourself to this. You don't know what it means. You know—you know instinctively—that none of this is for you. You know this before you are told. And who is it for and who is paying for it? And why isn't it for you?

Later on when you become a grocery boy or messenger and you try to enter one of those buildings a man says, "Go to the back door." Still later, if you happen by some odd chance to have a friend in one of those buildings, the man says, "Where's your package?" Now this by no means is the core of the matter. What I'm trying to get at is that by this time the Negro child has had, effectively, almost all the doors of opportunity slammed in his face, and there are very few things he can do about it. He can more or less accept it with an absolutely inarticulate and dangerous rage inside—all the more dangerous because it is never expressed. It is precisely those silent people whom white people see every day of their lives—I mean your porter and your maid, who never say anything more than "Yes, Sir" and "No, Ma'am." They will tell you it's raining if that is what you want to hear, and they will tell you the sun is shining if that is what you want to hear. They really hate you—really hate you because in their eyes (and they're right) you stand between them and life. I want to come back to that in a moment. It is the most sinister of the facts, I think, which we now face.

There is something else the Negro child can do, too. Every street boy—and I was a street boy, so I know—looking at the society which has produced him, looking at the standards of that society which are not honored by anybody, looking at your churches and the government and the politicians, understands that this structure is operated for someone else's benefit—not for his. And there's no reason in it for him. If he is really cunning, really ruthless, really strong—and many of us are—he becomes a kind of criminal. He becomes a kind of criminal because that's the only way he can live. Harlem and every ghetto in this city— every ghetto in this country—is full of people who live outside the law. They wouldn't dream of calling a policeman. They wouldn't, for a moment, listen to any of those professions of which we are so proud on the Fourth of July. They have turned away from this country forever and totally. They live by their wits and really long to see the day when the entire structure comes down.

The point of all this is that black men were brought here as a source of cheap labor. They were indispensable to the economy. In order to justify the fact that men were treated as though they were animals, the white republic had to brainwash itself into believing that they were, indeed, animals and *deserved* to be treated like animals. Therefore it is almost impossible for any Negro child to discover anything about his actual history. The reason is that this "animal," once he suspects his own worth, once he starts believing that he is a man, has begun to attack the entire power structure. This is why America has spent such a long time keeping the Negro in his place. What I am trying to suggest to you is that it was not an accident, it was not an act of God, it was not done by well-meaning people muddling into something which they didn't understand. It was a deliberate policy hammered into place in order to make money from black flesh. And now, in 1963, because we have never faced this fact, we are in intolerable trouble.

The Reconstruction, as I read the evidence, was a bargain between the North and South to this effect: "We've liberated them from the land—and delivered them to the bosses." When we left Mississippi to come North we did not come to freedom. We came to the bottom of the labor market, and we are still there. Even the Depression of the 1930s failed to make a dent in Negroes' relationship to white workers in the labor unions. Even today, so brainwashed is this republic that people seriously ask in what they suppose to be good faith, "What does the Negro want?" I've heard a great many asinine questions in my life, but that is perhaps the most asinine and perhaps the most insulting. But the point here is that people who ask that question, thinking that they ask it in good faith, are really the victims of this conspiracy to make Negroes believe they are less than human.

In order for me to live, I decided very early that some mistake had been made somewhere. I was not a "nigger" even though you called me one. But if I was a "nigger" in your eyes, there was something about you—there was something you needed. I had to realize when I was very young that I was none of those things I was told I was. I was not, for example, happy. I never touched a watermelon for all kinds of reasons that had been invented by white people, and I knew enough about life by this time to understand that whatever you invent, whatever you project, is you! So where we are now is that a whole country of people believe I'm a "nigger," and I *don't,* and the battle's on! Because if I am not what I've been told I am, then it means that you're not what you thought you were *either!* And that is the crisis.

It is not really a "Negro revolution" that is upsetting the country. What is upsetting the country is a sense of its own identity. If, for example, one managed to change the curriculum in all the schools so that Negroes learned more about themselves and their real contributions to this culture, you would be liberating not only Negroes, you'd be liberating white people who know nothing about their own history. And the reason is that if you are compelled to lie about one aspect of anybody's history, you must lie about it all. If you have to lie about my real role here, if you have to pretend that I hoed all that cotton just because I loved you, then you have done something to yourself. You are mad.

Now let's go back a minute. I talked earlier about those silent people—the porter and the maid—who, as I said, don't look up at the sky if you ask them if it is raining, but look into your face. My ancestors and I were very well trained. We understood very early that this was not a Christian nation. It didn't matter what you said or how often you went to church. My father and my mother and my grandfather and my grandmother knew that Christians didn't act this way. It was as simple as that. And if that was so, there was no point in dealing with white people in terms of their own moral professions, for they were not going to honor them. What one did was to turn away, smiling all the time, and tell white people what they wanted to hear. But people always accuse you of reckless talk when you say this.

All this means that there are in this country tremendous reservoirs of bitterness which have never been able to find an outlet, but may find an outlet soon. It means that well-meaning white liberals place themselves in great danger when they try to deal with Negroes as though they were missionaries. It means, in brief, that a great price is demanded to liberate all those silent people so that they can breathe for the first time and *tell* you what they think of you. And a price is demanded to liberate all those white children—some of them near forty—who have never grown up, and who never will grow up, because they have no sense of their identity. What passes for identity in America is a series of myths about one's heroic ancestors. It's astounding to me, for example, that so many people really appear to believe that the country was founded by a band of heroes who wanted to be free. That happens not to be true. What happened was that some people left Europe because they couldn't stay there any longer and had to go someplace else to make it. That's all. They were hungry, they were poor, they were convicts. Those who were making it in England, for example, did not get on the *Mayflower*. That's how the country was settled. Not by Gary Cooper. Yet we have a whole race of people, a whole republic, who believe the myths to the point where even today they select political representatives, as far as I can tell, by how closely they resemble Gary Cooper. Now this is dangerously infantile, and it shows in every level of national life. When I was living in Europe, for example, one of the worst revelations to me was the way Americans walked around Europe buying this and buying that and insulting everybody—not even out of malice, just because they didn't know any better. Well, that is the way they have always treated me. They weren't cruel, they just didn't know you were alive. They didn't know you had any feelings.

What I am trying to suggest here is that in the doing of all this for one hundred years or more, it is the American white man who has long since lost his grip on reality. In some peculiar way, having created this myth about Negroes, and the myth about his own history, he created myths about the world so that, for example, he was astounded that some people could prefer Castro, astounded that there are people in the world who don't go into hiding when they hear the word "Communism," astounded that Communism is one of the realities of the twentieth century which we will not overcome by pretending that it does not exist. The political level in this country now, on the part of people who should know better, is abysmal.

The Bible says somewhere that where there is no vision the people perish. I don't think anyone can doubt that in this country today we are menaced—intolerably menaced—by a lack of vision.

It is inconceivable that a sovereign people should continue, as we do so abjectly, to say, "I can't do anything about it. It's the government."

The government is the creation of the people. It is responsible to the people. And the people are responsible for it. No American has the right to allow the present government to say, when Negro children are being bombed and hosed and shot and beaten all over the Deep South, that there is nothing we can do about it. There must have been a day in this country's life when the bombing of the children in Sunday School would have created a public uproar and endangered the life of a Governor Wallace. It happened here and there was no public uproar.

I began by saying that one of the paradoxes of education was that precisely at the point when you begin to develop a conscience, you must find yourself at war with your society. It is your responsibility to change society if you think of yourself as an educated person. And on the basis of the evidence—the moral and political evidence—one is compelled to say that this is a backward society. Now if I were a teacher in this school, or any Negro school, and I was dealing with Negro children, who were in my care only a few hours of every day and would then return to their homes and to the streets, children who have an apprehension of their future which with every hour grows grimmer and darker, I would try to teach them—I would try to make them know—that those streets, those houses, those dangers, those agonies by which they are surrounded, are criminal. I would try to make each child know that these things are the result of a criminal conspiracy to destroy him. I would teach him that if he intends to get to be a man, he must at once decide that he is stronger than this conspiracy and that he must never make his peace with it. And that one of his weapons for refusing to make his peace with it and for destroying it depends on what he decides he is worth. I would teach him that there are currently very few standards in this country which are worth a man's respect. That it is up to him to begin to change these standards for the sake of the life and the health of the country. I would suggest to him that the popular culture—as represented, for example, on television and in comic books and in movies—is based on fantasies created by very ill people, and he must be aware that these are fantasies that have nothing to do with reality. I would teach him that the press he reads is not as free as it says it is—and that he can do something about that, too. I would try to make him know that just as American history is longer, larger, more various, more beautiful, and more terrible than anything anyone has ever said about it, so is the world larger, more daring, more beautiful, and more terrible, but principally larger—and that it belongs to him. I would teach him that he doesn't have to be bound by the expediencies of any given administration, any given policy, any given morality; that he has the right and the necessity to examine everything. I would try to show him that one has not learned anything about Castro when one says, "He is a Communist." This is a way of his learning something about Castro, something about Cuba, something, in time, about the world. I would suggest to him that he is living, at the moment, in an enormous province. America is not the world and if America is going to become a nation, she must find a way—and this child must help her to find a way to use the tremendous energy which this child represents. If this country does not find a way to use that energy, it will be destroyed by that energy.

"Nice White Lady" is a skit from the television sketch-comedy program *MADtv*. It lasts just over three minutes, and it begins ominously.

The scene: a group of tough-looking and unruly teenagers—black, Latino, Asian—gathered in a rundown classroom, lounging on desks and admiring their lethal-looking weaponry.

The stentorian voiceover: "Inner-city high schools are a dangerous place. A place where hope has lost out to hate, where your homework isn't about math, it's about staying alive."

Cut to a Latina student with maximum attitude, close-up, full face: "Yo, at this school, if you black, Latino, or Asian, you *will* get shot—that's a fact."

Voiceover: "There's only one thing that can make these kids learn—"

Before we finish that sentence, let's locate ourselves in the narrative thus far: we know that teenagers are trouble, that African American and Latino kids are particularly problematic—more than indifferent and self-absorbed, they are prone to mindless violence. And while city schools are chaotic and dilapidated, there is a single, straightforward solution somewhere close at hand: "only one thing can make these kids learn. . . ." And what is that miracle, that one thing? The narrator finishes with a flourish: "a nice white lady."

Most of us could have written that script ourselves—our culture, after all, is steeped in the cliché. Practically every teacher film from *Blackboard Jungle* to *Dangerous Minds* and *Freedom Writers* follows the formula faithfully: tough kids, a savior teacher willing to sacrifice everything to rescue students from the sewers of their circumstances, triumph, transformation, redemption. Even in the rare films with a mythical hero educator who is black or Latino—think *Lean On Me* or *Stand and*

Deliver—the narrative arc seldom varies. The plot points are all so well worn, the outcome so predictable, that for many teachers they end up trumping our own lived experiences, making us wonder why our efforts don't quite measure up, why the heroic outcome eludes us. Never, what's wrong with this picture, but, rather, what's wrong with me?

"Nice White Lady" is short and silly, but somehow manages to pack it all in:

- A young, innocent teacher—Amy Little in this case—introduces herself to the jeering students, as the narrator intones, "With the odds against her, she'll do the unthinkable."
- An older colleague, eager to temper her idealism and wake her up, barks, "Forget it! These are minorities—they can't learn and they can't be educated." She won't be deterred: "With all due respect, sir, I'm a white lady—I can do anything."
- She implores her students to let her teach them, but they resist, one girl giving her an impassioned street lecture: "What you think is gonna happen here? You think you gonna inspire me? Break through my tough girl act and see the beauty that's within? Is that what you think?" The teacher shoots the girl an intense look, pulls out a pen and a notebook and pushes it toward her saying, "Write that down!"
- Soon everyone is writing up a storm, weapons are holstered, and their troubles are gone. Before long Amy and her students are dancing in the aisles as the narrator intones, "When it comes to teaching inner-city minorities, you don't need books and you don't need rules—all you need is a nice white lady."

"Nice White Lady" works as satire, of course, because every part is so familiar. And for us, every part rubs the wrong way. All of it stands on a foundation of unexamined beliefs, and all of it stands, as well, as an obstacle to effective teaching and meaningful effort. It represents a bit of domineering common sense about city schools—and there is nothing more resilient than common sense, nothing more dogmatic and resistant to change. But resist we must; we will.

We resist the portrayal of city kids, their families, and communities as all deficit, all dread, all danger. While the cartoonish teen thugs in

"Nice White Lady" provoke laughter—sharpening knives on the barrels of their handguns at the back of the class—the portrayal is uncomfortably close to the view of urban youth that saturates the popular imagination. Ask a random group of adults or college students what they know about city kids, and their responses will likely include a resounding chorus of negatives: rough, dangerous, low achieving, unmotivated, illegal, prone to dropping out, gang involved, violent. All these are part of the mythology that surrounds urban youth—a mythology that, to outside observers, can feel more authentic than the dazzling complexity of real kids' lives.

Still, one reason these distorted images resonate and continue to be rolled out time and again is that they seem to capture an element of "truth." Data does suggest that urban students are more likely to obtain low test scores and drop out of school, and are less likely to graduate from high school or attend college. They are also more likely to be incarcerated, to have babies while teenagers, to become victims of assault or homicide. Bombarded by these dismal statistics, no wonder society embraces the image of hopeless hoodlum teenagers, students whose only chance for salvation lies with missionary teachers dispatched like Peace Corp workers to an impoverished Third World Country.

But the clichés fail utterly to illuminate how the broader society is implicated in the wide array of problems that beset urban youth. A recent report by UNESCO ranked the United States twenty-fourth among twenty-five wealthy nations on an array of social indicators related to child health, education, and well-being. Such a ranking suggests that there may be more to the problems that confront urban youth than media images or education statistics suggest. Urban youth do not determine which schools they will attend, the competency of the teachers they will have access to, or how much public money will be spent on their educations. They also do not control which neighborhoods they'll live in, whether or not a particular community will be safe, whether the air they breathe will be clean, or whether they'll have access to resources that support their health. The fact that the forces that shape their lives—deindustrialization, redlining, environmental racism, political indifference—are rarely named or interrogated, points to a widespread practice of scapegoating urban youth for larger failings in American society.

We insist on a more complex, more nuanced, and ultimately a more realistic view of city kids, families, and communities. While we recognize that the struggles of impoverished urban neighborhoods and their residents are all too real, we also understand that the familiar markers that have come to represent them in the mainstream—graffiti-covered walls, wailing sirens, aimless youth striking menacing poses—paint only a tiny corner of a much larger canvas. Pain and despair may live on city streets, but so, too, do resilience, hope, and possibility.

If we open our eyes, that is. In Sharon Dennis Wyeth's poignant children's book, *Something Beautiful*, a young black girl walks outside her city apartment to find broken bottles on the ground, a garden with no flowers, and the word "die" scrawled on her building's front door. Taking in the sights, she remembers her mother's notion that all people need beauty in their lives, so she decides to search her neighborhood for her own "something beautiful." What she discovers is beauty all around, in everyday nooks and unexpected crannies: a fish sandwich at the corner diner, kids jumping Double Dutch on the sidewalk, shiny red apples at Mr. Lee's fruit stand, a smooth stone, a dance move, a baby's laugh. *Something Beautiful* is fiction, but for us it has more to say about the multiple truths of city lives than does the torrent of deficit-minded writing on "at-risk" children or the "culture" and "mind-set" of poverty.

We reject, too, the idea that teaching moves in a linear and hierarchical way, from all-knowing teacher to ignorant student. Children in urban areas, like children everywhere else in the world, do not come to schools with empty heads, devoid of ideas, knowledge, skills, experiences, or dreams. Like other children, they engage in complex reasoning, have the ability to problem solve and use logic, and have no shortage of imagination or creativity. Certainly, many have critical, unmet needs for adequate housing, health care, nutrition, and even safety. But they are not broken or damaged goods, nor should they be thought of as so deprived and depraved that only a miracle worker could save them. What they lack, most of all, is opportunity—the opportunity to live healthy, productive lives, to attend safe, nurturing, intellectually stimulating schools, to have a chance to grow up to become adults who can help themselves, their families, their communities, and the world.

Because we reject the distorted media images and because we look beyond the dismal statistics, we see teaching as recursive, interactive, dynamic, and potentially transformative for teacher, student, and society. It is for this reason that we put so much faith in education: not because we are unaware of the numerous challenges confronting urban public schools—a systemic lack of funds and resources, an unresponsive, overly bureaucratic leadership, and an entrenched set of institutional practices that make success the exception and failure the norm—but because we know that education has been, and for many continues to be, a powerful vehicle for personal growth and collective forward motion.

We resist, as well, the image of the hero teacher. First, because it operates in the patronizing conceit of child saving—the venerable mission into the wilderness to uplift the savages—and second, because it denigrates the steady commitment of hard-working teachers who don't experience daily miracles in their classrooms. But more important, we oppose the hero-teacher notion because it perpetuates the lie that the only thing needed to bring about equality of opportunity and outcomes in city schools is a caring individual—a nice white lady. Never mind crushing poverty or persistent racism, hypocritical immigration laws or the relentless hammer of high-stakes testing. If we could just hire a few more kindhearted teachers, the fantasy goes, decades of social inequities would melt away and everything would be right with the world.

We propose instead a broader, deeper vision—teaching not as heroism but as commitment, teaching not in a vacuum of ego or personality but amid the whirlwind of contexts in which schooling is enacted and performed: historical flow, economic condition, cultural surround, linguistic construction. For example, the inequitable funding of schools—and the accumulated weight of oppression that that inequity creates—cannot be ignored when examining teaching and learning in city schools. Nor can we close our eyes to an economic system that generates both great wealth and great poverty. Nor to the particularly nasty American system of white supremacy which has survived revolution, civil war, and popular upheaval, remaining remarkably intact in its effects. To begin to see city teaching more fully, all this and more must be kept in view.

■ ■ ■

The received wisdom about city teaching and schools, about city kids and their families, isn't simply the province of fiction and film. Memoirs and how-to books written by urban teachers often perpetuate the same tired story line, shamelessly playing to the stereotypes of mainstream readers. "One heroic schoolteacher has saved hundreds of lives with unconditional love and zero tolerance for rule-breakers," reads the jacket of a recent book by a teacher at an alternative school in Los Angeles. "His students are the worst of the worst—drug addicts, gang members, and violent criminal offenders. . . . They have one thing in common: they have been rejected by everyone. . . ." Everyone, of course, except the book's author, who—surprise, surprise—is able to transform their lives with "ten simple rules."

Common-sense beliefs about urban education are also pervasive in the language of social science and policy, law and journalism, the nightly newscast and the front page. In these venues their presence can be even more pernicious, their impact even more damaging. While moviegoers may plunk down $10 to see *Freedom Writers* with little more in mind than being entertained for two hours, most of us turn on the news, check internet news sites, or read the paper with far different expectations. What we often find, though, is the same prevailing narrative—a narrative that is telling not only for what is emphasized, but for what is ignored or obfuscated, and lies, then, beyond critical examination.

A recent case in point: in 2004 the *Chicago Tribune* published a three-part, front-page special report ostensibly focused on the impact of the No Child Left Behind Act (NCLB) on Chicago's schools. The protagonist of the series was nine-year-old Rayola Carwell. Rayola's mother, Yolanda, had taken advantage of the school-transfer provision of NCLB by pulling her daughter out of a south-side school described as "among the worst in the city" and enrolling her at Stockton Elementary, thirteen miles from home. Over 270,000 students were eligible to transfer citywide, but because of a lack of openings at successful schools, Rayola was one of only a handful who actually did.

The story that unfolded over three days and ten full pages in the *Tribune* turned out to be less about a tragically flawed and underfunded educational policy than about perpetuating stereotypes of low-income parents. The spotlight shined not on NCLB, but on Yolanda Carwell, who was described as "a single mother of three who dropped out of high school . . . [and] spent her life moving from one low-paying job to another." According to the report, Carwell frequently allowed her children to stay up past midnight watching TV, and when they were too tired to get up, she let them miss school. When Rayola and her siblings got into arguments, readers were told that their mother couldn't hear them because "she [was] upstairs on the phone." We also learned that Carwell had "enrolled in, but not completed, three GED training courses at three different community colleges." Paragraph after paragraph, vignette after vignette, day after day, the articles underscored the mother's apparent poor choices and disregard for her children's welfare.

By the end of the series, which culminated with Rayola leaving Stockton and returning to a school near home, little attention had been given to the lack of federal funding to help schools address NCLB mandates. Nothing had been said about how NCLB's intensified focus on high-stakes accountability measures had handcuffed teachers around the country, especially in big-city systems that serve large numbers of poor and immigrant children. And barely a mention was given to the sheer folly of the transfer provision when the ground-level reality in Chicago was that schools had 1,000 available spots for 270,000 eligible transferees. Wasn't that the big story?

But readers weren't asked to consider any of that—at least not for long. Instead, they were left with the impression that the main thing holding Rayola back was a negligent, irresponsible mother. And if there was any doubt about reaching that conclusion, a *Tribune* editorial commenting on the series drilled the point home. While gingerly criticizing NCLB, the editorial reserved its harshest words for Carwell:

> Yolanda Carwell had the best of intentions when she took advantage of the No Child Left Behind Act. . . . But good intentions aren't always enough to educate children. . . . Carwell couldn't get her children out of bed early. She wouldn't make them turn off the TV. She couldn't manage to get herself to work and her kids to school. . . . The No Child Left Behind Law has focused welcome attention on a critical issue that schools have long avoided

confronting: the achievement gap between minority and non-minority students. . . . [But] no well-intentioned law, no well-intentioned school can succeed without the follow-through of a child's parent.

Just like that, all of us—except for Yolanda Carwell—were let off the hook, absolved from any collective responsibility for the failure of city schools to provide a quality education to children like Rayola. Forget rehauling No Child Left Behind, the paper's editors seemed to say. What really needs fixing is poor people. It's all their fault.

While this is a lone example from one newspaper, it's symbolic of the silences that often pervade mainstream reporting about urban schools—even when the account is supposed to be a positive one. In October 2006, *Chicago* magazine's cover story trumpeted what seemed like cheerful news: "The Best Elementary Schools: 140 Winners in the City and Suburbs and What Makes Them Good." The article's authors explained that they "tunneled into a mountain of data" (all, it turns out, from one source: the Illinois State Board of Education) to unearth "all-around top performers" among schools in Chicagoland. While they claimed that evaluating schools based solely on numbers is "too reductionist," that's exactly what they did. Their chart listing Chicago's thirty best public elementary schools compared them in six areas: average class size, student-teacher ratio, teachers' average years of experience, teachers' average salary, per-student spending, and the percentage of students who meet or exceed state standards in core subjects.

But a more complex—and troubling—picture emerges if we compare numbers that were missing from the magazine's chart: data on the racial and socioeconomic composition of the chosen schools and of Chicago Public Schools (CPS) as a whole. Systemwide, 86 percent of the 421,000 students in CPS are African American or Latino; only 8 percent are white. Yet white students are the predominant racial group in twenty of the thirty schools that *Chicago* called "the best in the city," and in seven of those schools, whites make up 68 percent or more of the student body. Equally glaring, in sixteen of the thirty best schools the percentage of low-income students is less than 33 percent, and in nine it's less than 20 percent. This in a system where 86 percent of students come from low-income families.

These numbers begin to unveil the stark reality of the city's schools: a dual system, offering vastly different educational opportunities, and largely divided along lines of race and family income. Yet that story is nowhere to be found in *Chicago*'s report. The only references to class in the twelve-page lead article are either throwaway sentences or attempts to talk around the subject. Race isn't mentioned once. The single veiled reference comes when the authors ponder the benefits of the "extra layers of worldly education" students at one Chicago school receive "by growing up in an urban mix." But even that seemingly harmless euphemism obscures more than it reveals: neighborhoods continue to be segregated by race and class, and over half of the schools in CPS are racially isolated, with 90 percent or more of their students being either black or Latino.

While most city dwellers have at least a faint awareness of such disparities, they often speak of them in coded terms. "My school is in the city," a teacher from an exclusive private school in Chicago once explained. "But it's not an urban school." What he meant, of course, is that the building's ceilings aren't crumbling, it isn't located in a "bad" neighborhood, and—above all—that most of the kids in its classrooms aren't black, brown, or poor. To him, and to many of us, "urban" has become a sort of shorthand. But the reality is not so simple: schools in many small towns and inner-ring suburbs have increasingly diverse student populations, and in cities like Chicago, New York, and San Francisco, where gentrification and selective redevelopment are rampant, neglected, decaying neighborhoods exist alongside expanding pockets of privilege and opulence. What we know for sure is this: cities are where the inequities and injustice of our society are brought into starkest relief. Yes, the characteristics we typically associate with urban schools exist, to one degree or another, in most places in this country, but in the city they present themselves with fire and intensity.

In this book, we aim to provide a context for understanding the challenges and possibilities of education in our nation's cities. We look backward to draw upon the wisdom of elders, and forward to harness the dreams of youth. We begin, in Part I, where all good teaching should—with students themselves: their hopes and struggles, their dreams and disappointments, the polyrhythms of their lives both inside and outside schools. Part II offers up-close portraits of teachers and teaching in urban contexts, narratives that honor the complexity and wonder of a life in schools. Part III examines critical issues within city classrooms and schools—resegregation, culturally relevant teaching, student-centered curriculum, and others—while Part IV illuminates some of the contexts beyond the school's walls that good teachers must take into account: racism, poverty, immigration, gentrification, the criminalization of youth.

Our hope is that, as we explore the ways our society is implicated in the systematic failure of urban public schools, you won't be overwhelmed by the immensity of the problems nor the complexity of the responses they require. Instead, we hope that the stories, poems, essays, and articles contained in these pages give you reason to remain optimistic about the strength and resilience of the human spirit, and leave you with greater clarity about what must be done to create the schools that city kids—and all of our children—need and deserve.

CITY KIDS, CITY SCHOOLS

■ PART I ■

CITY KIDS

INTRODUCTION

William Ayers

During the 2000–2001 school year students at Communication Arts and Sciences, a small school-within-a-school at Berkeley High School in California, decided to create a dictionary of slang and idiom. The kids were studying linguistics, and the idea that they might put something together that spoke about their unique language experiences struck a chord. Soon everyone was busy interviewing friends and neighbors, copying down entries, debating the origins, the subtleties, and the etymology of speech. Is the word "sick" a good or a bad thing? It turns out that to these kids it all depends on the specific context: "Check out that outfit, it's so sick" (meaning not so cool), as opposed to, "Oh, man, that track is so sick!" (solid, awesome). Go figure.

They were off and running: "shiggity"—for sure, positively; "boo"—pet name for your significant other; "scraper"—an old-school car, usually a Buick, fixed up with a fancy stereo system. "Word" comes from the African American church, "yo" from hip-hop, "ese" from Spanish, and "yoink" from the Simpsons.

Initially the *Berkeley High School Slang Dictionary* was a mimeographed sheet for the class itself, but it morphed quickly into a must-read for young people all over the Bay Area and beyond. Now in its eighth year, the dictionary is updated and published every spring in a professional format and distributed nationally. The current edition runs to seventy pages, from "a'ight" to "zuke," and from front to back, it's an astonishing and energizing read.

There's a real commitment of time and verve from the kids when the rhythm of the day turns toward the dictionary. They form small groups, interview friends and neighbors, participate in spirited debates, search for the perfect exemplary sentence for each entry, edit, refine, rewrite. Perhaps it's the relevance that buoys the rigor; perhaps a curriculum of "me!" serves the normal narcissism of adolescents; perhaps the opportunity to control and complete a project with a clear, material goal invites a deeper investment. Whatever the reason, the kids appear, to themselves and to others, intelligent, hard-working, and competent, the work is eagerly undertaken, the effort seemingly authentic, the focus laserlike, and the flow undeniable.

Rick Ayers (full disclosure: my younger brother), the teacher who nourished and powered this project from the start, says, "Naming the world, ordering the universe, is a fundamental human activity—it's an essential part of getting a purchase on our lives, having some power over the way things are. This is one of the ways I ask them to name their world." Rick tries to create an environment and a curriculum to which kids will bring their best energies, and that allows them to show off their "too-often-muted brilliance."

Language is slippery and dynamic, on the move and on the run, always a work in progress. For this reason Rick has tried to go beyond simply transmitting the language of power and authority to inert students; he has, instead, promoted multilingualism, the ability to negotiate between all kinds of languages and meaning systems. For him, the slang dictionary is but another iteration of his larger purposes and overarching goals as a teacher: to allow students to become more capable and more powerful in their pursuits and their projects, to open the possibility that they might better understand and perhaps even transform their worlds, to trudge toward enlightenment and liberation. It's a small book embodying a big idea.

Because education is always enacted within some social surrounding—a community or society—schooling always involves ushering the young into some social order or other, into an entire universe. So all of us, including students, must keep our eyes open: What is the existing social order? How do we warrant or justify the world as it is? What alternatives are possible? Who do we want to be in the world? What do we want to discover or understand more fully? What might we hope for?

The United Nations Convention on the Rights of the Child states that the education of all children throughout the world shall be directed to, "the development of the child's personality, talents, and mental and physical abilities to their fullest potential;" "the development of respect for human rights and fundamental freedoms;" "the development of respect for the child's parents, his or her own cultural identity, language, and values, for the national values of the country in which the child is living, the country from which he or she may originate, and for civilizations different from his or her own;" "the preparation of the child for responsible life in a free society, in the spirit of understanding, peace, tolerance, equality of sexes, and friendship among all peoples, ethnic, national, and religious groups and persons of indigenous origin;" "the development of respect for the natural environment."

This is an international standard, and yet it has a special resonance for those of us who teach in American cities. It should challenge us to think more deeply about the circumstances of the lives of city kids: How do we measure up? Is there something more to be done?

I want to see the city as a site of vigor and zip and possibility, to see young people in the city—like youth everywhere—as unruly sparks of meaning-making energy on a propulsive voyage toward discovery and surprise. I want to join them on that journey. I also want to measure my efforts—as well as the efforts of others—by goals like these: the preparation of the child for responsible life in a free society. I want to nourish citizens; I don't want to create bondsmen or vassals.

I begin, then, with faith that every child and every student appears as a whole and multidimensional being—a gooey biological wonder, pulsing with the breath and beat of life itself, evolved and evolving, shaped by genetics, twisted and gnarled by the unique experiences of living. Every human being has, as well, a complex set of circumstances that makes his or her life understandable and sensible, bearable or unbearable. Each is unique, each walks a singular path across the Earth, each has a mother and a father, each with a distinct mark to be made, and each somehow sacred. This recognition asks me to reject any action that treats students as objects, any gesture that "thingifies" young people. For starters, it demands that I struggle constantly to embrace the full humanity of everyone who walks through the classroom door.

I have to know my students well enough to connect with them, of course, in the project of their ongoing growth and continuous learning. Like all teachers I run the risk of not taking enough into account—every student is unique, none are exactly the same—but I also run the risk of taking too much into account, of leaping to shaky conclusions based on surface or superficial evidence. Even the phrase "city kids" can be reductive: narrow, stereotyped, filled with images of dread and danger and deficit. I choose to go in a different direction.

I promote multicultural education as a response to reality: we are, after all, a multicultural, multilingual, diverse, and evolving society. What would schooling be if we rejected multiculturalism? Education for white supremacy? What does opposition to learning many languages lead to? Promotion of a barricaded ignorance? Teachers must learn to embrace the students who actually come into our classrooms—from a range of languages, cultures, backgrounds, abilities, and perspectives—and challenge them all to stretch, to reach, to connect, to soar from their own bases, to go further.

To me, a functioning, vital democracy requires participation, some acceptance of difference, some independent thought, some spirit of mutuality—a sense that we're all in this boat together and that we had better start rowing. Democracy demands active, thinking human beings—we ordinary people, after all, are expected to make the decisions that affect our lives—and in a democracy, education is designed to empower and to enable that goal. Education in a democracy requires imagination, initiative, engagement, and courage. This is what city kids want and need.

No school exists outside of history or culture, of course—schools shape societies; societies shape schools. Our schools belong to us, and they also tell us who we are and who we want to become. Authoritarian societies are served by authoritarian schools, just as free and democratic schools support free and democratic societies. It's worth wondering what city schools tell city kids about society and themselves.

I oppose the manipulative reduction of lives into neatly labeled packages. I resist the easy embrace of oversimplified identities—a reliance on a single aspect of a life to say it all—and the corrosive gesture of fragmenting lives into conceptually crude categories. Our stance must become identification *with*, not identification *of*—our approach, one of solidarity not service.

Knowledge may be a form of power that can transform individual lives as well as whole communities and societies, but to do so it must be freely sought, explicitly linked to moral purposes, and tied to conduct. It must stand for something. In these pages we want to stand with city kids for humanization—for increased human capacity, for creativity, intelligence, and enlightenment, for human freedom.

1

FROM *OUR AMERICA: LIFE AND DEATH ON THE SOUTH SIDE OF CHICAGO*

LeAlan Jones with David Isay

In the mid-1990s, David Isay, founder of Sound Portrait Productions, gave two Chicago teens, LeAlan Jones and Lloyd Newman, a tape recorder and asked them to compose audio diaries of their lives growing up in and around the Ida B. Wells public housing development. The resulting public radio doc-umentaries, Ghetto Life 101 *and* Remorse: The 14 Stories of Eric Morse, *were widely acclaimed and won numerous national and international awards. In 1996, the three published a book based on the documentaries,* Our America: Life and Death on the South Side of Chicago, *which included new material recorded by Jones and Newman. The following is excerpted from a section by Jones, now a freelance writer for* N'Digo, *a weekly paper in Chicago.*

We live in two different Americas. In the ghetto, our laws are totally dif-ferent, our language is totally different, and our lives are totally different. I've never felt American, I've only felt African American. An American is supposed to have life, liberty, prosperity, and happiness. But an African American is due pain, poverty, stress, and anxiety. As an African American I have experienced beautiful things, but the majority of the things I've ex-perienced are not beautiful. And I don't even have it as bad as most—there are millions of young men and women living the struggle even harder than me. As children, they have to make day-to-day decisions about whether to go to school or whether to go on the corner and sell drugs. As children, they know that there may not be a tomorrow. Why are African American children faced with this dilemma at such an early age? Why must they look down the road to a future that they might never see? What have my people done to this country to deserve this?

And yet I am supposed to feel American. I am supposed to be patriotic. I am supposed to love this system that has been detrimental to the lives of my people. It's hard for me to say how I'm an American when I live in a second America—an America that doesn't wave the red, white, and blue flag with fifty stars for fifty states. I live in a community that waves a white flag because we have almost given up. I live in a community where on the walls are the names of fallen comrades of war. I live in a second America. I live here not because I chose to, but because I have to. I hate to sound militant, but this is the way I feel.

I wonder sometimes, "Why am I alive? What is my purpose?" And I can always find a reason. But for a kid whose mother is a crack addict and who doesn't have a father and doesn't have a meal at night and has holes in his shoes when he walks the streets and can barely read and can barely communicate his feelings (which is almost the usual characteristics of a child from the ghetto), when he asks himself the question "What is my reason for being? What is my purpose?" what can he tell himself? These are the thoughts that go on in my mind and really mesmerize me.

Some people might look at me and say, "He's just some little nigger from the ghetto that knows some big words." Well, true. That might be. But listen to what I'm saying. I know you don't want to hear about the pain and suffering that goes on in *that* part of the city. I know you don't want to hear about the kids getting shot in *that* part of the city. But little do you know that *that* part of the city is your part of the city, too. This is our neighborhood, this is our city, and this is our America. And we must somehow find a way to help one another. We must come together—no matter what you believe in, no matter how you look—and find some concrete solutions to the problems of the ghetto. Right now we are at the point of no return. We've got to make a change, because if we don't we'll go into the millennium in total disarray. But I believe it's going to be all right. Somehow, some way, I believe in my heart that we can make this happen. Not me by myself. Not you by yourself. I'm talking about all of us as one, living together in our America.

This is LeAlan Jones on November 19, 1996. I hope I survive. I hope I survive. I hope I survive. Signing off. Peace.

2

FROM *HOLLER IF YOU HEAR ME*

Gregory Michie

Holler If You Hear Me is Gregory Michie's memoir of his experiences teaching seventh- and eighth-graders in a Mexican-immigrant neighborhood on Chicago's south side. In addition to telling his own story in the book, Michie catches up with ten of his former eighth-grade students and talks with them about their lives both inside and outside school classrooms. Following are two of the student portraits.

JUAN

On a warm spring evening I'm at the Chopin Theatre, a performance space in Chicago's Wicker Park neighborhood, to attend a screening of winners in a citywide youth video competition. Juan Coria and Anthony Flores, two of my former students who are now both high school juniors, have three pieces in tonight's show. The first two are well received by the audience, but the true hit of the evening turns out to be *The Catch-Up*, a chase-sequence parody they made during their freshman year. Playing off a potentially threatening situation, the video takes a shot at the stereotyping of young Latino males. A surprise ending causes the crowd to explode in laughter; then they offer an extended ovation. One of the competition's judges tells Juan and Tony that he liked their work so much he had his video classes examine it shot by shot.

I first met Juan and Tony nearly five years earlier, at the beginning of their seventh-grade year, when they signed up for an after-school video production program I was trying to get off the ground. It didn't take long to see that shooting video came naturally for Juan. "I'm built for it," he once told me. "My body's a good tripod." But it was more than just a physical predisposition. Once I'd taught him the basics of camera movement and composition, he was on his way. He had an instant rapport with the camcorder and a keen visual sense—an ability to see specific shots, or even entire sequences, in his mind. He viewed storyboards as an unnecessary step. "I've got it all up here," he'd say, pointing to his head. By the time Juan graduated from eighth grade and headed off to high school, I would've put his work up against that of most college-level videographers. The kid had skills.

After the screening, we walk down Division Street. Juan and Tony are on a high—for the first time, they've seen and heard an audience outside of school react to their work. But it doesn't last long. When I ask Juan how he felt hearing all those people applaud, he turns melancholy. "It felt good," he says, "but that piece is two years old already. We can't live off *The Catch-Up* for the rest of our lives."

Juan's response brings us back to the present. He and Tony have produced only one new video during the entire school year, and that was back in the fall. Somewhere along the way they've lost some of their passion, and it's hard to pinpoint what's gone wrong. For Juan, the course work has always been a struggle; but during his first two years in high school, video classes were his island in a sea of boredom and frustration. Lately, however, they've provided no relief. He's been falling further and further behind on his credits, and it's beginning to look doubtful that he'll graduate on time, if at all. A part-time job cleaning windows doesn't put much money in his pocket, and at home, Juan says, things are "hectic."

My father was born in Uruapan, Michoacan, and my ma was born here in Chicago. My father came here when he was nineteen or twenty years old, and once he got here, he started working for a roofing company. Before that, he used to be what they call a "coyote," bringing people from Mexico over here. He came from a family of eleven children, and I don't think anybody from his brothers and sisters graduated from school. He came the closest, but he quit before he graduated, and I think that's one reason he nags on me to keep going to school. My mom graduated from high school here, and right now she's taking classes at Daley College.

I don't have the greatest relationship with my parents. Part of it, I think, is my fault. Sometimes I just don't want to have anything to do with them. I have a lot of anger toward my father. And that's one thing I'm afraid of. When I have kids, I don't want to be like my father was with me. I mean, I guess my parents did all right bringing me up. I think I'm a good kid, 'cause at least I'm not into drugs, or I'm not out looking for fights or anything. I'm not hanging out late at night. I'm not in juvie or anything—not that the kids in juvie are bad.

I guess you could say I was one of the lucky ones. Gangbanging never really caught my attention. When I was younger, I was afraid that if I joined a gang, my dad was gonna kill me. Then in seventh and eighth grade, I was in the video program, so I had something to do after school. And the day I graduated from eighth grade—the day I graduated—my mom took me to get a job. So those were my priorities: working and going to school.

I think what worries me most in my life is the economy. I'm broke as a joke. I mean, it's like, when you got money, it's not even there. When you're broke, you're like, "Damn, I wish I had five bucks"—you know, thinking that's money. But then when you have the five dollars, it's not enough. You want more. Basically this whole world revolves around money. Like right now, I owe somebody sixty bucks. I owe you ten. I mean, I owe people money and I'm not even making enough to pay them back. I make sixty a week cleaning the windows at the laundromat, and out of that sixty, fifteen goes for bus tokens, fifteen I give to my grandmother, and fifteen I give to my ma. So that leaves me fifteen for two weeks. That's a dollar a day. That sucks.

I've never really liked school that much. I remember one time in third grade, I was sitting in class wondering who it was that invented school. I thought it must have been somebody who hated kids. But sometimes it's OK. Right now for history, I got this student teacher, and I can see he's getting frustrated. He's looking around, and I can see he's coming up with ideas to try to make the class more interesting. 'Cause like, the first day, he was all shaking. He was scared. He picks up the chalk, and you see his hand shaking, and his voice is cracking crazy style. But he's cool, though. I think he's doing a pretty good job. At least he's trying. The other teacher would just stand there at the podium, and talk and talk and talk. And the kid next to me, he's snoring, you know?

Before the student teacher came, that teacher didn't even know my name. She kept confusing me with a guy across the room from me. She'd call me Francisco. She'd turn and look at me and go, "Francisco, read that." But the student teacher, he knows me. He picked my name up from the beginning.

To me what makes a good teacher is someone who understands the students. If the teacher knows how the students are thinking, you can teach a class more easily. I mean, if you see the kids are dead, common sense will tell you you better change your strategy, you know? If all these kids are looking at you like a bunch of zombies, common sense will tell you you're doing something wrong.

The way I look at it, teachers are strict 'cause they're afraid of their students. They're afraid that the students are gonna take over them, for example, my English teacher. I know she knows what she's doing, but it's the way she approaches it that kills the class. She's real strict. She sits there, and I swear, all she does is look at the class. She doesn't make the class interesting. It's so quiet in there, you can hear a pin drop, but it's 'cause everybody's afraid of her. The kids are doing the work just to do it so they won't get hassled by the teacher. But I know they ain't learning nothing.

Right now I'm confused. I want to do good in school, but then I think to myself, "Well, what am I gonna do? Am I gonna go to college?" 'Cause if I go to college, I want to go to film school. But am I gonna make it? And even if I do, am I gonna find a job? Will I be able to be independent? It gets frustrating sometimes. I worry about it. Sometimes I think the only thing that's keeping me in school is to prove something to my dad. But fine, I stay in school, I graduate—and then what? What happens? If I decide to go to college, is my dad gonna help me out with some money?

I want to be a respected man. A man of integrity. But in a way I feel scared because if I don't make it in becoming a director or getting into something that has to do with video, the only thing left for me is doing what my dad does—roofing. And that's kind of messed up. It's like my dream could come crashing down, you know? Everything.

LOURDES

Dressed in black boots, black jeans, and a black leather jacket, Lourdes Villa throws a purse over one shoulder and climbs out of her father's freshly washed Ford Ranger. She waves good-bye, then goes to ring the buzzer of the basement apartment where her weekly singing lesson is about to begin. Lourdes shivers slightly as she waits for her no-nonsense instructor, a Chilean she addresses as Maestro Gomez, to answer the door. "One time I rang it twice and he came out here yelling at me," Lourdes tells me. "He's pretty strict. Good, but strict."

The maestro finally appears, dismissing his 8:30 student as he admits us into a small waiting room. On the paneled walls are four corkboards, framed and behind glass; each contains photos of Gomez's students, most smiling proudly while holding tall trophies aloft. Near the entranceway to the rehearsal space, a cardboard sign serves notice to students and their parents: "Always pay *before* your class." Familiar with the drill, Lourdes digs into her purse for the $25 class fee as Gomez waits silently, his arms crossed. He counts the wad of money Lourdes hands him, pockets it, then leads her into the next room without so much as a word passing between them.

Since starting the singing lessons, Lourdes had noticed a marked improvement in the range and quality of her voice. But she had been offended when her instructor told her that she shouldn't waste time singing the songs she had grown up listening to—songs of the mariachi. They were folk songs, Gomez told her. Songs of the common people. If she wanted to be a real singer, then she had to train her voice by singing real songs. Eager to learn, Lourdes did as her teacher asked. Yet he hadn't changed her mind. For now, she would study and sing the music Maestro Gomez prescribed. But once she felt confident enough to go out on her own, she would return to the songs that, as a child, she had so often heard wafting through her family's apartment. No matter what the maestro said, Lourdes thought that was real music, too.

The voice lessons had been a surprise birthday present to Lourdes from her father. She began them during her freshman year in high school, the same year her parents gave Lourdes and her younger brother another surprise: After years of squirreling away money earned from various neighborhood businesses—a jewelry store, a restaurant, and most recently a flower shop—the Villas had finally saved enough to buy a house of their own. They moved from their modest apartment in Back of the Yards, a predominantly Mexican enclave on Chicago's south side, to a sturdy brick single-family home in a mostly white subdivision on the western edge of the city.

Though Lourdes's new neighborhood was calmer, somewhat cleaner, and perhaps safer than Back of the Yards, it had none of the Mexican flavor or vibrant life of that community. Gone were the *paleteros* selling ice cream from their pushcarts in the summer, sidewalks full of children on bicycles, and the posadas celebrations that wound their way through the streets each Christmas. Gone, too, were the smaller touches that made Back of the Yards feel so distinctly Mexican, like the rear window stickers that proudly proclaimed a car owner's home state back in Mexico, or the rancheros music that blared from countless storefronts. The new neighborhood was a completely different world—a world that, to Lourdes, seemed sterile, bland, and lifeless by comparison.

When I moved to my new neighborhood, I was in shock. I couldn't believe that I was in Chicago, that I was actually in the city, because I didn't hear anything at night. There was no people out. I miss my old neighborhood a lot. I go to choir practice over there every Thursday, and I just love being in the neighborhood. You're around Mexican people, you're outside, there's a lot of people out, there's traffic, a lot of activity. I'm a people person. I like being around where there's a lot of people, talking to them. But where I live now it's more closed up. Neighbors just say hi and that's about it. They won't open their door to you and ask if you want to come in or anything.

When we moved in, as soon as we met one of the next-door neighbors, he was like, "Oh, Mexican people used to live here." And we said, "Yeah, we met them when we came to look at the house." And he was like, "Well, they were always having parties, playing loud music, and I would really appreciate it if you would keep the music a little lower." Trying to assume that just because we were Mexican, we were gonna do the same thing and be like them. And that was the first day we were at the new house! So I knew I wasn't gonna like it. I understand my parents' point of view, and why they wanted to move here, but I'm just not used to it.

I remember once when I was in fourth grade, someone who had just come from Mexico got put in our classroom, which wasn't bilingual. And I remember the teacher got real angry and started saying, "Why should I start trying to learn your language when you're coming to my country? You're in America and here we speak English. Why should I learn yours?" She said all this right there in front of all of us. And I just don't think that's a good attitude. I thought America was supposed to be a place where all different cultures can come and learn from each other.

I have a lot of respect for the people who are immigrating because I've never suffered like they have to suffer. They have to go through a lot just to come here and survive. Now they're thinking about closing the border so Mexican people can't come in, and I don't really understand why. Mexican people are coming here for the same reason white people came here. So why should the doors get closed now?

I think all Mexican people experience some racism. Say you take a Mexican person that went to college, got a diploma, and is working at a good job. I think he's still going to get a taste of racism. Not as much as the migrant worker or factory worker who didn't go to school and has worked in the factory all his life, but he's still gonna experience it. No matter what you do, there's gonna be people out there who look down on you. I try real hard not to do that. I've always tried to avoid judging a group of people based on one. I've heard friends and even some of my relatives say negative things about black people. Like we'll be riding past a black neighborhood and you will just hear the car locks click. And I don't see any reason for that. I always try to remember that if something bad ever happens to me with a black person or a white person, that I've met other people of that race who aren't like that. You just can't make a judgment based on one person or one incident. I remember when my father's restaurant got robbed, it was Mexican people that robbed us. And I'm not gonna go by that and say, "Oh, all Mexican people are bad—including me!"

My father is real supportive of me. He asks me what I want to do, and then tries to help me with whatever I need. I like acting and singing, and he's always supported me in that. He got me into singing lessons. He's always trying to look for opportunities for me and pushing me. So I am lucky, I know. But sometimes I think he wants so much for me to succeed that he goes overboard and pressures me. I go to school all day, then I go to work for him at the flower shop until eight, then come home and do my homework and then I still have to practice my singing. And sometimes I just want to explode, I just want to do something else. It gets me frustrated sometimes. But

I feel good about my future. Right now, I'm not thinking anything negative. It's hard sometimes, but I'm not gonna give up just like that. My father told me once that I was the hope for bringing the family up, to be the first one to graduate from college. So that's what I want to do.

As far as school goes, I've never liked history or social studies. The way they teach it is—it's a history book. You open it, and it says Columbus did this, Columbus did that, he went back to Spain, he came back over here—and I just think it's another example of the white man's thinking about what went on, from their point of view. I'm not trying to sound like a racist—I'm not prejudiced against all white people or anything—but that's the way it is. And they're putting it in a book and trying to make it seem like that's all that happened. You don't get other people's stories. They just narrow it all down to one side. Why don't we hear it from the Indian's side? I don't see how they can say, "This is what happened." Because we can't be sure that's how it was. That's why I think I don't like history. Teachers need to make it more of a discussion instead of just learning all these facts, page by page and book by book.

The teacher should tell the kids, "You can learn from me, but I can learn from you, too." Because it gets the kids more interested. Last Monday I got a new teacher in English. She's just out of college—a Caucasian—and she's pretty cool. She makes us write journals. And one day she told us to write down three things from our culture and how we recognize them. So one of the things I wrote about was the music, about mariachi and all that. And after she read mine, she started asking me questions. She said she had seen a group like mariachis, except it was all guitars. And I explained to her that that was *rondalla*. And she was like, "Yeah, I like that." And she brought over a piece of paper and she made me write it down. 'Cause she really wanted to learn, you know?

When your culture is brought into a class at school, it makes you feel good because you know that your culture isn't just being recognized for, "Oh, today they caught five immigrants crossing the border," or whatever. And it's interesting because you want to know more about your roots. Awhile back, we were doing a report in school on the country we were from, and one of the questions I asked my father was what were some of the traditions he lost coming over here. And there was a couple of things he named that I didn't even know existed. There's a Children's Day in Mexico.

There's *Dia de los Muertos,* and that isn't really celebrated here, either. And when he was telling me about these things, that's when I started to realize that that's part of the price of coming here—you lose part of your culture.

I don't want that to happen to me. I consider myself Mexican. I grew up in the United States, I was born here, I pretty much live the life of an American. But I don't care. Mexican is what I am. It's in my blood. And I don't think I'll ever lose that. It's very important to me to hold on to it.

FROM *PUSH*

Sapphire

Sapphire is a performance poet and author of American Dreams *and* Push. *The protagonist of her intense and moving novel,* Push, *has endured a life of unimaginable abuse at home and unconscionable neglect at school. Sixteen years old and unable to read or write, Precious Jones is pregnant with her second child—both by her father—when she is kicked out of her Harlem junior high and referred to Each One Teach One, an alternative education program. This excerpt follows Precious on her first day at the new school, where she meets Ms. Rain, a teacher unlike any she's had before.*

———

I always did like school, jus' seem school never did like me. Kinnergarden and first grade I don't talk, they laff at that. Second grade my cherry busted. I don't want to think that now. I look across the street at McDonald's but I ain't got no money so I unwrap ham and take a bite. I'm gonna ask Mama for some money when she get her check, plus the school gonna give me a stipend, thas money for goin' to school. Secon' grade they laffes at HOW I talk. So I stop talking. What for? Secon' thas when the "I'mma joke" start. When I go sit down boyz make fart sounds wif they mouf like it's me fartin'. When I git up they snort snort hog grunt sounds. So I jus' stop getting up. What for? Thas when I start to pee on myself. I just sit there, it's like I paralyze or some shit. I don't move. I *can't* move. Secon' grade teacher HATE me. Oh that woman hate me. I look at myself in the window of the fried chicken joint between 127th and 126th. I look good in my pink stretch pants. Woman at Lane Bryant on one-two-five say no reason big girls can't wear the latest, so I wear it. But boyz still laff me, what could I wear that boyz don't laff? Secon' grade is when I just start to sit there. All day. Other kids run all around. Me, Claireece P. Jones, come in 8:55 A.M., sit down, don't move till the bell ring to go home. I wet myself. Don't know why I don't get up, but I don't. I jus' sit there and pee. Teacher ack all care at first, then scream, then get Principal. Principal call Mama and who else I don't remember. Finally Principal say, Let it be. Be glad thas all the trouble she give you. Focus on the ones who *can* learn, Principal say to teacher. What that mean? Is she one of the ones who can't?

My head hurt. I gotta eat something. It's 8:45 A.M. I gotta be at school at 9 A.M. Ham gone. I ain't got no money. I turn back to chicken place. Walk in cool tell lady, Give me a basket. Chicken look like last night's but people in there buying it ol' or not. Lady ax, Fries? I say, Potato salad. Potato salad in the refrigerator in the back. I know that. Lady turn roun' to go in back, I grab chicken and roll, turn, run out, and cut down one-two-six stuffing chicken in my mouth. "Scarf Big Mama!" this from crack addict standing in front abandoned building. I don't even turn my head—crack addicts is *disgusting*! Give race a bad name, lost in the hells of norf america crack addicts is.

I look at watch, 8:57 A.M.! But shit I'm almost there! Coming around the corner of 126th onto Adam Clayton Powell Jr Blvd. I throws the chicken bones into the trash can on the corner, wipe the grease off my mouth with the roll then stuff rest of roll in my mouf, run across 125th, and I'm there! I'm in the elevator moving up when I realize I left my notebook and pencil in the chicken place! Goddam! And it's 9:05 A.M. not 9:00 A.M. Oh well teacher nigger, too. Don't care if she teacher, don't no niggers start on time. The elevator goes Bing! I step out. My class last door on left. My teacher Miz Rain.

I'm walking across the lobby room real real slow. Full of chicken, bread; usually that make me not want to cry remember, but I feel like crying now. My head is like the swimming pool at the Y on one-three-five. Summer full of bodies splashing, most in shallow end; one, two in deep end. Thas how all the time years is swimming in my head. First grade boy say, Pick up your lips Claireece 'fore you trip over them. Call me shoe shine shinola. Second grade I is fat. Thas when fart sounds and pig grunt sounds start. No boyfriend no girlfriends. I stare at the blackboard pretending. I don't know what I'm pretending—that trains ain' riding through my head sometime and that yes, I'm reading along with the class on page 55 of the reader. Early on I realize no one hear the TV-set voices growing out blackboard but me, so I try not to answer them. Over in deepest end of the pool (where you could drown if not for fine lifeguard look like Bobby Brown) is me sitting in my chair at my desk and the world turn to whirring sound, everything is noise, teacher's voice white static. My pee pee open hot stinky down my thighs sssssss splatter splatter. I wanna die I hate myself HATE myself. Giggles giggles but I don't move I barely breathe I just sit. They giggle. I stare straight ahead. They talk me. I don't say nuffin'.

Seven, he on me almost every night. First it's just in my mouth. Then it's more more. He is intercoursing me. Say I can take it. Look you don't even bleed, virgin girls bleed. You not virgin. I'm *seven*.

I don't realize I've gone from walking real real slow to standing perfectly still. I'm in the lobby of first day of school Higher Education Alternative/Each One Teach One just standing there. I realize this 'cause Miz Rain done peeked her head out last door on the left and said, "You all right?" I know who she is 'cause Miss Cornrow with the glasses had done pointed her out to me after I finish testing and show me my teacher and classroom.

I make my feet move. I don't say anything. Nothing in my mouth to say. I move my feet some more. Miz Rain ask me if I'm in the A.B.E. class. I say yes. She say this is it and go back inside door. The first thing I see when I step through door is the windows, where we is is high up, no other buildings in the way. Sky blue blue. I looks around the room now. Walls painted lite ugly green. Miz Rain at her desk, her back to me, her face to the class and the windows. "Class" only about five, six other people. Miz Teacher turn around say, Have a seat. I stays standing at door. I swallow hard, start to, I think I'm gonna cry. I look Miz Teacher's long dreadlocky hair, look kinda nice but look kinda nasty, too. My knees is shaking, I'm scared I'm gonna pee on myself, even though I has not done no shit like that in years. I don't know how I'm gonna do it, but I am—I look at the six chairs line up neat in the back of the room. I gotta get there.

The whole class quiet. Everybody staring at me. God don't let me cry. I takes in air through my nose, a big big breath, then I start to walk slow to the back. But something like birds or light fly through my heart. An' my feet stop. At the first row. An' for the first time in my life I sits down in the front row (which is good 'cause I never could see the board from the back).

I ain' got no notebook, no money. My head is big 'lympic size pool, all the years, all the me's floating around glued shamed to desks while pee puddles get big near their feet. Man, don't nobody know it but it ain' no joke for me to be here in this school. I glance above teacher's head at the wall. Is a picture of small dark lady with face like prune and dress from the oldern days. I wonder who she is. Teacher sit at desk marking roll sheet, got on purple dress and running shoes. She dark, got nice face, big eyes, and hair like I already said. My muver do not like niggers wear they hair like that! My muver say Farrakhan OK but he done gone too far. Too far where I wanna ax. I don't know how *I* feel about people with hair like that.

The teacher is talking.

"You'll need a notebook like this," she hold up a black 'n white 79-cent notebook just like what I left in chicken place. As she talking girl walk in.

"It's nine-thirty-seven," teacher say. "Jo Ann you *late*."

"I had to stop and get something to eat."

"Next time stay where you stop. Starting tomorrow this door will be locked at nine o'clock!"

"I better be on the side that's in," grumble Jo Ann.

"We agree on that," say teacher, she look Jo Ann in eye. She not scared of Jo Ann. Well gone, Miz Rain.

"We got some new people—"

"I found something!" Jo Ann shout.

"I beg your pardon," say teacher but you can see she ain' beggin' nothin', she mad.

"No, I'm sorry Ms Rain"—I see right now Jo Ann is clown—"but I jus' want to say, do anyone need an extra notebook I foun' in the chicken place?"

"It's mine!" I say.

"Git a grip," Jo Ann say.

"I got one." I shocks myself saying that. "I left that book at Arkansas Jr. Fried Chicken on Lenox between one-two-seven and one-two-six this morning."

"Well I'll be a turkey's asshole!" Jo Ann screamed. "Thas where I found it."

I reaches my hand she smile me. Han' me my book, look at my stomach, say, "When you due?"

I say, "Not sure."

She frown, don't say nothing, and go sit a couple seats away from me in the row right behind me.

Miz Rain look pretty bent out of shape then melt, say, "We got more new people than old people today, so let's just go back to day one and git to know each other and figure out what we gonna do here together." I look at her weird. Ain' she spozed to *know* what we gonna do. How we gonna figure anything out. Weze ignerent. We here to learn, leas' I am. God I hope this don't be another . . . another . . . I don't know—another like before, yeah another like the years before.

"Let's try a circle," teacher say. Damn I just did sit myself down in front row and now we getting in a circle.

"We don't need all those chairs," teacher say waving at Jo Ann who dragging chairs from second row. "Just pull out five or six, however many of us it is, and put 'em in a little circle and then we'll put 'em back in rows after we finish introducing ourselves." She sit herself in one of the chairs and we all do the same (I mean she the teacher 'n all).

"OK," she say, "let's get to know each other a little bit uummm, let's see, how about your name, where you were born, your favorite color, and something you do good and why you're here."

"Huh?" Big red girl snort. Miss Rain go to board and say, "Number one, your name," then she write it, "number two, where you were born," and so on until it all on board:

1. name
2. where you were born
3. favorite color
4. something you do good
5. why you are here today

She sit back down say, "OK, I'll start. My name is Blue Rain—"

"Thas your real name!" This from girl with boy suit on.

"Um hmmm, that's my for-real-hope-to-die-if-I'm-lying name."

"Your first name *Blue*?" same girl say.

"Um hmm," Ms. Rain say this like she tired of mannish girl.

"Splain that!"

"Well," say Ms. Rain real proper. "I don't feel I have to explain my name." She look at girl, girl git message. "Now as I was saying my name is Blue Rain. I was born in California. My favorite color is purple. What do I do good? Ummm, I sing purty good. And I'm here because my girlfriend used to teach here and she was out one day and asked me to substitute for her, then when she quit, they asked me did I want the job. I said yeah and I been here ever since."

I look around the circle, it's six people, not counting me. A big redbone girl, loud bug-out girl who find my notebook at chicken place, Spanish girl with light skin, then this brown-skin Spanish girl, and a girl my color in boy suit, look like some kinda butch.

Big Red talking now, "My name Rhonda Patrice Johnson." Rhonda big, taller than me, light skin but it don't do nuffin' for her. She ugly, got big lips, pig nose, she fat fat and her hair rusty color but short short.

"I was born in Kingston, Jamaica." Ain' that something! She don't talk funny at all like how coconut head peoples do. "My favorite color is blue, I cook good."

"What?" somebody say.

"Name it!" Rhonda shoot back.

"Peas 'n rice!"

"Yeah, yeah," like why even mention somethin' so basic.

"Curry goat!"

"Yeah, you name it," Rhonda say. "My mother usta have a restaurant on Seventh Ave before she got sick, she taught me everything. I'm here," she say serious, "to bring my reading up so I could get my G.E.D."

The skinny light-skin Spanish girl speak, "My name is Rita Romero. I was born right here in Harlem. I'm here because I was an addict and dropped out of school and never got my reading and writing together. My favorite color is black." She smile messed up teef. "I guess you could tell that." We could looking at her clothes 'n shoes, all black.

"What you do good?" Rhonda ax.

"Hmm," she say, then in shaky voice real slow, "I'm a good mother, a very good mother."

Brown girl talk. We about the same color but I think thas all we got the same. I is *all* girl. Don't know here.

"My name is Jermaine."

Uh oh! Some kinda freak.

"My favorite color—"

"Tell us where you born first," Rhonda again.

Jermaine give Rhonda a piss-on-you look. Rhonda cut her eyes at Jermaine like jump bad if you want to. Jermaine say she was born in the Bronx, still live there. Red her favorite color. She a good dancer. She come here 'cause she want to get away from negative influence of the Bronx.

Spanish girl Rita say, "You come to *Harlem* to get away from bad influence?"

Jermaine, which I don't have to tell you is a *boy's* name, say, "It's *who* you know and I know too many people in the Bronx baby."

"How did you find out about the program?" Miz Rain ax.

"A friend."

Miz Rain don't say nothin' else.

Girl foun' my notebook next. "Jo Ann is my name, rap is my game. My color is beige. My ambition is to have my own record layer."

Miz Rain look at her. I wonder myself what is a record layer.

"Where was you born and why you at this school," Rhonda ax. OK, I see Rhonda like to run things.

"I was born in King's County Hospital. My mother moved us to Harlem when I was nine years old. I'm here to get my G.E.D., then, well I'm already into the music industry. I just need to take care of the education thing so I can move on up."

Next girl speaks. "My name is Consuelo Montenegro." Ooohhh she pretty Spanish girl, coffee-cream color wit long ol' good hair. Red blouse. "Why I'm here, favorite color—what's-alla dat shit?" She look Ms. Rain in face, mad.

Miz Rain calm. Rain, nice name for her. Ack like she don't mind cursing, say, "It's just a way of breaking the ice, a way of getting to know each other better, by asking nonthreatening questions that allow you to share yourself with a group without having to reveal more of yourself than might be comfortable." She pause. "You don't have to do it if you don't want to."

"I don't want to," beautiful girl say.

Everybody looking at me now. In circle I see everybody, everybody see me. I wish for back of the class again for a second, then I think never that again, I kill myself first 'fore I let that happen.

"My name Precious Jones. I was born in Harlem. My baby gonna be borned in Harlem. I like what color—yellow, thas fresh. 'N I had a problem at my ol' school so I come here."

"Something you do good," Rhonda say.

"Nuffin'," I say.

"Everybody do something good," Ms. Rain say in soft voice.

I shake my head, can't think of nuffin'. I'm staring at my shoes.

"One thing," Ms Rain.

"I can cook," I say. I keep my eyes on shoes. I never talk in class before 'cept to cuss teacher or kids if they fuck wif me.

Miz Rain talking about the class. "Periodically we'll be getting into a circle to talk and work but let's put our chairs back in rows for now and move on with our business. Well, first thing, this is a basic reading and writing class, a pre-G.E.D. adult literacy class, a class for beginning readers and writers. This is *not* a G.E.D. class—"

"This not G.E.D.?" Jermaine ax.

"No, it's not. This class is set up to teach students how to read and write," Miz Rain say.

"Shit I know how to read and write, I want to get my G.E.D.," Jo Ann say.

Miz Rain look tired, "Well then this class isn't for you. And I'd appreciate it if you watch your language, this *is* a school."

"Ain' shit to me—"

"Well then go, Jo Ann, why don't you just tip," Miz Rain seem like, you know, well *leave* bitch.

Spanish girl, Rita, say, "Well this here *is* for me. I can't read or write."

Rhonda come in, "I can a little, but I need help."

Jermaine look unsure.

Miz Rain, "If you think you want to be in the G.E.D. class, all you have to do is come back to this room at one p.m. for placement testing." Jermaine don't move. Consuelo look to Jermaine but don't say nuffin'. Jo Ann say she be back at one, fuck this shit! She ain' illiterit. Miz Rain look at me. I'm the only one haven't spoken. I wanna say something but don't know how. I'm not use to talkin', how can I say it? I look Miz Rain. She say, "Well Precious, how about you, do you feel you're in the right place?"

I want to tell her what I always wanted to tell someone, that the pages, 'cept for the ones with pictures, look all the same to me; the back row I'm not in today; how I sit in a chair seven years old all day wifout moving. But I'm not seven years old. But I am crying. I look Miz Rain in the face, tears is coming down my eyes, but I'm not sad or embarrass.

"Is I Miz Rain," I axes, "is I in the right place?"

She hand me a tissue, say, "Yes, Precious, yes."

4

DESCENDANCY

Mayda del Valle

Los Angeles–based spoken word poet Mayda del Valle grew up on the south side of Chicago and began performing her own writing while in high school. In 2001, she won the Individual National Poetry Slam Championship at the National Poetry Slam, becoming the youngest poet and the first Latino person to win the title. Much of Mayda's work grows out of her own experiences, and in "descendancy" she weaves her words around questions of identity that echo within all young people: Who am I? Where am I from?

It's nice
that you can claim your clan to purebred pedigree
      descendancy
but the middle passages mark the makeup of my
      amalgamated
Afro-Boricua ancestry.
I know it's kinda hard to see the motherland
      legitimacy in me
but I can't deny the fact that Youruba songs
lay in the lines of my mother's palms
as
offerin' up Psalms
seekin' the calm offered by God's son
'cause
when the day is done
the color of my skin still

marks me as an alien in the country of my birth.
I can't check myself into a box
I'd be ignoring mami's straight and papi's nappy locks
        in me
the chi-town Midwest windy city in me
the be-bop
hip-hop
non-stop
salsa con sabor
queen of soul in me
the growing up next door to mexicanos
with
Orale cabrones
tacos and tamales in me
The descendancy that doesn't deny the darker
        shades of skin in me
the what in me
yes the THAT in me
what you claim you can't see
so descend and see
descend and see me for what I be
'cause I be a Rican
a Chi-town not a Nuyorican
a Chi-town south-side Rican simply seekin' to see if I
        can fit in
I dare you to sit still in your chair and
intellectualize what I can only make sense of by
        feelin'
I see
you're being blind not seein' past the kinds of
        fabricated fictional fables
assaulted ancestral accounts
I should be callin' your historical scribes Aesop
the way they stop
the truth from being illuminated
using tactics

Trying to force my assimilation
causin' me to question my creation
You must've mistaken me for Hansel and Gretel
thinkin' I'd jump into the meltin' pot
always trying to place me in constant categorizations
        of populations
You calling this shit civilization?

My so-called pre-Columbian savage
unenlightened ancestors
had more humanity
than your Microsoft
Macintosh technology
Monopoly information highway riding bareback
on the backs of underpaid third world women and
        children
85 cents a day for makin' hundred dollar nike's
nuclear bomb droppin'
immigrant stoppin'
death by lethal electrocution
injectin' lies-of-let-me-get-my-piece-of-the-American-
        apple-pie-dream-into-our-children's-minds society
LET ME order your new world and paint the White
        House brown coz
I'M GOING DOWN
yes I'm goin' down to the earth searchin' my roots
        like Hailey's
and I'm ridin' comets back to the past
back to the past that becomes my future that is my
        present that is my now
I'm goin' back seekin'
My Descendancy

5

FROM *THE PACT: THREE YOUNG MEN MAKE A PROMISE AND FULFILL A DREAM*

Sampson Davis

Sampson Davis, George Jenkins, and Rameck Hunt grew up poor in Newark, New Jersey, where they struggled to steer a positive course for their lives and to resist the lure of the streets. They recount in the memoir The Pact *that, as teenagers, they promised each other that they would all go to college, graduate, and become doctors—which all three ultimately did. In the following excerpt, Sampson Davis, now a Board Certified Emergency Medicine Physician in Newark, relates a critical turning point in his young life.*

––––––––––

When we were kids, sports saved us many times from the dangers in our neighborhood. We'd play ball behind the school or in the courtyard of the projects while gunshots rang out around the corner. Sometimes, though, the danger unfolded right in front of us.

One day, Noody and I bought a sponge ball from a neighborhood store for a dollar and headed back to the projects to play. We stopped at Building 6, where Noody lived. The fading "X" spray-painted on the wall next to the stairwell marked the strike zone for the pitcher.

As we played, we saw a familiar drug dealer enter the stairwell with a man we didn't recognize. The man wasn't from the neighborhood, which probably meant he was a customer. Seconds after he got inside, another drug dealer sneaked in from behind and began to beat the man with a bat. The two dealers then snatched the man's money and ran. Noody and I watched the whole scene, then went back to playing sponge ball. We had seen it many times before.

The sounds of gunshots and screeching cars late at night and before dawn were as familiar to us as the chirping of insects must be to people who live in the country. In broad daylight we often saw young guys, barely old enough to see over the steering wheel, speeding down Ludlow Street in stolen cars. Sometimes, a trail of speeding police cars would be on their tail.

I was in the sixth grade when I awakened one morning to a loud crash outside. Minutes later, the wail of sirens filled my room. I jumped up and rushed outside. Down the street, about a block from my house, a car had crashed into a utility pole. The pole lay across the smashed front window and hood of the car. As paramedics pulled the driver from the car, I recognized him as a guy who had gone to my school—he was no more than twelve years old. He had been speeding down the street in a stolen car when he lost control. Now he was dead.

This is the backdrop against which I lived. You see it enough, and it becomes normal. Some parts of the life even become exciting. How can a mother's pleas compete with the thrill of having wads of cash handed to you when your pockets are empty and the pantry is bare? Sure, you see cats your age dying all the time, but you figure that's the price you pay for being born poor. And you accept your fate, unless someone or something convinces you that you have the power to change the script.

Even as early as elementary school, the pressure was on me to do what the other neighborhood boys were doing. The pressure was subtle: participate, or feel like a chump and risk being isolated. When I was about seven, the big thing was to run into Jack's, a neighborhood grocery, and steal Icees. My friends were always bragging about how easy it was. I was in the store one sweltering summer day with a friend and decided I wanted a large cherry-flavored Icee, which cost fifty cents. The problem was, I had no money. I opened the freezer, slipped the big, cold cup into my shorts, and walked casually toward the door with my friend. Suddenly, I felt a pair of huge hands on the back of my arm. One of the store's owners, a big, burly Hispanic man over six feet tall, pulled my friend and me to the back of the store.

"Open your pants," he demanded.

"No," I shot back.

He grabbed my shorts and the Icee clunked to the ground. My heart was thumping. I thought for sure I was about to die. The next thing I knew, I was face-to-face with two snarling dogs. They were German shepherds, and they looked big enough to eat me alive. I screamed for mercy. In his thick Spanish accent, the owner was shouting something about letting the dogs tear me to pieces if I ever tried to pull that trick again. I could have sworn the dogs were licking their chops when the owner suddenly let us go. We flew out of the store. I didn't have much of a taste for stolen Icees after that.

But it wouldn't be the last time I followed friends into trouble. It would take years for me to learn that friendship can lift you up, strengthen and empower you, or break you down, weaken and defeat you. In the meantime, though, I kept getting mixed up with neighborhood guys who had lost all hope that their lives would ever be different from what we all saw around us every day.

At thirteen, I was arrested for the first time and charged with shoplifting. A friend set me up. That must sound like the lamest excuse on the books, but it was true. I had walked up Ludlow Street to the Food Town grocery in the bordering city of Elizabeth with a seventeen-year-old friend who told me that he was planning to start a carpet-cleaning business. As we were leaving the store, he said he had paid for a high-powered vacuum cleaner-steamer and needed my help getting it home.

"Grab that for me, man," he said, motioning to a large vacuum cleaner against the wall near the exit. "My hands are full."

We had split up for a few minutes in the store, so it never occurred to me that he was lying. I casually walked over to the machine and pushed it out of the store. I was halfway down the street with it when a police officer rolled up behind me, jumped out of the car, and snapped a pair of handcuffs on me. My friend took off running. I was dumbfounded.

I was detained for a few hours at the Elizabeth police station and then released when the same guy who had been with me in the store and planned the scheme sent his older brother to bail me out. Eventually, the charges were dropped. But the crazy thing is, I kept hanging with the guy who had set me up. I didn't know any better. To my friends, my arrest was one big joke. I never told any of them how scared I was sitting in that police station. That wouldn't have been cool. I just played along. Yeah, man, real funny.

When I look back over my life, I realize that at the most critical stages, someone was there to reach me with exactly what I needed. A martial-arts teacher named Reggie was one of those people. My brother Andre had taken kung fu lessons from Reggie and had introduced me to him when I was ten. Reggie was in his early twenties himself, and he worked as a security guard in the cemetery across the street from my house. I looked up to him. He made an honest living, didn't do drugs, and took good care of himself. He was cool and the only man I knew who was respected by some of the toughest guys in the community for doing good. He was looked up to in that bigger-than-life way more often reserved for drug dealers. In Reggie, I saw what I wanted to be: a good guy who commanded respect from the streets in a way that was different from everything I had seen.

Kung fu was popular at the time. I watched it on television every Saturday morning. Reggie was a highly ranked black belt, good enough to star in a movie, and he taught lessons free of charge at the cemetery to any kid in the neighborhood eager to learn. I never knew anything about Reggie's background, but I wonder now where he got the insight at such a young age to provide a diversion to kids who could so easily drift into trouble.

On Sundays, a small group of us—Lee, Cornell, Crusher, Eric, and some other drifters—walked through huge, mahogany doors and gathered in an empty room that converted to a chapel for memorial services. Reggie worked behind a desk there. Sometimes he wore his security-guard uniform as he led us in practice; other times he practiced with us. We started with warm-up exercises, then spent at least an hour perfecting old sparring moves and learning new ones. Then Reggie led us in meditation. He taught us how to remove ourselves from our environment through deep concentration. As we sat on the floor with our eyes closed and minds blank, Reggie delivered little messages. They were mostly clichés, like "If the blind leads the blind, both of them will fall into a hole." Or, "If you feel weak, you will be weak." But something about sitting there with your mind clear, totally focused on what he was saying, gave his words power.

At the end of each session, we exercised again for an hour, jogging around the cemetery several times or through the neighborhood. We looked like soldiers, jogging in unison with stone faces, right past the tall granite tombstones inside the cemetery gates or the drug dealers and hustlers hanging around outside. The sessions made me feel physically and mentally strong. They had another benefit: they kept me from roaming the streets. I looked up to Reggie and didn't want to disappoint him.

For four years I was dedicated to learning everything I could about martial arts from my mentor-teacher. But by age fifteen, I had started to slip. I was hanging out until one A.M. with guys who were four to seven years older. We sat around drinking forty ounces of malt liquor and talking trash. At first, I just listened as they shared war stories about their dealings around Dayton Street. In time, though, I would have stories of my own.

A year later, I stopped going to kung fu lessons. I'm sure it's no coincidence that about the same time, my life shifted gears and began speeding toward trouble.

No matter how much I hung out with my friends and pretended not to care about school, I always managed to excel. Moms couldn't help me with homework, but she stayed on me to do well.

"Go to school," she said so seriously, as if my life depended on it.

I saw close-up how she suffered without an education, and I didn't want the same thing to happen to me. I aimed as far as I could see: finishing high school. Beyond that, I had no ambition. My teachers seemed to like me. As tough as I acted outside school, I paid attention to them in class and usually did what they asked. Sometimes, though, I had to be creative in explaining a good grade to friends. I lied to them frequently. "I cheated," I'd say, trying to minimize any accomplishment. Kids who did well in school were considered nerds. I wanted to be cool. And more than anything, I wanted to fit in.

Moms had placed many of her dreams on me. She had sacrificed her education for her family, and she pushed to make sure I took advantage of the opportunity she never had.

Most students in our neighborhood attended Dayton Street Elementary until the eighth grade, then went on to high school. In the sixth grade, I was looking forward to returning to Dayton Street as a seventh-grader, an upperclassman, running things. But my sixth-grade teacher, Ms. Sandi Schimmel, approached me and recommended that I take an examination to apply to a magnet program at University High School the following year. University High was one of the more prestigious high schools in the Newark school system and the only one that accepted seventh- and eighth-graders.

I didn't want to be bothered with going to another school. Everyone I knew had stayed at Dayton Street until eighth grade.

"Why?" I asked the teacher.

She explained that attending University High would give me a better shot at getting into college and making something of my life. College was far from my mind. But Ms. Schimmel and the principal talked to my mother. They told her that I was reading on a ninth-grade level and needed to be at a school where I would be academically challenged. Moms pushed me to take the test.

It helped that I wasn't the only one handpicked from my school to apply. One of my boys, Craig Jordan, was encouraged to take the test, too. On test day, we rode the bus together to University High School, a boxy two-story structure in the middle of a working-class residential neighborhood. It took us an hour and a half on two public buses to get to the South Ward, where the school was located.

At University High, we walked into a room of unfamiliar faces. George was in the room somewhere, but we would not meet until later. I felt uncomfortable, but practically everybody there was from somewhere else, so we all looked a bit out-of-place. I tried hard to concentrate on the test. It wasn't as difficult as I expected. A few weeks later, I got the news: I had made the cut. I was about to become a student at University High.

MORNING PAPERS

Marlon Unas Esguerra

A second generation Filipino American and Chicago-born poet, Marlon Unas Esguerra co-founded the critically acclaimed pan-Asian spoken word ensemble, I Was Born with Two Tongues, which from 1998 to 2004 performed in over 300 colleges and venues across the country. Currently, Esguerra is a special education teacher in the South Bronx as part of the New York City Teaching Fellows program. His poem "morning papers" deals with issues of language, culture, prejudice, and assimilation that many immigrant children in urban areas—and their parents—must confront.

---

words.

every morning at the living room table
for fifteen years
my papa lettered boxes.
he filled the squares in the sun-times
and tribune crosswords
back in the pages where family circle comics
mingled with word jumbles and crisscrossed.
he would always sift swiftly
through front page headlines
bypass the bi-lines.
he would always sit there
until he got every last word.
he always did.
sometimes, with a little help from me:

anak, what's a four letter word that goes with horseshoe?
toss, i said.

a seven letter word with counter _____?
culture, i said.

we tossed culture with words.

every morning for fifteen years
he created a brew
mixed sanka and syntax
american common knowledge with coffee.
my mother told me later
they have a habit of always telling you so damn later—
that when he came here in 1969
he worked as a bellhop at the palmer house.
she said his accent was so thick
and he being so tongue tied
they laughed him clear out of the lobby
out of the graveyard shift
into our living room table
into a secondhand dictionary
into the back of a newspaper
into a crossword puzzle.

anak, what's a four letter word for "to hit a snag"?
slip, i said.
maybe trip, i said.

sometimes fall
over words.

one morning at the corner store
my father was buying lottery tickets.
some guy in line shoves him over and jabs:

aw, sooo! the jap wants to buy a lotto ticket!
don't you think you've already bought everything, you greedy japs?

the more refined, acculturated sidekick of his adds:

he's not a jap, stupid. look at him!
he must be a rican-chink-mut or somethin'.
so what of it spic? what the hell do you need a lotto ticket for?
ain't you got it all? our jobs? our country?

and i wanted papa to bust out kali sticks
slice them clear into bridgeport
pull every last four letter word in the book to accent his revenge.
tell them our family history!
pull a gun!
a sarcastic one-liner!
throw a punch!
a yawp!
the visa papers!
the five years of pictures
he sent momma while he petitioned for us!
our home!
his union card!
my good english!
poetic license!

anything.
the proof.

a single word.
nothing.

he grabbed his tickets
said nothing.
walked briskly back to the house
nothing.
opened his newspaper
picked a ballpoint out of his pocket
said nothing.
except a sigh.
then a tear
on crumpling newspaper.
his fist to the table

he cried for everything that day.
for every failure
for every mispronounced syllable
for me

without words.

7

FOUR SKINNY TREES

Sandra Cisneros

Sandra Cisneros's classic, acclaimed coming-of-age novel, The House on Mango Street, *tells the story of Esperanza Cordero, a young Mexican American girl growing up in a working-class Chicago neighborhood. The book's evocative vignettes reveal the sometimes difficult realities of a child-hood in the city, but Cisneros also pays close attention to moments of beauty and transcendence, and to the surprising places where hope and strength can be found.*

A winner of the MacArthur Foundation Fellowship, Cisneros's most recent book is the novel Caramelo.

They are the only ones who understand me. I am the only one who understands them. Four skinny trees with skinny necks and pointy elbows like mine. Four who do not belong here but are here. Four raggedy excuses planted by the city. From our room we can hear them, but Nenny just sleeps and doesn't appreciate these things.

Their strength is secret. They send ferocious roots beneath the ground. They grow up and they grow down and grab the earth between their hairy toes and bite the sky with violent teeth and never quit their anger. This is how they keep.

Let one forget his reason for being, they'd all droop like tulips in a glass, each with their arms around the other. Keep, keep, keep, trees say when I sleep. They teach.

When I am too sad and too skinny to keep keeping, when I am a tiny thing against so many bricks, then it is I look at trees. When there is nothing left to look at on this street. Four who grew despite concrete. Four who reach and do not forget to reach. Four whose only reason is to be and be.

8

TO "SEE" AGAIN[1]

Luis J. Rodriguez

Best known for Always Running: La Vida Loca: Gang Days in L.A., *his unflinching memoir of gang life in Los Angeles, poet and author Luis J. Rodriguez has also published several volumes of poetry, two children's books, and the novel* Music of the Mill. *In addition, Rodriguez is a longtime youth worker and community activist. In his book* Hearts and Hands: Creating Community in Violent Times, *he reflects on his experiences working with gang members and other marginalized youth, while providing a potent critique of society's unwillingness to look beyond the "gangbanger" label and provide opportunities for kids who need them most.*

When more and more young people plan their funerals and not their futures,
it spells alarm for the rest of us.
—Father Greg Boyle

Alberto walked out of his apartment building in the Pico-Union neighborhood of Central Los Angeles. He had a round mustached face and was bald, except for a long "homeboy" braid that began at the top of his head. His long-sleeve shirt covered the intricate lines and shades of tattoos on his arms. He backed out of the entrance pulling a baby carriage that held his ten-month-old daughter, Angela, whom he was taking to a neighborhood babysitter. Her mother, Sonya, followed. Sonya, a slight and cute girl in her late teens, had reddish peroxided hair and intense chola-style makeup.

Alberto would later hop a bus to an auto shop in South Central L.A.

where he apprenticed with his brother. Sonya would wait for a friend to drive her to a small garment plant in Koreatown where she worked.

Alberto had emigrated to L.A. in his early teens. As a child during the civil war in El Salvador, he learned how to use a rifle in a guerrilla outfit. He had witnessed many deaths among his comrades in the villages they were protecting before he grew out of puberty. Perhaps this knowledge allowed Alberto access to L.A.'s gang culture, gaining him respect and notoriety. But it also made him a frequent target of rival gangs.

Sonya earned her "gang stripes" on L.A.'s streets. She entered the country as an infant, living with her mother in a crowded Pico-Union apartment complex. She eventually dropped out of school, moving in with Alberto when she got pregnant. Sonya often worked in downtown dance halls where immigrant girls from Mexico and Central America were given tickets to dance with strangers, some of whom desired sexual favors. A forged identification card made her twenty-one when she was clearly in her teens. Eventually Alberto put a stop to this when the nightly drinking and dangerous situations proved too draining for the young mother. They were hardworking and thoughtful people. When Alberto worked under the hood, tuning up a car in the shop, he seemed like a regular working stiff, happy, for the moment, to be out of the battle zone.

Alberto and Sonya were members of 18th Street, the city's "deadliest street gang," according to a 1996 series of articles on the gang in the *Los Angeles Times*: headlines such as "A Look Inside at 18th Street's Menace" were used to demonize a segment of mostly Mexican and Central American youth.[2] Alberto once dealt drugs. He had a massive "Eighteen" in old English lettering across his back. There were times when the couple would lay deathly still on a mattress, their infant daughter between them; then Alberto would edge up to the window to check for possible snipers.

But 18th Street is not a monolith. There are caring and intelligent people among their members, just as there are those who don't give a damn.

I got to know Alberto, Sonya, and some of their homies. I also met with some of their rivals in La Mara Salvatrucha. In the Normandie section of the barrio, there are multistoried art deco buildings amid streets crowded with brown-faced mothers and unemployed men, and noisy with the horns and roar of traffic and the squeals of children. The apartment hallways are dense with people lounging on fold-up chairs near their doors, with toys for their kids nearby—they'd rather not be outside and possibly get caught in a crossfire. Street parties are held next to neatly scripted barrio graffiti, below the fire escapes of smog-sooted dark buildings. Several young men in wheelchairs, casualties of the *pleitos* (gang battles), bob their heads to the incessant beat of a Spanish-laced hip-hop sound. With their scars, bullet wounds, harsh makeup, and mad-dog looks, you know many of them are hurting.

When U.S. immigration officials raided the auto shop, Alberto got deported. He called Sonya from Tijuana once or twice, but eventually he stopped calling. The last time I heard, the couple had broken up, leaving Sonya to fend for herself—a single mother in a place where single mothers abound, with little or no resources.

Politicians and demagogues often reduce the complex interactions and situations confronting most people, particularly those ensnared in poverty, to soundbites and quick fix solutions. Everything is a moral failing—"It's not about rich or poor, but about right or wrong." This thinking opens the door for "get tough" legislation.

Most of these people are not in the community as teachers or elders because they are not willing to fully address the problems. They are not vested to do anything real and lasting because they are more concerned about their career, their financial standing, or their own neck. Instead they build campaign coffers and ratings on the legitimate fear people have of violence and uncertainty. With the problems becoming increasingly aggravated and left unsolved, panic begins to grip the highest levels of city, state, and federal power. Most official responses are repressive: more laws, more police, more prisons.

In 1999, in the heavily Mexican–Puerto Rican Chicago-area township of Cicero, some of the most severe antigang ordinances were enacted: officials could confiscate vehicles and evict people from their homes if they believed them to be members of a street gang. These measures were changed later that year after the ACLU threatened to challenge the ordinances in court. New ordinances were then established that would allow police to confiscate a young person's vehicle if he or she had no legitimate purpose to be out after nine P.M.[3]

Equally troubling is the notion—which helps give life to these repressive measures—that we don't know what to do about the escalating violence. Judith Steele, a City Hall public safety analyst, was quoted in a *Los Angeles Times* article as saying, "We don't know what works. . . . It's like trying to catch Niagara Falls in a teacup."

Maybe we don't know because we are asking the wrong people. Instead why don't we ask the parents? Why don't we ask longtime community activists? Or the young people themselves? Aren't they the "experts" on their lives? If policy is targeting them, shouldn't they be participating in the formulation of that policy?

In 1999 there was a dialogue organized by the Jane Addams School of Social Work at the University of Illinois, Chicago, concerning child protective services in the state. One official, representing the Illinois Department of Children and Family Services, asserted that "prior domestic abuse is no justification for abusing one's own child." Of course, abusing a child has no "justification." However, if a parent was abused when he or she was younger, it is an important part of the equation. Such things can help us understand the patterns of broken relationships that contribute to the abuse of children. Why would anyone not want this to be part of the dialogue?

We must deal deeply with the circumstances and the environment in which child abuse exists and not just deal with it in a limited and punitive manner, such as the practice of taking children away from the mostly poor—and mostly African American—families that have been targeted by such agencies. It is a way to involve such families, regardless of their economic status or skin color, to become active shapers of the policies and remedies that involve them. Looking at the history and conditions that give rise to such violence can help us to prevent it.

Michael Meade has often stated that the work of community elders is "holding the ground while youth make their glorious mistakes."[4] What brings youth and elders together is trouble. When society at large fails to develop true eldership and mentoring at the most basic community level, and when the elders are not there to provide compassion, wisdom, experience, and meaningful and lasting skills knowledge, the young usually "sacrifice" themselves to drugs, violence, gangs, and prison, many times paying with their lives.

Repeatedly administrators in youth detention centers or community programs say they want their young charges to go through a process of awareness and change, of opening up and maturing, but without any trouble. But there is no such process. Unfortunately these "troubles" lead the people with the resources to turn away from the individuals who need them most. Alberto and Sonya, and youth like them, are often lost because too many churches, recreation centers, and employers have closed their doors to them. Too many people have given up. I've heard parents plead to the courts, "Take my child—I don't know what to do anymore." But the problem is not just unsure parents. The whole community is fragmented in their response, and many children are falling through the cracks.

Young people need a place—both at home and in the community—of unconditional acceptance, where they are honored, where their natural gifts are nurtured and they can live out purposeful lives. Children and youth need the guidance and support of community as their psychological-social development occurs. Self-esteem can't be achieved by telling oneself over and over "I'm okay." One also needs confirmation from the outside to more or less accurately estimate one's place and abilities. Such confirmation can only come from a community that surrounds young people with "hearts and hands," and provides them the initiatory experience necessary for their proper growth and tempering.[5] Properly helped, young people learn not to be helpless; properly disciplined, they can become self-disciplined; properly cared for, they care for themselves.

All youths, troubled or otherwise, have these needs. A violent and fractured community will produce violent and lost children. We need to look at the big issues: Have we abandoned our elders? Are we pushing our young people aside? Unless we address such concerns, megalopolises like Los Angeles or Chicago cannot sustain the kind of grassroots community-building that is necessary.

This is not about "rescuing" young people. We can't rescue them, because they have to save themselves, tapping into their own creative energies. They have to become masters of their own lives—with their autonomy and integrity strengthened in the process. Finding their places in this world is an intensely personal endeavor. But where is the community that prepares them, sets clear and consistent parameters, and, when the ordeal is over, welcomes them home?

We must ask ourselves the following questions:

- Where are the centers and the schools where young people can be creative, respected, and safe?
- Where are the meaningful social activities, including community-organized and community-sanctioned recreation, as well as the empowering, socially charged, community improvement projects?
- Where are the loving family environments? Where these environments don't exist, is it fair—or wise—to blame the families?[6]
- Where are the sanctuaries, the safe and sacred spaces, where their spiritual quests are attended to, their psychological and social concerns are met, and where the law, which often works against them, can be accessible and understandable so it can work for them?
- Do the young have the sense that their floundering steps, even the missteps, are part of their growth and advancement?
- How can youths contribute to social change, to bettering their homes and community, and know that their contributions are essential?

Other societies have long recognized that young people need proper initiatory experiences, rites of passage profound enough to match the fire in their souls. If not, they will turn that fire outward, burning everything around them, acting out in violent ways, or consuming themselves in such false initiations as drugs or alcohol.

As renowned social-psychologist James Hillman has pointed out, these initiations must be linked to discovering one's life purpose, one's daimon or genius. All of us have to find our own special calling. The Mexika people of ancient Mexico, also known as "the people with an umbilical to the moon," believed that every child had his or her own *tonalli*, or soul-direction, calculated by the movements of the sun, moon, planets, and constellations. They believed that there are personal and specific group destinies tied to the cosmos and integral to the web and movement of all life. The *tonalli* was kept secret by the parents and the diviners until the child was old enough to make conscious steps to-ward it—and to prevent anyone from blocking the child from his or her predestined path. *Tonalli* was a direction, but not unalterable; a person had to consciously participate in his or her own destiny to get there. Hillman has written that a life is similar to that of a tiny acorn in which the image of a mighty oak tree is already imprinted.[7] Like the acorn, human beings have innate attributes and faculties that, properly nur-tured, can reach fruition. Our life task is to go in the direction of this calling, the pull of destiny. What eventually gets us there is character. Destiny therefore is not just about a future. Destiny is here, now. It is something you have to make happen.

Unfortunately in a postindustrial capitalist society our internal pur-poses are too often demeaned, denied, or crushed in the helter-skelter scramble to survive (similar to when a plague, conquest, natural disas-ters, or war destroys whole peoples). Today much of this creativity is ex-pressed as madness. It appears that many of our sons and daughters have gone insane, whether they are shooting their classmates, using drugs, or becoming precocious consumers.

Any society that does not take care of the material, spiritual, and ed-ucational needs of its children has failed. A community out of balance turns out unbalanced people. So when one sees the young dying before their elders, when there are more and more violent responses to problems—whether from the powerful or the powerless—we know so-ciety has lost its vision. "Conservative," "liberal," or "moderate" are not terms that express the real content of our times, the revolutionary promise that most people are crying out for: a society humane enough to take the wondrous inventions, the advanced resources, and unleash them to heal and protect the lives of its people.

As Michael Meade has often said, the problem is not the gang; the problem is the lack of interest in the gang. We need to look at people like Alberto and Sonya again. At its root this is what the word "respect" means, from the Latin *respectus*: "to look back at, to reconsider, to see again." If Alberto and Sonya, with their wisdom born of barriers, blocks, and battering, had been given the proper support, teachings, op-tions, and centering, they would have been more capable of becoming good parents, hard workers, and creative people. But when things looked good, when both were working, renting their own place and avoiding some of the hazards of where they lived, the law came in and undermined this partnership while it was in its formative stages, eventually forcing them to go their own ways.

The general attitude toward gangs is that they are a social disease ("they're worse than a cancer," a so-called gang expert recently declared), that gang youth have nothing positive to give. But when their needs are addressed, these youth will give plenty. Many have already done so despite the negligence. What can determine the difference is an aware, resourceful, authentic, committed, and spiritually rich community. Under favorable conditions, anyone can become a confident, competent, and autonomous person.

NOTES

1. Based on the essay "Treating L.A.'s Gang Problem: We Need 'Root' Doctors," *Los Angeles Times*, Feb. 9, 1997.

2. Rich Connell and Robert J. Lopez, "The 18th Street Gang," *Los Angeles Times*, Nov. 17–19, 1996.

3. Sarah Downey, "Cicero Turns Its Failed Anti-gang Ordinance into a Curfew Law," *Chicago Tribune*, Aug. 25, 1999.

4. Michael Meade, *Thresholds of Change: Finding Purpose and Inner Authority in Troubled Times* (Pacific Grove, Calif.: Oral Traditions Archives, 1995), audiotape, read by author.

5. Joseph Campbell, *The Hero with a Thousand Faces* (Princeton, N.J.: Princeton University Press, 1949). In this section of his most well-known book Campbell illustrates the vital role of persons (women, mentors, elders), angels, deities, or spirits in assisting the protagonists of hero adventures, what James Joyce termed the monomyth, which is the archetypal narrative line of most of the world's folktales and myths. In the story of the "Labyrinth and the Minotaur," the hero Theseus was aided through the maze with the help of a thread of linen that the labyrinth's creator, the artist-scientist Daedalus, gave him to tie at the entrance, and that he unwound as he maneuvered through the labyrinth's treacherous twists and turns. Campbell then, writes, "The flax for the linen of his thread was gathered from the fields of the human imagination. Centuries of husbandry, decades of diligent culling, the work of numerous hearts and hands, have gone into the hackling, sorting, and spinning of this tightly twisted yarn. Furthermore, we have not even to risk the adventure alone; for the heroes of all time have gone

before us; the labyrinth is thoroughly known; we have only to follow the thread of the hero-path" (pp. 24–25).

6. The biggest issue cited about the fractured family structures of today, particularly in poor urban communities, has been the lack of fathers. However, I contend that poor men, particularly fathers, have been highly marginalized in society—first by the economy, then by social services, and finally by people who accept the perilous notion that "we don't need men."

Public services tended to push this concept for years by penalizing welfare recipients for having men in the house, forcing men to seek work outside the community, not having more men assist with children in schools or social agencies (as if they can't be trusted with children), and increasingly detaining and removing men who are idle, active in gangs, or in illegal trades.

Unfortunately this means that women carry the physical, financial, and emotional burdens of raising the children and keeping the community intact (and for the most part they've done a massively heroic job). It's true that many men buy into this and act accordingly: we don't need any more abusive, irresponsible, and cowardly men (a situation that, ironically, in many subtle and not-so-subtle ways is given a green light in this culture). But we can't walk away from men, either. We need compassionate, astute, and courageous men. We need strong men and strong women.

7. James Hillman, *The Soul's Code: In Search of Character and Calling* (New York: Random House, 1996).

■ PART II ■

CITY TEACHERS

INTRODUCTION

Gregory Michie

From the opening frames, it's evident that *Half Nelson* isn't going to be a conventional "urban teacher" film. It begins on the hardwood floor of a bare apartment, where Dan Dunne sits in his underwear, legs outstretched, a scraggly beard creeping down his neck, a dazed, spacey look in his eyes. An alarm clock buzzes insistently in the background. It's time for Dan to leave for school, but he's struggling to peel himself off his living room floor. Soon, we understand why: in addition to being a social studies teacher and the girls' basketball coach at a Brooklyn junior high school, he's a crack addict, a basehead.

Dan wants to be a good teacher, and even when he's coming unglued personally—which is often—he does his best to hold it together for his students. In his classroom he ditches the prescribed curriculum and asks his black and Latino kids to wrestle with tough questions. His methods are part Socratic seminar, part didactic ramble, but his lessons push students to think, to make connections, to see history as something that can be shaped by everyday people working together and taking action.

Yet we're never tempted to see Dan as the savior, the white hero—and not just because of his drug habit. While it's clear that he despises the forces that keep his students down ("the machine," he calls it), the filmmakers remind us that he's not an innocent. When he asks his kids during class one day to name the obstacles to their freedom, their answers come easily: "Prisons." "White [people]." "The school." Then Stacy chimes in from the back row: "Aren't you part of the machine then? You white. You part of the school."

As committed as Dan tries to be to his students, it's obvious that he's holding on by a thread. He succumbs to his addictions at night and is distracted and tired in class the next day. It seems inevitable that his two lives will collide, and one evening following a girls' basketball game, they do. One of his students, Drey, a player on the team, finds him cowering in a bathroom stall, soaked in sweat, crack pipe in hand. She glares at him, more hurt than surprised; he looks terrified.

"Can you help me up?" Dan finally mutters.

Drey gets him to his feet, then wipes his forehead with a wet paper towel. For a moment, we forget who's the teacher and who's the student. If anybody needs saving here, it's Dan.

But no miracle turnarounds or stand-and-cheer moments are to come. *Half Nelson* is too smart for that—subtle, understated, every note played in a minor key. It's a quiet film that takes the trite conventions of Hollywood teacher-hero movies and turns them inside out, revealing troubling contradictions and real-life shades of gray. Dan Dunne is bright, sensitive, politically aware, and has a genuine rapport with his students. He's also immature, unfocused, impulsive, and self-absorbed. Is he a good teacher? In some ways, yes; in others, probably not. That alone makes him far more believable than the saintlike, cardboard protagonists of most urban teacher films.

Even in its smallest details, *Half Nelson* seeks complexity and plays against popular stereotypes. As Dan arrives at school one morning and gets out of his car, we don't hear sirens, gunshots, or a thumping hip-hop soundtrack. Instead, we hear the chirp of a lone songbird. Who knew the city had any? Later in the film, when Drey rides her bike past a row of desolate lots in her neighborhood, the overwhelming feeling is not one of menace or impending danger but of utter isolation and abandonment. It's the crippling aftermath of deindustrialization: factories shuttered, opportunities vanished, work disappeared.

What's freshest about *Half Nelson*, though, is its depiction of the reciprocal nature of the teacher-student relationship. Dan teaches and is taught, guides and is guided, receives as much as he gives. His students have much to learn from him, and they do—lessons about the clash of opposing social forces, about historical turning points, and how change happens—but he, too, is a continual learner. Drey and the other kids help make Dan a better person than he would be without them. And in watching him, we learn that good teaching is not only about changing the world or changing the lives of others—it's about changing ourselves, a transformation from within.

For city teachers, it's also about functioning within—and challenging—a system that in many ways works to undercut and even thwart your best efforts. While the tyranny of high-stakes testing has made life difficult for teachers from the tiniest towns to the toniest suburbs, teachers in big-city schools often face additional hurdles and hardships. They must navigate added layers of administrative nonsense, do more with fewer resources, create community in buildings where alienation and anonymity are accepted elements of school life. Teachers in city schools are far more likely than their counterparts elsewhere to have fewer desks than students, to have no planning periods (or even bathroom breaks) during an entire school day, to lack daily access to a school counselor or photocopier, or to be handed a scripted curriculum and told how and when it must be taught. To teach in a big-city school system is to recognize, as former New York City Teacher of the Year John Taylor Gatto once said, that the institution itself has no conscience. And it is to understand, as Dan tells his students, that you sometimes have to throw your body on the gears of the machine.

In the documentary film *The First Year*, novice teacher Maurice Rabb gets a crash course in how the needs of a child can be crushed by the entrenched bureaucratic machinations of a mammoth school system. "I feel the pain of my students," says Maurice, who is black, of his five-year-olds in South Central Los Angeles. As we watch his futile efforts to obtain help for Tyquan, a student with a severe speech impediment, we feel it, too. Maurice agitates to get Tyquan assessed by the school's frequently absent speech therapist, but months pass with no results. While his principal is sympathetic to his plight, she claims her hands are tied. The bigger picture, she says, is that the district is short forty speech therapists, so their school is lucky to have one at all. Maurice makes phone calls to public clinics to try to get services for Tyquan, but there, too, he runs into a wall: the child's government insurance will cover only two hours of therapy per month. Frustrated and angry, but undeterred, Maurice begins one-on-one tutoring sessions with Tyquan three days a week after school. Progress is slow but certain. It's not enough, to be sure. But it's something.

Maurice's story demonstrates that resistance to schooling-as-usual doesn't have to take the form of grand or symbolic gestures. It can also be found in steady, purposeful efforts to make the curriculum more meaningful, the classroom community more affirming, the school more attuned to issues of equity and justice. Sometimes it means starting small: visiting the home of a troubled child, ignoring a senseless mandate, improvising to create a lesson that connects to students' lives. Other times it means joining with like-minded educators to form a study group, advocate for a policy change, or speak out at a board meeting. Either way, committed urban teachers learn that while they can't always tear down the wall that stands between their students and a truly humanizing education, they can chip away at it brick by brick.

Of course, not all city teachers face identical challenges because not all city schools are the same. In Chicago, where I taught for nine years, magnet schools and college-prep academies are inundated with résumés from qualified teachers and lavished with attention from community partners and politicians. Many schools in poor neighborhoods, meanwhile, struggle to stay alive amid threats of "takeover," and strain to attract the attention of outside partners or prospective teachers. A few elite Chicago public schools boast state-of-the-art facilities and technology; many others have sparsely stocked libraries, lack a functional science lab, or have no recreational space for students. These differences don't mean the selective and elite schools aren't really "urban." But they're a reminder that vast differences and inequities exist even within big-city systems, and for teachers in the most forgotten and forsaken schools, the journey toward equitable outcomes for children is an even steeper, more precarious climb.

Even so, urban teaching is not all toil and struggle—not by a long shot. It's nurturing a community among teenagers who've experienced too much pain in their young lives. It's the comfortable rhythm of Mr. B's classroom at the juvenile detention center. It's getting a surprise birthday present from thirteen-year-old Ellis, coming out to your fifth-graders, helping Jasmine begin to heal. It's protesting against a dreadful standardized test—and winning. For those teachers who remain in city schools long enough to get their bearings, the instances of utter frustration are tempered—and on the best days eclipsed—by moments of joy and transcendence.

The obstacles are no doubt formidable for city teachers but, to borrow from James Baldwin, the work is more various and more beautiful than anything anyone has ever said about it.

See for yourself. Class is in session.

9

BUILDING COMMUNITY FROM CHAOS

Linda Christensen

Linda Christensen is a founding editor of Rethinking Schools, *the activist teacher magazine focused on justice and equity, and director of the Oregon Writing Project at Lewis & Clark College. A longtime high school English teacher in Portland, Christensen grounds her vision of radical school reform in the complexity, dynamism, and sometimes chaos of real classroom life.*

———————

Recently, I read a book on teaching that left me feeling desolate because the writer's vision of a joyful, productive classroom did not match the chaos I faced daily. My students straggled in, still munching on Popeye's chicken, wearing Walkmen, and generally acting surly because of some incident in the hall during break, a fight with their parents, a teacher, a boyfriend or girlfriend. This year, more than any previous year, they failed to finish the writing started in class or read the novel or story I assigned as homework. Many suffered from pains much bigger than I could deal with: homelessness, pregnancy, the death of a brother, sister, friend, cousin due to street violence, the nightly spatter of guns in their neighborhoods, the decay of a society.

For too many days during the first quarter, I felt like a prison guard trying to bring order and kindness to a classroom where students laughed over the beating of a man, made fun of a classmate who was going blind, and mimicked the way a Vietnamese girl spoke until they pushed her into silence.

Each September I have this optmistic misconception that I'm going to create a compassionate, warm, safe place for students in the first days of class because my recollection is based on the final quarter of the previous year. In the past, that atmosphere did emerge in a shorter time span. But the students were more homogeneous, and we were living in somewhat more secure and less violent times. While students shared the tragedies of divorce and loss of friendships, their class talk was less often disrupted by the pressure cooker of society—and I was more naive and rarely explored those areas. We were polite to each other as we kept uncomfortable truths at bay.

Now, I realize that classroom community isn't always synonymous with warmth and harmony. Politeness is often a veneer mistaken for understanding, when in reality it masks uncovered territory, the unspeakable pit that we turn from because we know the anger and pain that dwells there. At Jefferson High School in Portland, Oregon, where the interplay of race, class, and gender creates a constant background static, it's important to remind myself that real community is forged out of struggle. Students won't always agree on issues, and the fights, arguments, tears, and anger are the crucible from which a real community grows.

Still, I hate discord. When I was growing up, I typically gave up the fight and agreed with my sister or mother so that a reconciliation could be reached. I can remember running to my "safe" spot under my father's overturned rowboat whenever anger ran loose in our house.

Too often these days I'm in the middle of that anger, and there's no safe spot. My first impulse is to make everyone sit down, be polite, and listen to each other, a great goal that I've come to realize doesn't happen easily. Topics like racism and homophobia are avoided in most classrooms, but they seethe like open wounds. When there is an opening for discussion, years of anger and pain surface. But students haven't been taught how to talk with each other about these painful matters.

I can't say that I've found definitive answers, but as the year ended, I knew some of the mistakes I made. I also found a few constants: to become a community, students must learn to live in someone else's skin, understand the parallels of hurt, struggle, and joy across class and culture lines, and work for change. For that to happen, students need more than an upbeat, supportive teacher; they need a curriculum that teaches them how to empathize with others.

SHARING POWER AND PASSION

Before I could operate on that level, I had to find a way to connect with my students. Ironically, violence was the answer. This year none of the get-acquainted activities that I count on to build a sense of community worked in my fourth-block class. Students didn't want to get up and interview each other. They didn't want to write about their names. They didn't want to be in the class, and they didn't want any jive-ass let's-get-to-know-each-other games or activities. Mostly, our ninety-minute blocks were painfully long as I failed daily to elicit much response other than groans, sleep, or anger. It's hard to build community when you feel like you're "hoisting elephants through mud" as my friend Carolyn says. I knew it was necessary to break through their apathy and uncover something that made these students care enough to talk, to read, to write, to share—even to get angry.

My fourth-block class first semester was Senior English, a tracked class where most of the students were short on credits to graduate—as T.J. said, "We're not even on the five-year plan"—but long on humor and potential. They came in with their fists up and their chins cocked. They had attitudes. Many of them already had histories with each other.

To complicate matters, our year opened with a storm of violence in the city. The brother of a Jefferson student was shot and killed. Two girls were injured when random bullets were fired on a bus. A birthday party at a local restaurant was broken up when gunfire sprayed the side of the restaurant. So violence was on the students' minds. I learned that I couldn't ignore the toll the outside world was taking on my students. Rather than pretending that I could close my door in the face of their mounting fears, I needed to use that information to reach them.

In the first days, the only activity that aroused interest was when they wrote about their history as English students'—what they liked, what they hated, and what they wanted to learn this year. Many of these students skulked in the low-track classes and they were angry—not at tracking, because they weren't aware that another kind of education might be possible, but at the way their time had been wasted on meaningless activity. "The teacher would put a word on the board and then make us see how many words we could make out of the letters. Now what does that prepare me for?" Larry asked. But they also hated reading novels and talking about them because novels "don't have anything to do with our lives." The other constant in many of their written responses was that they felt stupid.

For the first time, they got excited. I knew what they didn't want: worksheets, sentence combining, reading novels and discussing them, writing about "stuff we don't care about." But I didn't know what to teach them. I needed to engage them because they were loud, unruly, and out of control otherwise. But how? I decided to try the "raise the expectations" approach and use a curriculum I designed for my Contemporary Literature and Society class, which receives college credit.

During those initial days of listening to these seniors and trying to read the novel *Thousand Pieces of Gold*, by Ruthann Lum McCunn, I discovered that violence aroused my students. Students weren't thrilled with the book; in fact, they weren't reading it. I'd plan a ninety-minute lesson around the reading and dialogue journal they were supposed to be keeping, but only a few students were prepared. Most didn't even attempt to lie about the fact that they weren't reading and clearly weren't planning on it.

In an attempt to get them involved in the novel, I read aloud an evocative passage about the unemployed peasants sweeping through the Chinese countryside pillaging, raping, and grabbing what was denied them through legal employment. Suddenly students saw their own lives reflected back at them through Chen, whose anger at losing his job and ultimately his family led him to become an outlaw. Chen created a new family with this group of bandits. Students could relate: Chen was a gang member. I had stumbled on a way to interest my class. The violence created a contact point between the literature and the students' lives.

This connection, this reverberation across cultures, time, and gender challenged the students' previous notion that reading and talking about novels didn't have relevance for them. They could empathize with the Chinese but also explore those issues in their own lives.

This connection also created space to unpack the assumption that all gangs are bad. Chen wasn't born violent. He didn't start out robbing and killing. Lalu, the novel's main character, remembered him as a kind man who bought her candy. He changed after he lost his job and his family starved.

Similarly, kids in gangs don't start out violent or necessarily join gangs to "pack gats" and shoot it out in drive-bys. Because the tendency in most schools is to simultaneously deny and outlaw the existence of gangs, kids rarely talk critically about them.

A few years ago, scholar Mike Davis wrote an article analyzing the upsurge of gang activity in L.A. He found it linked to the loss of union-wage jobs. I hadn't explored Portland's history to know whether our situation is similar to L.A.'s, but I suspected economic parallels. When I raised Davis's research, kids were skeptical. They saw other factors: the twin needs of safety and belonging.

Our discussion of gangs broke the barrier. Students began writing about violence in their own lives and their neighborhoods. T.J. explained his own brushes with violence:

> [T]he summer between my sophomore and junior years, some of my friends were getting involved in a new gang called the Irish Mob. . . . My friends were becoming somebody, someone who was known wherever they went. The somebody who I wanted to be. . . . During the next couple of weeks we were involved in six fights, two stabbings, and one drive-by shooting. We got away on all nine cases. The next Saturday night my brother was shot in a drive-by. The shooters were caught the same night.

Kari wrote that she joined a gang when she was searching for family. Her father lost his job; her mother was forced to work two jobs to pay the rent. Kari assumed more responsibility at home: cooking dinner, putting younger brothers and sisters to bed, and cleaning. While at middle school, Kari joined the Crips. She said at first it was because she liked the "family" feel. They wore matching clothes. They shared a language and nicknames. In a neighborhood that had become increasingly violent, they offered her protection. She left the gang after middle school because she was uncomfortable with the violence.

Students were surprised to learn that Hua, a recent immigrant from

Vietnam, was also worried about her brother who had joined a gang. Her classmates were forced to reevaluate their initial assessments of her. While she had seemed like an outsider, a foreigner, her story made a bond between them.

At first, I worried that inviting students to write about violence might glorify it. It didn't turn out that way. Students were generally adamant that they'd made poor choices when they were involved in violent activities. As T.J. states in his essay, "I wanted to be known wherever I went. . . . But I went about it all wrong and got mixed in. . . . It was nothing I had hoped for. Sure I was known and all that, but for all the wrong reasons."

More often students shared their fears. Violence was erupting around them and they felt out of control. They needed to share that fear.

Through the topic of violence I captured their interest, but I wanted them to critique the violence rather than just describe it. I had hoped to build a community of inquiry where we identified a common problem and worked to understand it by examining history and our lives. That didn't happen. It was still early in the year, and students were so absorbed in telling their stories and listening to others it was difficult to pull them far enough away to analyze the situation. I didn't have enough materials that went beyond accusations or sensationalism, but the topic itself also presented practical and ethical problems, especially around issues of safety and confidentiality.

I want to be clear: bringing student issues into the room does not mean giving up teaching the core ideas and skills of the class; it means I need to use the energy of their connections to drive us through the content.

For example, students still had to write a literary essay. But they could use their lives as well as Lalu's to illustrate their points. Students scrutinized their issues through the lens of a larger vision as James did when he compared the violence in his life to the violence in Lalu's:

Lalu isn't a gang member, but some of the folks, or should I say, some of the enemies she came in contact with reminded me of my enemies. Bandits in the story represented the worst foes of my life. In some ways bandits and gangs are quite similar. One would be the reason for them turning to gang life. Neither of them had a choice. It was something forced upon them by either educational problems or financial difficulties. It could have been the fact that their families were corrupt or no love was shown. Whatever the reasons, it was a way of survival.

Finding the heartbeat of a class isn't always easy. I must know what's happening in the community and the lives of my students. If they're consumed by the violence in the neighborhood or the lack of money in their house, I'm more likely to succeed in teaching them if I intersect their preoccupation.

Building community means taking into account the needs of the members of that community. I can sit students in a circle, play getting-to-know-each-other games until the cows come home, but if what I am teaching in the class holds no interest for the students, I'm just holding them hostage until the bell rings.

A CURRICULUM OF EMPATHY

As a critical teacher I encourage students to question everyday acts or ideas that they take for granted. But I also teach them to enter the lives of characters in literature, history, or real life whom they might dismiss or misunderstand. I don't want their first reaction to difference to be laughter or withdrawal. I try to teach them how to empathize with people whose circumstances might differ from theirs. Empathy is key in community building.

I choose literature that intentionally makes students look beyond their own world. In the class I teach with Bill Bigelow, we used an excerpt from Ronald Takaki's *A Different Mirror* about Filipino writer Carlos Bulosan. Bulosan wrote, "I am an exile in America." He described the treatment he received, good and bad. He wrote of being cheated out of wages at a fish cannery in Alaska, being refused housing because he was Filipino, being tarred and feathered and driven from town.

We asked students to respond to the reading by keeping a dialogue journal. Dirk, who is African American, wrote, "He's not the only one who feels like an exile in America. Some of us who were born here feel that way, too." As he continued reading, he was surprised that some of the acts of violence Bulosan encountered were similar to those endured by African Americans. In his essay on immigration, he chose to write about the parallels between Bulosan's life and the experiences he's encountered:

> When I was growing up I thought African Americans were the only ones who went through oppression. In the reading, "In the Heart of Filipino America," I found that Filipinos had to go through a lot when coming to America. I can relate with the stuff they went through because my ancestors went through sort of the same thing.

Dirk went on to describe the parallels in housing discrimination, lynching, name calling, being cheated out of wages that both Filipinos and African Americans lived through.

Besides reading and studying about "others," we wanted students to come face-to-face with people they usually don't meet as a way of breaking down their preconceived ideas about people from other countries. For example, during this unit, we continued to hear students classify all Asians as "Chinese." In the halls, we heard students mimic the way Vietnamese students spoke. When writing about discrimination, another student confessed that she discriminated against the Mexican students at our school. Our students were paired with English-as-second-language students who had emigrated from another country—Vietnam, Laos, Cambodia, Eritrea, Mexico, Guatemala, Ghana. They interviewed their partner and wrote a profile of the student to share in class. Students were moved by their partners' stories. One student whose brother had been killed at the beginning of the year was paired with a student whose sister was killed fighting in Eritrea. He connected to her loss and was amazed at her strength. Others were appalled at how these students had been mistreated at their school. Many students later used the lives of their partners in their essays on immigration.

Besides making immigration a contemporary rather than a historical topic, students heard the sorrow their fellow students felt at leaving "home." In our "curriculum of empathy," we forced our class to see these students as individuals rather than the ESL students or "Chinese" students, or an undifferentiated mass of Mexicans.

A curriculum of empathy puts students inside the lives of others. By writing, interior monologues, acting out improvisations, taking part in role plays, and creating fictional stories about historical events, students learn to develop understanding about people whose culture, race, gender, or sexual orientation differs from theirs.

"Things changed for me this year," Wesley wrote in his end-of-the-year evaluation. "I started respecting my peers. My attitude has changed against homosexuals and whites." Similarly, Tyrelle wrote "I learned a lot about my own culture as an African American but also about other people's cultures. I never knew Asians suffered. When we wrote from different characters in movies and stories I learned how it felt to be like them."

SHARING PERSONAL STORIES

Building community begins when students get inside the lives of others in history, in literature, or down the hallway, but they also learn by exploring their own lives and coming to terms with the people they are "doing time" with in the classroom. Micere Mugo, a Kenyan poet, recently said, "Writing can be a lifeline, especially when your existence has been denied, especially when you have been left on the margins, especially when your life and process of growth have been subjected to attempts at strangulation." For many of our students their stories have been silenced in school. Their histories have been marginalized to make room for "important" people, their interests and worries passed over so I can teach Oregon history or *The Scarlet Letter.*

To develop empathy, students need to learn about each others' lives as well as reflect on their own. When they hear personal stories, classmates become real instead of cardboard stereotypes: rich white girl, basketball-addicted black boy, brainy Asian. Once they've seen how people can hurt, once they've shared pain and laughter, they can't so easily treat people as objects to be kicked or beaten or called names. When students' lives are taken off the margins, they don't feel the same need to put someone else down.

Any reading or history lesson offers myriad opportunities for this kind of activity. I find points of conflict, struggle, change, or joy and create an assignment to write about a parallel time in their lives. We've had students write about times they've been forced to move, been discriminated against or discriminated against someone else, changed an attitude or action, worked for change, lost a valuable possession. Obviously, losing a treasured item does not compare to the Native Americans' loss of their land, but telling the story does give students a chance to empathize with the loss as well as share a piece of themselves with the class.

When I was a child, my mother took me to the pond in Sequoia Park on Sundays to feed the ducks. They'd come in a great wash of wings and waves while I broke the bread into pieces to throw to them. I loved to watch them gobble up the soggy loaf, but I began noticing how some ducks took more than others. In fact, some ducks were pushed to the side and pecked at. I've noticed the same thing happens in classrooms. Students find someone who they think is weak and attack them. In my fourth-block class, the victim was Jim. He'd been in my class the year before. I'd watched him progress as a writer and thinker. In his end-of-the-year evaluation, he drew a picture of himself as a chef; his writing was the dough. In an essay, he explained how writing was like making bread. He was proud of his achievements as a writer.

In both classes, Jim was a victim. He was going blind because of a hereditary disease. It didn't happen overnight, but he struggled with terror at his oncoming blindness. Because he was steadily losing his eyesight, he was clumsy in the classroom. He couldn't see where he was going. He knocked into people and desks. He accidently overturned piles of books. Students would respond with laughter or anger. Some days he cried silently into the fold of his arms. He told me, "I know the darkness is coming." Several male students in the class made fun of him for crying, as well. One day, Amber was in a typically bad mood, hunched inside her too-big coat and snarling at anyone who came near. When Jim bumped her desk on the way to the pencil sharpener and her books and papers tumbled on the floor, she blew up at him for bumbling around the room. Jim apologized profusely and retreated into his shell after her attack.

A few days later I gave an assignment for students to write about their ancestors, their people. First, they read Margaret Walker's poems,

"For My People" and "Lineage," and others. I told them they could imagine their people as their immediate ancestors, their race, their nationality or gender. Jim wrote:

To My People with Retinitis Pigmentosa

Sometimes I hate you
like the disease
I have been plagued with.
I despise the "sight" of you
seeing myself in your eyes.
I see you as if it were you
who intentionally
damned me to darkness.
I sometimes wish
I was not your brother;
that I could stop
the setting of the sun
and wash my hands of you forever
and never look back
except with pity,
but I cannot.
So I embrace you,
the sun continues to set
as I walk into darkness
holding your hand.

Students were silenced. Tears rolled. Kevin said, "Damn, man. That's hard." Amber apologized to Jim in front of the class. At the end of the year she told me that her encounter with Jim was one of the events that changed her. She learned to stop and think about why someone else might be doing what they're doing instead of immediately jumping to the conclusion that they were trying to annoy her.

My experience is that, given a chance, students will share amazing stories. Students have told me that my willingness to share stories about my life—my father's alcoholism, my family's lack of education, my poor test scores, and many others, opened the way for them to tell their stories. Students have written about rape, sexual abuse, divorce, drug and alcohol abuse. And through their sharing, they make openings to each other. Sometimes a small break. A crack. A passage from one world to the other. And these openings allow the class to become a community.

STUDENTS AS ACTIVISTS

Community is also created when students struggle together to achieve a common goal. Sometimes the opportunity spontaneously arises out of the conditions or content of the class, school, or community. During Bill's and my first year teaching together, we exchanged the large student desks in our room with another teacher's smaller desks without consulting our students. We had forty students in the class, and not all of the big desks fit in the circle. They staged a stand-in until we returned the original desks. One year our students responded to a negative article in a local newspaper by organizing a march and rally to "tell the truth about Jefferson to the press." During the Columbus quincentenary, my students organized a teach-in about Columbus for classes at Jefferson. Of course, these spontaneous uprisings only work if teachers are willing to give over class time for the students to organize, and if they've highlighted times when people in history resisted injustice, making it clear that solidarity and courage are values to be prized in daily life, not just praised in the abstract and put on the shelf.

But most often I have to create situations for students to work outside of the classroom. I want them to connect ideas and action in tangible ways. Sometimes I do this by asking students to take what they have learned and create a project to teach at nearby elementary or middle schools. Students in Literature and U.S. History write children's books about abolitionists, the Nez Perce, Chief Joseph, and others. After students critique the media, they are usually upset by the negative messages children receive, so I have them write and illustrate books for elementary students. They brainstorm positive values they want children to receive, read traditional and contemporary children's books, critique the stories, and write their own. They develop lesson plans to go with their books. For example, before Bev read her book about John

Brown she asked, "Has anyone here ever tried to change something you thought was wrong?" After students shared their experiences, she read her book. Students also created writing assignments to go with their books so they could model the writing process.

Students were nervous before their school visits. As they practiced lesson plans and received feedback from their peers, there was much laughter and anticipation. They mimicked "bad" students and asked improper questions that have nothing to do with the children's book: Is she your girlfriend? Why are your pants so baggy? Why does your hair look like that?

When they returned, there were stories to share: children who hugged their knees and begged them to come back; kids who wouldn't settle down; kids who said they couldn't write. My students proudly read the writings that came out of "their" class. They responded thoughtfully to each student's paper.

James, a member of my English 12 class, was concerned by the number of young children who join gangs. He and several other young men wrote stories about gang violence and took them to our neighborhood elementary school. He strode into the class, wrote "gangs" in big letters on the board and sat down. The fifth-grade class was riveted. He and his teaching mates read their stories and then talked with students about gangs. As James wrote after his visit:

> For a grown person to teach a kid is one thing. But for a teenager like myself to teach young ones is another. Kids are highly influenced by peers close to their age or a little older. I'm closer to their age, so they listen to me. . . . Some of these kids that I chatted with had stories that they had been wanting to get off their chest for a long time. . . . When I came to class with my adventures of being a gangster, that gave them an opportunity to open up. Spill guts. [No one] should object to me teaching these shorties about gang life, telling them that it's not all fun and games. It's straight do or die. Kill or be killed.

The seriousness with which the students understand their lives was in sharp contrast to the seeming apathy they displayed at the year's beginning. Through the year, I came to understand that the key to reaching my students and building community was helping students excavate and reflect on their personal experiences, connecting it to the world of language, literature, and society. We moved from ideas to action, perhaps the most elusive objective in any classroom.

Community and activism: these are the goals in every course I teach. The steps we take to reach them are not often in a straight path. We stagger, sidestep, stumble, and then rise to stride ahead again.

10

MR. B

William Ayers

William Ayers teaches at the University of Illinois at Chicago and writes about teaching and social justice. The following is a portrait of a remarkable teacher from Chapter 1 of his book, A Kind and Just Parent: The Children of Juvenile Court, *an ethnography of the oldest and largest juvenile jail in the world.*

———————

The door crashes open suddenly. "Morning, Mr. B." Rasheed springs into the classroom with a bright greeting.

"Good morning, Rasheed."

"Good morning, Ito."

"Morning, Mr. B," Ito mumbles, shuffling along to his desk. He collapses noisily into his chair, head in arms, and looks to be instantly asleep.

"Good morning, Jeff." Jeff hops in and moves manically around the room.

"Morning, Mr. B."

"Good morning, Freddie."

"Morning, Mr. B."

Eight young men burst or file or stumble into class today, each wearing dark green cotton pants and a white T-shirt with a simple drawing of an owl or a bluebird or a cardinal printed on the front, the standard-issue uniform for all residents in juvenile lockup. Only their gym shoes are distinctive, with status and style statements run rampant: Ito's shoes are old and beat-up; Rasheed's are red, white, and dazzling; Freddie's are full of gadgets, lights, and pumps; Jeff's are entirely spent.

Alonzo and LeMarque have excused absences today—each has a court date. Merce will be late—it's haircut day on his unit, and he'll come down in an hour. Oscar is on punishment—locked up on the unit for being drunk last week. Where did the liquor come from? No one knows for sure, perhaps his mother or another visitor, an attendant, a teacher. Alcohol and drugs are not prevalent here, but they are always a concern because, as in every other American high school, alcohol and drugs are available.

Today is opening day for the Chicago public schools, and so for the Juvenile Temporary Detention Center School it is also the official start of a new year. School has a predictable rhythm in our common memory: there is the opening in September, the holiday period from Thanksgiving through Christmas and the New Year, then the coming of Spring and graduation. The facts of life at Audy Home can overwhelm the familiar rhythms: court dates, students suddenly leaving, new kids abruptly arriving, transfers to adult prison. This opening, then, is neither as festive nor as promising as it might be: the school meets year round, the students are locked up in living units upstairs, and the break, never particularly restful for the kids, has been only a few days.

Mr. B is a big man with a square head and a chunk of body to match—massive chest, huge arms, rugged shoulders, and thick neck. Horn-rimmed glasses perch on the outcropping of his nose, a full salt-and-pepper beard provides a forest surround. Dressed in his customary uniform—dark slacks, flannel shirt, brown industrial apron—and settled at his desk in the center of the classroom, Mr. B is a volcano at rest.

Mr. B nods a greeting to me and there is the hint of a welcoming smile, mostly in his eyes. Mr. B wastes no movement, certainly no word. As is customary for him, he has been here since seven this morning and it is now almost nine. He works along silently. I take my place at a corner desk and begin to get organized . . . notebooks, folders, pens.

A slate-topped counter and storage island runs the length of the room and splits the body of the classroom from a smaller work area. Twelve indestructible plastic desks with matching chairs—bright blue, yellow, green—are set in rows; two more are isolated off to themselves in front of the counter. Windows run high along the far wall, but the light is not quite natural; it filters through the metal mesh that muffles every opening.

To the right, one door leads to a toilet and sink, another to a larger anteroom that serves as closet storage area, weight room, and relaxation center. Posters of cities at night (Chicago, New York, Los Angeles, San Francisco), each outlined and set off with an African kente cloth pattern, dominate one wall. A large chalkboard, a classroom clock, student essays and artwork, a neglected American flag in one corner, all the trappings of the imagined typical classroom, share space with an emergency phone system and a heavily secured door—a solid reminder that we are in detention. Temporary lockdown.

Willie Baldwin—Mr. B—has been here since the school opened in 1973. In twenty-two years of teaching he has fashioned an identity and a routine that suit him—solid, genuine, predictable. Participating in a writing exercise with the kids, he lists his last name as "Baldwin" and his first name as "Mr. B." The word among the kids upstairs in the living units is that Mr. B makes you work but that he also lets you play, that he listens carefully to you and that he wants you to learn, that he is firm but fair. A teacher and his classroom can resemble one another, and this space is unmistakably Mr. B's—businesslike, focused, and orderly, with bursts of color and latent possibilities.

The brief school vacation, while not protracted, does mean a few long days of unbroken time on the units. With nothing much to do, everyone watches TV for hour upon hour—almost six hours a day, twice the average for American teenagers. Boredom, depression, purposelessness, gloom covering rage accumulate. Twenty-two young men draped across chairs around the tube is an invitation to a collision, and everyone knows it. "I got in seven fights in ten days," laughs Ito. "Mostly I was locked up, which was OK with me."

"The place is a madhouse," says Mario, fine-featured with long, narrow sideburns and a soft pointy goatee, like a young Ahmad Jamal, "and I'm one of the lunatics." This is no vacation.

There is a palpable sense of relief as the students trickle into Mr. B's class. Coming back to school from their units is a break from the madhouse. There is nothing demonstrative, no lavish displays of affection, but Jeff seems incapable of *not* smiling at Mr. B, a big Cheshire-cat grin covering his face, and Andrew, serious, low-keyed, likable, carrying a large look of sadness wherever he goes, has more energy than he's had in months.

"Bathroom, Mr. B," says Jeff, heading toward the toilet.

"Bathroom," responds Mr. B.

"Counter, Mr. B," says Freddie.

"Counter," comes the seemingly automatic response as Freddie slips behind the counter to sharpen his pencil. Rasheed and Mario hover by the door, watching eagerly as the other students come down the hallway to their classes.

Andrew has pulled out a folder at his desk and is leafing through his papers, settling on a piece that he reads thoughtfully. Jesus is applying paint to a plaster mask he made earlier, before break.

"Back room," calls out Mario, aiming himself toward the weights.

"No," says Mr. B in the same quiet register, low-keyed, flat. "No, Mario."

"Yo, Mr. B. Why I can't go lift for a bit?"

"Remember what you told me Friday before the break?"

"What?"

"You said you'd finish your regular work for the day after painting," he says, referring to the ongoing, everyday assignments in math, science, English, and history he designs specifically for each student. "But your work isn't here. I want to see some work. I want you to finish your regular work, then take a break. Do you know what to do?"

"I ain't got my card, Mr. B," says Mario, pouting. "And that was so long ago."

"OK. It was long, long ago, but it's still got to be done. Do you know what to do?"

"Chapter twelve in science, I think. Chapter fourteen in history. Which numbers in history?"

"Do all the Roman numerals at the end. There aren't many in this chapter. Numbers one to three or one to four." Mr. B turns quickly to chapter fourteen. "Here it is. One to four."

"OK, Mr. B. I'll get it. Then can I lift?"

"Of course, Mario," he says, touching his shoulder.

The classroom is calm—peaceful—filled with a sense of quiet expectations. Ito has roused himself and is filling in a simple crossword. Rasheed has moved to a small utility table where he is working on a massive jigsaw puzzle that is only beginning to take shape. Jeff has returned from the bathroom, taken out some colored pencils, and is bent over a large piece of white construction paper creating what looks to be a vivid, flamboyant altar or memorial.

"Mr. B," says Jeff without looking up from his work.

"Yes, Jeff."

"Help, Mr. B." It is neither a question nor a demand, but a quiet declaration delivered in the same tone as "Bathroom," "Counter," "Back room." Mr. B moves over to Jeff's desk and kneels down beside him, his steady hugeness highlighted beside the slight and discombobulated Jeff, their heads bent together over Jeff's work, their voices in quiet conference.

"Should the top of these flowers be red, Mr. B?"

"What do you think?"

"I think yes, but I don't know if it look right."

"Mr. B," says Ito from his desk.

"Just a minute, Ito. I'll be over when I'm finished with Jeff's question." He turns back to Jeff's project. "Well, I like the red set off by this blue, and if you think yes, then I guess I agree with you."

"OK, Mr. B. What about these letters here?" He indicates a row of ballooning graffiti letters: "R.I.P. Lary."

"Now you're making me do most of the work," he smiles. "I thought you had a plan for it." Mr. B. strikes a neat balance between nurturance and challenge.

"OK, Mr. B," Jeff smiles back. "It's cool. They're black."

Mr. B moves on to Ito and again settles on to his knees beside him, one arm around the back of Ito's chair, the other on his desk. He envelopes Ito, leans close and listens.

"What's this mean, Mr. B? A-S-S-E-T-S? I looked in the dictionary and they had 'capital,' 'property,' and 'possessions.' I want a word that starts with 'M'."

"Did you look in the thesaurus?"

"No."

"Try that and I'll check back with you."

Mr. B gets up and checks in with Mario who is working away. He looks over Rasheed's shoulder at the jigsaw, puts his hand to his chin and furrows his brow in concentration for a moment, picks up a tiny piece and tries unsuccessfully to fit it in, quietly shakes his head, chuckles, and moves back to his desk.

"Gentlemen," he announces in his deepest voice, "ten more minutes of free time, and then we'll be reading *The Piano Lesson*." He pauses. "I will assign parts for today's reading in ten minutes." Rasheed looks up for a moment and then returns to his puzzle; everyone else simply continues.

The Piano Lesson, a play by August Wilson, had been the focus of English class for much of the summer. "I had hoped to have it finished before summer break," says Mr. B, "but one thing or another interfered. We'll finish it this week."

The story is straight and simple enough to begin: Boy Willie and a friend have driven from Sunflower, Mississippi, to Pittsburgh to Boy Willie's Uncle Doacker's house with a pickup filled with watermelons that they hope to sell off the back of the truck. Boy Willie wants to get enough money together to buy Sutter's farm back home. He has some money saved up; he should have just enough if he can add to that the money he will make selling watermelons, plus the profit he hopes to realize from his share of the family heirloom—an elegant upright piano with legs intricately carved in the manner of African sculpture, standing in Doacker's parlor.

Here is the conflict: Boy Willie's sister, Berniece, lives with her daughter in Doacker's house. Berniece is proper, staid, and careful while Boy Willie is raucous, wild, and mildly criminal. Berniece distrusts and dislikes Boy Willie, indirectly blaming him for the death of her husband three years earlier; when some men stealing firewood were interrupted by the sheriff, her husband had pulled a pistol. She adamantly refuses to sell the piano, which originally came into the family that owned her ancestors—the Sutter family—when they traded Doacker's grandmother and father for it. Doacker's grandfather, in his grief, carved likenesses of his wife and son on the piano's legs, and then kept carving until he had etched in wood every detail of the family's history—marriages, births, deaths, funerals. Years later, long after formal emancipation, Berniece and Boy Willie's father stole the piano to "free the slaves." After he hid the piano, he was cornered trying to escape town in an empty railway freight car; the boxcar was set ablaze by his captors and he and four hobos were killed.

"Gentlemen," Mr. B breaks in once more just as Merce arrives from upstairs. "Gentlemen, put your things away. We'll be reading from *The Piano Lesson* now. Later this week we'll be viewing the video of the play."

Rasheed and Andrew straighten their desks and pull out their books. Jeff calls out "Bathroom" and heads for the toilet again. Mario detours past the door to the hallway and stretches a look before cruising to his desk. Ito is drooping once more.

"OK." Mr. B pulls the collective attention to himself. "Let's sum up what's happened thus far."

"Sutter got drowned in his well," says Mario.

"Yes."

"And Boy Willie don't know who pushed him," he continues. "Could have been the Ghost of the Yellow Dog"—a reference to the men burned in the boxcar—"or someone else."

"And now," says Rasheed, "Boy Willie needs to sell that piano to buy Sutter's land. But Berniece wants to keep it."

"Why?"

"Because of the carvings in the legs, and because people died in that piano."

"People died in the piano?"

"Well, they died in the pictures," says Rasheed.

"And her daddy died stealing it," adds Andrew excitedly, "which wasn't really stealing."

"It wasn't?"

"Not the same as *stealing*, since the piano legs was carved by *their* family. In a way it was already theirs."

"And what are Berniece and Boy Willie to each other?" asks Mr. B.

"Brother and sister," says Andrew.

"Uh-huh," a chorus of assent.

"Mr. B?"

"Yes, Merce?"

"Mr. B, Berniece been mourning for her husband for three years. Is that too long?"

"Some would think so, and others would think not."

"It's not long," Antoine says quietly but firmly. His face, always tense, draws tight. "Three years is not too long if you love someone. You might mourn that the rest of your life. It could be a good thing. It could be good for her." Perhaps it is the seriousness with which Antoine asserts his position, or the fact that he rarely speaks at all, and now he has spread words across several sentences, or some shared sense of grief or rage, but no one disagrees. Several students nod, some to themselves, others openly in his direction.

"Yo, you right, man," says Jesus. "My little shorty's friend got killed more than three years ago, and I ain't never going to forget. Never. I don't want to forget him. It's a way of respecting him. Woo, woo, woo."

Mr. B points to a line in the play where Avery, the young man courting Berniece, asks her how long she intends to grieve for her dead husband, and she responds: "I'll decide." Again a chorus of assent from the students. "Right," says Jesus. "Me, I'm going to grieve. Others can do what they want. Each one's got to decide for theyselves."

"So you agree?" asks Mr. B.

"Sure, Mr. B," says Andrew. "She can decide, and, like Antoine said, it might be good for her to go on being sad for quite a while."

The students have come to like Berniece, to identify with her struggles even as they see parts of themselves more vividly in Boy Willie. Boy Willie is bad, he struts and swaggers, but they no longer object to playing Berniece and reading her lines, in part because her role is substantial and provides major spotlight time, and in part because she is, in her way, vigorous and plucky and tough—qualities they admire and long for. When Freddie had been Berniece he read in his labored way one of her rebukes of Avery:

> You trying to tell me a woman can be nothing without a man. But you alright, huh? You can just walk out of here without me—without a woman—and still be a man. That's alright . . . that's alright for you. But everybody gonna be worried about Berniece. "How Berniece gonna take care of

herself? How she gonna raise that child without a man? Wonder what she do with herself. How she gonna live like that?" . . . Everybody telling me I can't be a woman unless I got a man. Well, you tell me, Avery—you know—how much woman I am?

As he finished he broke into a huge smile and exclaimed proudly, "Whom! She zooms it back on him! She's equal, right?"

Today Mr. B says, "Here, Merce," pointing to a piece of dialogue in which Avery pleads with Berniece, and aiming, I think, to complicate matters, "read this."

Merce reads haltingly: "You got to put all of that behind you, Berniece. . . . Everybody got stones in their passway. You got to step over them or walk around them. You picking them up and carrying them with you. All you got to do is set them down by the side of the road. You ain't got to carry them with you."

The passage alludes to the great bluesman Robert Johnson's "Stones in my Passway," a reference these kids will miss. Still, the theme is apparently potent for them, for several voices rise up at once: "He right." "Yeah, but he's forgetting her pain." "Sometimes it's true."

"Merce," Mr. B interrupts again. "Merce, what do you think of what Avery says there?"

"Well," Merce frowns deeply, pulling the book close to his face. "There are some things you need to forget and there are some things you need to remember. It depends on the person, and I say let Berniece decide for her, and let Avery decide for him, and I'll decide for me."

"So which is it, gentlemen?" asks Mr. B. "Should you bring the past along with you or should you leave it behind?"

"You can't really leave it all behind," says Mario. "Because whatever happens, it's part of you. You got to deal with it some way."

"Naw," says Freddie, "you got to get up each day and say, 'Here I am world, a brand-new day.'"

"In your dreams, man," Mario responds. "In your dreams it's a brand-new day, but you're waking up in jail—the same old thing and what you did sitting right there with you."

"Yo," says Freddie, feigning hurt, "why you got to bring that up? I told you I didn't do it."

"Man," says Jeff quietly, "let's leave the past behind. Let's go on."

"All right, let's leave it at that for now," says Mr. B. "Let's see what parts we need for today's reading."

Mr. B assigns parts quickly and the reading begins. Mario is Boy Willie today, and he reads with flair and style: "She trying to scare me. Hell, I ain't scared of dying. I look around and see people dying every day. You got to die to make room for somebody else. . . . See, a nigger that ain't afraid to die is the worse kind of nigger for the white man. He can't hold that power over you."

After the reading I ask the students to write a short poem or poetry fragment focusing on themselves. I give them a structure to help them get started: the first line is your first name; next, write three words to describe yourself; then list in sequence something you love, something you hate, something you are afraid of, and something you hope or wish or long for; the last line is your last name. I give an example: Martin / courageous, nonviolent warrior / I love all people / I hate no one / I am afraid of war and violence / I hope for freedom / King.

This is how Mr. B responds: I am Mr. B / patient, observant, sincere / I love fishing / I hate meetings / I fear shortsightedness / I hope for success for all my students / Baldwin.

Merce, whose name is short for "Mercedes," "a sharp car my father hoped to buy one day, but never did," writes: My name is Merce / dark and tall / I love my freedom / I hate being locked up / I'm afraid of going back to the street and do what I was doing to get locked up / I wish I was out in the world and I hope for mercy / Hall.

And Rasheed: Rasheed / handsome, brave, silly / I love my family / I hate people telling me what to do / I fear death / I wish to be rich / Coburn.

Everyone reveals extravagant dreams for a future that is surely shrinking before their eyes: fame, fortune, fantastic moments. And just as uniformly, everyone fears the almost inevitable: conviction, time in prison, death.

Andrew / small, black, nice / I love my family / I hate fish / afraid of getting found guilty / I wish to go home / Johnson.

Ito / I love to girl love and be loved / I love freedom / I hate being down / I don't want to die in jail / I wish to be free / Lopez.

Oscar / I'm real quiet / I love my family / I hate being used / I'm afraid of nothing but guns / I wish to go home soon / Streeter.

The students feel the hold of history over their lives, live with ghosts and debts to be paid. The dream of going home soon is a constant companion, but its extravagance is measured in a simple fact: less than five percent of the scores of students who have passed through Mr. B's class in the past five years have gone directly home. They've mostly gone to "Little Joliet," to Cook County Jail, to Statesville, and to Menard to serve hard time, but not home, at least not right away.

These youngsters are all awaiting transfer to adult court, some petitioned by the state's attorney for transfer to adult court, others as automatic transfer students—or A.T.s—which means they are fifteen or sixteen years old and their charged offenses are felonies that the state of Illinois deems too serious for a juvenile proceeding; they warrant, instead, an automatic transfer to adult court. Until a few years ago such charges were murder, rape, armed robbery; now, with the list seeming to grow longer each year, dealing drugs near public housing projects, carjacking, carrying a gun to school. Going home? They seem at this moment to have a better chance of winning the lottery or being hit by lightning.

Here is Jeff: I am Jeff / black, scared, nervous / I love my mom / I hate being locked up / I am afraid of being long in prison / I wish for freedom / Baron.

11

ONE OF "THESE CHILDREN"

Monique Redeaux

Monique Redeaux is a doctoral student in Curriculum and Instruction at the University of Illinois at Chicago and a young public-school teacher in the city, not so far removed in age from the students in her classroom. When she witnesses the casual disregard for her students' lives, her identification with them is brought into sharp focus, and she comes face-to-face with struggles for recognition and justice—for herself as well as her students.

I am a black youth. I teach black youth. I am attentive to the way my students are described, portrayed, perceived. Because I teach "these children." And I am one of "these children."

I do not locate myself outside my practice. My experiences—as a black student in classrooms where race was never discussed except when we came to that one paragraph in the social studies book on the civil rights movement, as one of the only students of color in honors and advanced-placement courses, as one of five black students to graduate from a teacher education program designed to prepare teachers for "urban environments," as a teacher of low-income students of color tracked into the lower-level class—have influenced my cognitive and social development and inevitably seep into my teaching. But rather than distance myself from these experiences, I cling to them because they define me. They make me the teacher that I am and drive me toward the teacher I want to be. I embrace my vested interest in my work and argue that it makes me a more passionate and effective educator than someone who has only book knowledge.

As teachers and researchers, we are taught to be objective; to teach what we know, not who we are. But all teaching is autobiographical.

"Happy Birthday, Ms. Redeaux." Ellis handed me a small box.

"Oh, thank you," I said somewhat surprised. I was turning twenty-three, and was halfway through my first year of teaching seventh grade. It was only 8:00, but Ellis and I always arrived at school around 7:30. In fact, Ellis usually beat me to school. He would wait in the gym or by the security desk until I arrived to open our classroom. While we had a pretty good relationship due to our early-morning ritual, I had not expected a gift for my birthday. I was even more surprised as I opened the box and found a thin gold necklace with a diamond-shaped yellow topaz stone. It was beautiful. "Thank you," I said again, this time in a quiet, strained voice that was unsuccessfully trying to hold back tears.

Today, as I wear that chain, tears well up in my eyes for a different reason. Tears of sadness are immediately followed by tears of anger as I remember the newspaper headlines and the reports from TV journalists: "Police Investigation Says Officer Justified in Shooting Boy Who Pointed Gun at Officer;" "He refused to stop and take his hands out of his pockets and he subsequently raised the weapon and pointed it at the officer;" "The boy also matched the description of a robbery suspect."

The Cabrini-Green neighborhood was frantic. One of their residents, a thirteen-year-old boy named Ellis Woodland, had been shot three times by Chicago police. The police stated that Ellis was about to be questioned regarding a robbery that had recently taken place in the area. When he was asked to stop, they said, Ellis proceeded to raise a semiautomatic weapon at the officers, who then shot at him five times, hitting him three. On later review, the semiautomatic turned out to be a BB gun and witnesses argued that Ellis was not pointing the gun at the officers, but attempting to place the gun down on the ground. Whatever the case, a child was critically wounded, and a community with a history of bad relations with the Chicago police department was in an uproar.

When I heard the news, I looked down at the chain on my chest and imagined Ellis lying on the hot pavement as the police handcuffed his immobile body. I wondered if the Ellis I knew was, in fact, the one being described in the news. Was he the offender, the victim, the cause for what had happened? After all, as Police Superintendent Phil Cline remarked, "The police officer has seconds to make a decision when he sees that gun pointed at him." Regardless of whether the gun was pointed at the officers or if they simply saw Ellis reaching for the gun in an effort to put it down, the superintendent is correct: police officers only have seconds to make life-changing decisions. But something Ellis's father said while questioning the police board after the incident still rings in my ears: "As the father of that boy, I want to know one thing: Did his race or community play a part in that split-second decision?"

Ellis is black, young, male and a resident of a low-income housing project. To many in education, these criteria classify Ellis as an at-risk student: at risk of failing and/or dropping out of school, of being placed in special education, of being incarcerated, of being the victim of a homicide—the list of potential destinies continues. And statistically, these evaluative judgments are not without merit. It is a fact that black males drop out at higher rates than any of their counterparts, and the probability of school failure and/or dropping out increases exponentially when the black male is of low socioeconomic status. The same is true when examining the demographics of special-education placements and incarceration rates. These realities have led to increased efforts to supposedly help and assist this "endangered species."

Enter Ruby Payne. I first heard of Payne from a friend who teaches at a suburban high school that serves a high percentage of black youth from low-income backgrounds. My friend was quite disturbed by Payne's theories about the behaviors and characteristics of these particular students. According to my friend, Payne was a "self-proclaimed expert" on the "mind-set of poverty" using her limited personal experiences as the basis for broad generalizations.

As an educator within a school where 98 percent of the student body is low-income students of color, I decided I should take a look at education's latest phenomenon. I found that Dr. Payne holds workshops all over the country, has produced several bestselling books, and is the founder and president of her own publishing company, which distributes countless products—from CDs to audiocassettes to Simulated Classroom Scenarios (SIMS)—designed, she says, to help educators and professionals work effectively with children and adults who live in poverty. Her success demonstrates how much the field yearns for answers to the questions regarding how poverty and social class affect students in the classroom. But as I read Payne's work, I did not see answers—I saw insidious and pernicious problems. In fact, I was appalled. What had been accepted as doctrine by many teachers and administrators was Payne's assertion that there is a "culture" of poverty characterized by certain behaviors:

- **fun-loving** ("one of the main values of an individual to a group is the ability to entertain")
- **loud** ("the noise level is high, the TV is always on, and everyone may talk at once")
- **inherently criminal** ("the line between what is legal and illegal is thin and often crossed")
- **sexually deviant** (males are in and out in no predictable pattern)

Payne argues that since these behaviors hinder the success of people living in poverty, they must be taught how to behave in middle-class society. In addition, they must be taught to *want* to escape the grasps of poverty since, according to Payne, it is a position they choose to be in. As I read Payne's beliefs about how violence and prison are considered a part of life for people in poverty, I thought about Ellis. I thought of that split second in which the police officers had to make that decision. I wondered if they looked at Ellis and saw the person Payne describes: inherently violent, seeing "jail as a part of life that's not always bad." What if they, like educators all over the United States, were being fed Payne's stereotypes about children of poverty? And then one night as I casually surfed through Payne's Web site, through a list of workshops conducted by her and/or her representatives, I saw it. It virtually jumped off the page and held me in a choke hold: "Understanding Class for Law Enforcement: A Customized Workshop for Officers and Administrators." And I knew that I could no longer remain silent.

My subjectivity—the fact that I know and care for Ellis, worked with him on a regular basis, and am a black educator who works with the "culturally deficient" children Ruby Payne describes—does not weaken my work, but strengthens it. I occupy a unique position; I see things others cannot. While most can only read about Ellis and draw conclusions based on the media's portrayal of him, I am able to draw from my life, from everyday experiences with him. I can therefore locate inconsistencies that others cannot. While the papers describe a robbery suspect with gang affiliations and no respect for law enforcement, I can juxtapose this with the highly intelligent, soft-spoken young man who came to school at 7:30 every morning, carried my bags up the stairs, and drew cartoon characters for my bulletin boards. This insider's perspective, while not free of contradictions, makes for a more holistic and messy version of "reality"—where problems and solutions are not black and white and/or self-evident—but are different shades of gray, complicated, and subjective. It is this perspective that provides insight and understanding as it necessitates a cycle of inquiry, analysis, critique, and articulation.

This cycle must be perpetuated by us—city teachers. While Ruby Payne refers to the kids we teach as "those students," we understand that these are *our* students. And our students are indeed at risk: at risk of being labeled as "culturally deficient," at risk of receiving instruction that reinforces that they are inferior, at risk of being stifled by a system that would have us believe they need to be fixed because it is they and their communities that are broken. It is easier to diagnose them as having the problem than to indict the present social order, which is founded on the exploitation and exclusion of poor people of color.

As teachers, we must understand the history of American education. It has never been the goal of the American educational system to interrupt the cycle of poverty, alleviate crime, or equalize society. The educational system, like the criminal *in*justice system, is a billion-dollar industry. Ruby Payne, herself, is a self-made millionaire. She has made millions by situating poverty within the dominant narrative of cultural deficiency and individual choice. She is successful—not because her work has proven effective, but because it reconfirms the "reality" that it is, indeed, poor people of color who are the problem. Their situation, being poor and of color, makes them inherently at risk. But our students are not, in truth, inherently at risk of failure. They are, in fact, *the* risk. To provide these students, who are the majority in urban school districts, with a quality education runs the risk of educating a new generation of Malcolm Xs, Emiliano Zapatas, Assata Shakurs—a generation of critically literate persons who seek to eradicate systems of injustice rather than simply understand the framework.

Those who promote the master narrative of individual choice and accountability understand the framework. So they attack us first, the people who educate "these children." If they can influence our perceptions of who these students are and how they behave, they will inevitably affect students' beliefs of who they are and what they can achieve. So they convince us that our students are deficient, lacking completeness, but that we can help them out of their deprived state. They tell us that schools are the only places where students can learn the choices and rules of the respected middle class, and because we want so badly for our children to succeed, we busy ourselves with trying to assimilate them into a system that benefits from their exclusion and failure. We forget that it is the system that is flawed and attribute the defects to the children, their families, and their culture. We recognize these students as at risk and we vow to help them recover, to save them from their present condition, as long as they are willing to be saved. And in doing so, we forget that they are not sick. We forget that they are not lab rats or science experiments with universal characteristics and uniform behaviors. We forget that they are whole, not deficient or incomplete. And we forget that *these* children are *our* children.

Ellis's physical wounds have healed. His body has made a full recovery. But he will never be the same child as before. He has been robbed of his innocence, and his emotional wounds will take much longer to mend. Every day that I teach, I see potential Ellises and I am saddened.

I realize that as teachers, we can inflict wounds on our students that last longer than even Ellis's physical scars. We do this every time we teach to assimilate rather than liberate, every time we imagine our students to be broken and ourselves to be repairmen, every time we uncritically accept racist policies and ideologies, every time we forget that these children are our children.

We cannot afford to forget. Because we teach "these children." And we are "these children."

ARE THOSE REAL?

Anafaith Lubliner

Anafaith Lubliner is center director for SF Music Together in San Francisco and has been a teacher of theater, songwriting, and music in both public schools and community venues. Her coming-out story resonates with honest courage and the uncertainties that every teacher sometimes faces.

I can still remember the moment before I came out as a lesbian to my students. I was sitting on the dirty floor of the cafeteria/auditorium. There was that familiar strange aroma of garbage and kids. It was dark, with dingy faux-theater lighting. I looked around at their distracted faces, poking one another, thinking today would be just another day in acting class. I was anxious. But there was a little glimmer of hope. Hope that I was about to do something . . . good. Life-changing. They had no idea what was about to hit them.

How did I come to this decision? I came out because of a realization. I am an after-school theater teacher in the Mission District at César Chávez Elementary in one of the most gay-friendly cities in the country, possibly the world.

Now, let me tell you, scratch the surface of any school in San Francisco and you will find a large queer population—from the teachers, to any part of the administration. So many people have migrated to this gay mecca in order to be free and open about their sexual orientation. Yet here is the conundrum: while most of the people on the staff are out to one another, they are still closeted with the students and the parents. In general, we know who is a cross-dresser, who is a lesbian, and who is raising a son that has two daddies. But we're hush-hush when it comes to the students we see day in and out.

This may not seem so strange in Utah, but in San Francisco? Why would we be afraid here? This is the town where we see men in dresses and dyke lesbian leather daddies with their "boi" and we do not bat an eye. Yet the teachers and staff are still afraid to tell their students.

Why are we hiding from children? I believe the answer is internal. It is the inner child that still lives in the schoolyard—the child that has been bullied and pummeled into corners and hard pavement for being different. Too swishy, too butch, too, too, too anything . . . just too. We do not want to be teased, to be the weak one, to be taunted and humiliated again and again, or worse, to be the one totally left out. We are afraid if we are exposed, the parents, the teachers, and the kids will hate us. We won't be allowed to play with our friends anymore.

I came out because I finally decided that I did not want to let these old fears win. It was time for me to face the bully in the schoolyard. The day I made this decision, a student of mine made a gay slur toward another boy. Instead of responding immediately, I became numb and did not say anything at all. I froze.

Afterward, I was very disappointed in myself and tried to look at why I had been so unable to respond. Had the slur been toward any racial group, I would have acted immediately. Yet a gay slur hit my core: he was talking about me. This was when I realized the depth of my hiding. I had to take action. If I believe in freedom and equality for all, what better place to start than in my own classroom?

My first plan of action was to speak with the staff at Jamestown. I told my supervisor, Katie Brackenridge. I sat her down in the school therapy section, surrounded by little toys, African American and Latina dolls, and various stuffed animals. Katie was a phenomenal supervisor: sharp, strong, and an excellent educator. She still floored me with her response. Katie looked at me and immediately told me she would completely support me. She even offered to sit in with the kids when I came out. I was thrilled.

I also spoke with my teaching assistant, who was only fifteen and had been raised Catholic. She was intelligent and scrappy and the kids loved her, but her Catholic upbringing made me cautious. She quietly told me that she had been raised to accept everyone, that her uncle is gay, and that it was no big deal to her. She also offered to support me. This had been one of my anxieties around coming out in my school. So many children in the Mission District are raised in a Catholic or Christian environment, which I assumed was generally homophobic. Once again I was happily surprised. Together we picked a specific date.

When that day finally came, only half the kids showed up, so we decided to wait until my next teaching day. That was when the anxiety and tension began to build. I had to wait two more days!

Finally the day came. I sat in a circle with the kids, Katie, and my TA. My first line was "I need to talk to you all about something that upset me." They were immediately on alert, sure they were in trouble. I assured them they were not in trouble. Then I said, "There was something that one of you said that hurt my feelings. When I heard one student say to another student they were gay in a mean way, that hurt my feelings. Because you were talking about me; I am a lesbian."

Shocked looks, silence, gasps, and wide-open eyes.

"Who did it?" they asked, looking around.

"I am not going to say who did it, but does anyone have a question?" That is when the flood of questions began. Their curiosity was amazing.

Question: Who is the girl and who is the boy? Answer: We are both girls, no one plays the boy.

Question: Are you really a man? Answer: No.

Question: Do you kiss her? Answer: I don't talk about private things.

Question: At what age did you know that you liked girls? Answer: About eighteen.

Then, my favorite question: While pointing at my breasts, one girl asked, Are those real? Answer: Yes, my breasts are real, and I am a woman!

One student said, "That's OK, Ana, you are still the nice person you always were. . . ."

Then they asked why Katie was there. Katie said, "Because I want everyone to know I support Ana. She is gay, and it doesn't matter—she is still my friend."

Another student said, "My uncle is gay." A few others chimed in with stories about gay relatives, or how their parents relate to gay people. We were done.

Then the most extraordinary thing happened. Afterward, I was still anxious, my heart was tight, my breathing shallow. I was afraid that I would be rejected, thrown out of the house, so to speak. We went outside for our break, to let the kids play in the yard, and two of the girls kept on hugging me over and over, giving me "love bombs." It was as if they felt closer to me because I had opened up to them.

Then came the biggest surprise of all: the kids decided to improvise a play in a talk-show format. Here was the setup:

Title: *Bullies on the Playground*

Characters: An upper-class English girl, a Southern girl, a bully, best friend to the English girl, two talk-show hosts, a *gay character*, and the studio audience.

Story: Gay character and all the others had been mercilessly mistreated by the school bully. Characters come up to be interviewed by the hosts. One by one they tell the story of how they have been bullied. The bully comes onstage. The studio audience all began to boo. Then when the gay student is telling his story onstage, they all began to cheer. Then they all began to chant "Gay is good, gay is good." Then the bully apologizes to the gay kid and all of his other victims. The end.

It was unbelievable. I could not have planned it better myself. That was how the day ended.

The following week the resistance began. One of the children, Pablo (all of the children's names have been changed to protect their privacy), was absent the day I had come out. When he returned he came back to *Bullies on the Playground* being played out again. He began to turn the chant around into "Gay is bad," and some of the students joined in. We had to stop class to talk about it.

The honeymoon was over. It seemed like a metaphor for society. Often when there is an opening, there is also a closing down in fear.

It was not all easy after that. That same student, Pablo, was mysteriously and suddenly pulled out of my class. My own identity issues came up: I am married to a woman, and yet I consider myself bisexual. Should

I have come out as bisexual? Or would that have been too much for me? For the kids? I do not know. Maybe I was still hiding.

Still, the ice had been broken. They all expressed an interest in meeting my partner, Katrine. They were as intrigued with her being a juggler as with her being my partner. A week later I brought in Katrine to meet them, and as promised she taught them how to juggle. They all seemed both intrigued and shy. They were thrilled with the juggling.

My being out eventually faded into the background of plays and sets and regular day-to-day activities. I have since come out three other times, with varying degrees of drama.

Years later, the third time I came out, there was an interesting development. I told this new class that they could meet Katrine, as well. But Katrine was not able to make it that semester. Yet one student, Angelica, bothered me over and over. She was beyond fascinated: she was borderline obsessed. She bothered me every time she saw me. "When am I going to meet Katrine?" "When am I going to meet Katrine?" Finally Katrine came to a performance to meet her. When she met Katrine, Angelica was shy beyond belief.

Will Angelica be a lesbian? I do not know, but her level of interest made me believe that by coming out I had stirred some possible inner recognition in her. She also told me she wants to be a teacher. If she is a lesbian, she will have a role model of an out, gay teacher who was not ashamed of the fact that she loves a woman.

I believe without a shadow of a doubt this is the best lesson I have ever given.

THE CURIE 12: A CASE FOR TEACHER ACTIVISM

Katie Hogan

Katie Hogan teaches at the Social Justice High School in Chicago's Little Village neighborhood and is a tireless activist against racism and for immigrant, women's, labor, and queer rights. She is currently organizing an antiviolence campaign in her school's community. The following piece, in which Hogan reflects on her participation in an extended protest against a standardized test, shows that when justice is the question, there is always something urgent to be done.

"You know, we're all going to be sitting back here in three months grading these damn tests anyways."

That was Marty, getting some nervous laughter out of the group of twelve teachers gathered at the local Polish diner. Just one week earlier we had sat down in Sara Spachman's living room to write our justification for refusing to give the CASE, or Chicago Academic Standards Examination, to our students at the end of the semester. We had a solid argument against this mandated test, we had data to back us up, and we had the support of our department chair. What we didn't have was any known precedent for what we had just done. Teachers refusing to give a standardized exam mandated by the city? And in Chicago, a city with its education system run by the mayor? Come on. We were tiny bugs waiting to be stepped on. And we knew it. Yet what took place over the course of the last few months of 2002 was not a story of defeat. It wasn't a story of total triumph and transformation, either. It was just a simple story, one we might tell later to another colleague at a late-night bar. It started like this . . .

Beginning in 1998, ninth- and tenth grade core-subject teachers in the Chicago public schools were mandated by the city to give an end-of-semester test that supposedly assessed student progress. The idea for this exam was not necessarily a bad one. Systemwide students' scores on national exams like the ACT and SAT were dismal, and there was no common language around curriculum to help teachers to ensure quality instruction.

Enter the CASE exam. CASE was supposed to measure student learning according to state standards. Teachers and administrators, the board of education said, could use CASE scores as a means to gauge progress. Sounds good on paper, right? Yet CASE became another beast of standardized testing that measured not student progress, but the already existing inequities of the city's school system. Magnet school students did great. Non–magnet school students did poorly.

After watching my freshmen take the CASE during my first year of teaching at Curie, a 3,000-student high school on Chicago's southwest side, I felt the disillusionment and disappointment only a rookie teacher can feel. I knew my students were doing their best, and I knew they were all much better readers and writers than they'd been when they walked in my door the first day of class. Still, they looked at the test questions with confusion, and seemed to be panicking as they tried to get through the reading passages. What was going on?

I looked over the test and was shocked. Instead of a skills-based test using the Illinois learning standards, I saw a poorly written, content-based test that asked students seemingly random questions unrelated to the curriculum of survey literature. One question asked students to write an essay explaining the satire of a piece that was not satirical in the least. Who was writing this test? And who was benefiting from it? We had just spent four weeks of instructional time going over the material that was supposed to be on the CASE, and three days of actual test taking. How, I wondered, did this help my students? The answer was that it didn't.

I soon realized that I was not alone in my hatred of the CASE exam. Pretty much every teacher I knew loathed it. But when I asked why no one had done anything about it, I got at most a shrug, or a "You'll understand soon, kid." I was frustrated, angry, and most of all I felt like a fake. I had become a teacher to affect change and instead I was becoming complicitous in maintaining the systems of power that kept my students from achieving their dreams.

I began my second year in the classroom with a very clear desire to start fighting this test. One day in September another English teacher, Marty McGreal, and I had lunch. After joking around for a bit the conversation turned toward the CASE.

"Why doesn't someone just refuse to give it?" I asked Marty.

"We could." He smiled.

"No, I'm serious. We need some major movement or university to support us."

"It wouldn't be easy. You wouldn't be fighting just CPS, but the mayor's office, as well. Not to mention everyone who profits from this test."

"I just can't give it anymore," I said.

Marty stopped eating and looked at me. "Let's not give it," he said.

"Are you sure? We could be fired."

Marty's eyes flashed cold. "Yes, I'm sure."

From that lunchroom conversation our "movement" was born. I began mentioning to a few other teachers in the English department that Marty and I weren't going to give the test.

"What do you mean, you're not going to give the test? You have to give it," most responded.

"No, I'm serious. We're not going to give it. We're going to write up a press release with our evidence and send it to CPS and the papers."

The response was not quite as enthusiastic as we had hoped. While a few teachers quickly voiced their support, most looked away and pretended to do other work. And that's the part of this whole thing that I will never understand. Teachers stand up every day and inspire students with their words and presence. They work hours without pay beyond almost any other profession. They sacrifice their time, spirits, and energies for the education of youth, yet when it comes to expressing publicly their beliefs about testing you might as well be talking to a room full of sheep.

In the end only ten other teachers—all English teachers except for one social studies—decided to join our protest. I can remember clearly the moment we all signed our names to the paper. It was quiet in Sara's house. We were all scared. Those of us without tenure feared we could be fired without due process the day this letter hit the papers. For those with tenure it could clearly be seen as an act of insubordination and grounds for dismissal. Yet every teacher in that living room put their careers and livelihoods on the line that day. We weren't sure what to expect. The only thing we truly hoped for was a public discussion about the CASE.

The day the letter was received by CPS and hit every major Chicago newspaper our department was in chaos. People wanted to talk to the rebel teachers who wouldn't give the test. They wanted to know if we would handcuff ourselves to the doors if they tried to drag us out. CPS wanted an immediate meeting with our principal and those who had sent the letter. Students lined up by our desks to ask if that was really us in the newspaper and if we were really risking our jobs for them. My mother wanted to know if I was going to have to move back home after losing my job. I had never been so exhilarated.

Three factors clearly helped our claims. First, we had hard data supporting our assertion that the CASE exam did not improve instruction, but instead actually hurt student achievement. Second, we had let our administration know what we were planning to do ahead of time. Third, we elected Marty McGreal and Vera Wallace, two veteran teachers, as the spokespeople of the group to ensure we could not be attacked individually.

In the months that followed we had meeting after meeting with officials from Chicago public schools. They sent the heads of every department I could imagine over to the school to talk to us. But we refused to back down. We were prepared to be fired for this cause, so there was nothing they could threaten us with to which we couldn't say, "If that's what you need to do, then do it." We were on television, on the radio, and in local and national papers. Teachers from all over the country wrote and told us how proud they were. I stood in front of my students each day with a clear conscience.

"How do you know when to trust someone?" students have asked me.

"When their words and actions match," I would always reply.

For the first time in my short career as a teacher, my words of promoting justice and fighting for your rights matched my actions. The twelve of us were not fakes, and the students saw it.

In December, the central office suddenly issued a press release saying that the CASE exams were being discontinued—not just at Curie, but throughout CPS. And not just for the next round of tests, but permanently. In a system of over 600 schools, 26,000 teachers, and 400,000 students, twelve teachers had spoken out in a way that brought about systemwide change.

The new CEO of Chicago's schools, Arne Duncan, never gave credit to any movement to abolish the CASE, but we knew what it had taken. We celebrated at a local bar as we watched Vera and Marty on television responding to our victory. Even the librarian, who was never nice to anyone, put down a twenty for a round for the "Curie 12," as we had been dubbed. It was a good day to be a teacher in Chicago.

In the years since the fight to end the CASE, I have been asked to speak or write about my experience frequently. I have always maintained that teacher activism is the essential ingredient for student activism. We were not twelve overly sophisticated intellectuals who wanted to buck the system. We were not twelve angry teachers who wanted to tell CPS to shove it. We were just twelve regular teachers on different ends of the activism spectrum who wanted to end a really bad test. We never expected to win; we only expected to fight. Isn't that what we should teach our students every day?

For me, being a teacher is not a profession: it is my art, my craft, and my life. I want to walk through my life with thoughtfulness and courage. I want my students to see me acting in a manner that befits the sacredness of the profession. And I also want to remember that no job is worth having if it comes at the price of checking your beliefs at the door. If teachers are not willing to stand up for their students, who will?

14

DADDY IN JAIL

Tyehimba Jess

Tyehimba Jess is a poet, assistant professor of creative writing at the University of Illinois, and the author of leadbelly, *his first poetry collection. In this selection he brings an all-too-common reality to life with a spare but freighted dialogue between teacher and student.*

———————

the little boy was holding a 2×3 photo of a large black man dressed in blue. he was built, forearms and shoulders stretching the fabric of his jumpsuit, a wide grin under beard. eyes piercing beneath his dreads. he looked just like the crude pictures this fifth grader had drawn, a mix of squares, rectangle and line hunched over in solid colors. behind him and the open green of grass stood the gray brown towers, the bars, and wire. his father was in prison.

ma daddy sent me this picture. he always be writin me.

this boy is the best writer in the group of twenty, and the images he throws on paper sometimes threaten to stand up and breathe crayola color into the classroom, wreak a hurricane, and stomp out the door to face the city. the kid truly has a natural talent. and now he is showing me his world in kodak. photo framed by pink of his palm.

yep. he always be writin and stuff. he in california. i visited him last year.

i don't know what to say about dad in jail. i focus on the familiar. the writing.

so. what do you guys write about?

oh, he be talkin about history and stuff. he say always study yo history, and he talk about africa, how we was kings and queens, and how we was slaves. yup, he know a whole lot of stuff.

wow. well, that's good. that's good that you write back and forth and stuff.

uh huh. he say i need to learn to write better.

well, looks like you're doing a pretty good job.

the other boys at his table are leaning over looking at dad in jail.

damn. that nigga swole. he in cali?

yeah

my cousin in cali.

another voice cuts in

you know tyvonne? that boy in 206?

yeah, that big fo'head boy.

yeah. his daddy in cali too. in the joint

no he ain't. uh, i think it was joliet

o.k. you guys, what about your writing assignments? you can write about this if you want, but remember, you gotta write something.

i'm walking from their table, and i still see that small picture in that small hand. the boy's lips were smiling. he said: that's my daddy.

15

EVERYTHING FLOWERS

Lisa Espinosa

Lisa Espinosa is the mother of five, a seventh-grade teacher in Chicago's Pilsen neighborhood, and has published her work in Rethinking Schools. *She's an astute observer, an artist in the classroom, and a storyteller who can capture the transcendent magic in the dailiness of classroom life. In this piece, she traces her year-long efforts to connect with a particularly challenging student.*

"*Es la maestra!*" Jasmine yells up the stairs of her apartment building as soon as she opens the door and sees me. I can hear little feet scurrying around on the top floor and marvel that I really am "*la maestra*," the teacher. As I follow Jasmine up the dark, narrow staircase, I feel more like a tired and somewhat desperate student than someone who has come to teach. I am actually here hoping to learn.

Jasmine leads me into her family's crowded apartment with a look of embarrassment and curiosity. In my classroom she is a tough, angry seventh-grader; here she is suddenly transformed into a younger, softer self. The difference is startling. It's hard for me to reconcile this shy, timid girl with the fearless child I've struggled with so much in my class.

I wonder again what I'm doing here. Jasmine's family has a reputation in our school, and I've heard all the opinions and rumors from teachers, office personnel, and the parents of other students: "How could the mom let her daughters run around like that, fighting and doing no work?" "*Y tienen una boca.*" "I think there is another daughter who already has a baby." "Do they even have a father? I've never seen a dad." "If they were my daughters, I would. . . ." No one ever seems to finish that thought, but it's clear they all think they would do something different. They only have minimal interactions with Jasmine, though. I have her in my class all day, every day, along with twenty-nine other students, and right now I am mostly feeling mentally and physically exhausted.

Inside Jasmine's apartment, little kids seem to be coming from every direction. She has five brothers and sisters and a baby nephew who are all curious and excited about a teacher visiting them. I remember that I am carrying a bag of *pan dulce* I brought for Jasmine's family and I offer it to them. A quick suspicious look crosses Jasmine's face and I see the first sign of the girl I know: she detects B.S., bribery, and threats a mile away. Jasmine only respects honesty and openness, and even then you have to know her well to be able to spot her grudging respect. I can almost read her mind: *If she thinks I'm going to be nice to her because she brought bread . . .* No, Jasmine. I've learned. After four years of teaching I've learned that it's not like in the movies. There's no guarantee that things will get any better after this visit. They might, in fact, get worse.

When I started teaching, I was eager to meet the challenges presented by students like Jasmine. I chose to work in a predominantly Latino community because I feel a strong connection to it. Like the majority of the families of the kids I teach, my parents immigrated from Mexico. I was born and raised in Chicago and attended public schools. My elementary and high school experiences were not good ones, however. I had mostly unremarkable teachers with a couple of awful ones mixed in. In grammar school I was a successful student by many measures—I excelled on standardized tests, I was placed in the one elite gifted class, and I was the only student from my school to attend a selective magnet high school. My teachers deposited information, and I was able to spit it back out: no real thinking, just regurgitation.

It wasn't until I was in college that I became aware of, and then angered by, the way I'd been taught. Several classes and books helped me begin to critically analyze my own schooling. I noted the biased curriculum, which offered only one side of every story, the absence of lessons on the Chicano movement or other aspects of my history and culture, the various attempts to make me less Mexican and more white. Even more upsetting to me, though, was the absence of any meaningful connections with my teachers. I suppose I was easy to ignore—unlike Jasmine, who screams and stomps in order to be heard, I was a lonely, quiet girl. In high school I was lost in every sense of the word. I couldn't find my way around the immense school I attended, and I couldn't find my identity or my voice. I felt like an outsider and became disengaged, cutting and failing classes. Still, no teacher made an attempt to reach out.

So yes, when I became a teacher I was determined to do things differently. I would teach my students to think critically. I would validate their voices and experiences and expose them to different perspectives. But most of all I would get to know them. I would be a meaningful presence in their lives. Looking back on it now, I see that I was somewhat naive about the type of impact I might have with my students. I believed my personal experiences and passion would be enough. I underestimated the challenges I'd face working in city schools. My education classes hadn't prepared me for the overcrowded classrooms and lack of resources. And my professors hadn't told me that I would often feel shut out of the decision-making process in my school, that in meetings and mandated professional development I would be talked at, receiving information that too often made little, if any, educational sense.

By the time Jasmine entered my classroom in my fourth year of teaching, my idealism had been tempered by experience. I had learned that the results of my efforts with individual students were not going to be seen right away, or maybe at all. I had also begun to learn that I had overestimated my natural connection to this community. It was true that my students and I shared cultural connections and this provided me with important insights into their lives. But that didn't mean I always saw the whole picture. Paulo Freire writes of "entering into communion" with those you are trying to serve, and I had assumed that as a Latina woman I was already in communion with my students. Jasmine helped me see that I had a lot to learn.

Jasmine's mom welcomes me, and we sit at the table. She looks tired. She spends a couple minutes unsuccessfully trying to get all the younger children to move to another room so we can talk. Finally, one of Jasmine's older sisters, Marta, takes them all out. Jasmine sits close to her mom, their shoulders touching. It's obvious that they love each other and are comfortable with physical closeness, and this surprises me. I realize, suddenly, the depth of my assumptions about this mother. I had pictured a woman who couldn't connect with her daughter, who didn't give her the affection and attention she needed. But watching them, I realized that there was so much that I didn't understand.

"How is this girl behaving?" Juanita, the mom, asks in Spanish. She speaks no English, and I am thankful that I am fluent in both languages.

"Well, she's still having a lot of difficulties," I say, thinking to myself what a gross understatement that was. "She gets very angry."

"I know. I tell her that sometimes she looks like a crazy woman."

Jasmine starts to laugh. I am again taken aback by how different she is here. Her laughter is so carefree—far different from the laughter I heard in my classroom earlier that day.

When Jasmine is in a certain mood her laughter sounds angry and violent. She sounds like her mom often says, *una loca*, a crazy woman. I had been in the middle of helping another student, Nayeli, with her reading when Jasmine's loud laughter erupted. When I turned to look at her, she stopped laughing but shot me a defiant look. This is a game Jasmine and I have played many times before. Sometimes a look from me is enough to calm her down. Sometimes ignoring her works. Other times I threaten to call her mom or, as a last resort, send her to the office. It's exhausting. Still, the most serious episodes happen when I'm not around: a fight entering the school building, another one in the classroom on a day I was absent, a shouting match on the playground after school.

This time I decided to ignore Jasmine and keep working with Nayeli. But a few seconds later I heard the explosive laughter again, and the look on Jasmine's face told me that I *had* to give her my attention—she was going all out today.

"This is boring!" she yelled and threw her work on the floor. I told her to go with me into the hall, which doubles as my office, the place where I somehow manage to counsel students while half of my body—and one of my eyes—is still in the classroom monitoring the others. I knew I needed to get Jasmine there as quickly as possible before it got worse, but I made one fatal mistake: on the way out we passed Melvin's desk. Melvin, whose dad has left his family again, who has his own pain and anger, and is particularly good at pushing Jasmine's buttons.

"What?" Jasmine yelled at Melvin.

Melvin looked at me saying, "I didn't do anything."

Whatever he didn't do, he apparently did again, and Jasmine yelled, "Oooh, I swear I'm gonna kick your fucking ass."

"Jasmine—in the hall!" I said, placing my body in between her and Melvin. She looked at me, all the anger she has at the world contained in that one look, and finally left the room. "Jasmine, I'm going to call Mr. Simon," I said. "We had an agreement and you are not following it."

"Go ahead. I don't care."

I didn't really want to call the school disciplinarian, because Mr. Simon's main concern is following the system's uniform discipline code—a small booklet that contains all the infractions students might commit along with "appropriate" consequences. They are all labeled in code: 1-2, 2-3. Mr. Simon has memorized a lot of them and often speaks in code, making it sound like he's dealing with prisoners, not students. But as much as I didn't want to bring him in, I knew Jasmine couldn't go back into the room. Whatever had set her off, she wouldn't be able to regain control. And my other options for dealing with the situation were limited: this school of 1,000 students (that was built for 700) has one counselor who spends almost all her time working on testing, not seeing kids, and one social worker who works with three different schools and is only available after you've completed the "necessary paperwork." So my only resort was to call Simon.

"This is a four-dash-two," he told Jasmine after he arrived. "You can be suspended. Do you understand that, princess?" Jasmine stayed quiet. "Answer me—I don't have time for this. Do you want to be suspended?" At this point most kids would be crying or groveling but Jasmine is not like most kids. Simon understood this and began trying to back out of enforcing the suspension, probably because he realized he would be in charge of her. "Ms. Espinosa," he said, "what do you think we should do?"

I answered in my head: *I think there should be a safe place where she can go to calm down. And some regular counseling should be initiated to help her deal with all the issues she has. I also think I should have less students and more bilingual support and regular special-education services.* But I didn't say any of that. Instead I said, "I think Jasmine needs to be taken out of the room and she needs to come back when she's ready to learn."

Jasmine looked at me as if I'd said the stupidest thing in the world, and Simon took her down to his office. I understood that it was just a small Band-Aid on a gushing wound, but I didn't know what else to do. Later in the day, Jasmine returned. I tried to talk with her before she came into the classroom but she refused to make eye contact with me. She was quiet for the rest of the day, but I could see that she was hating me.

Now, in her apartment, she is sitting across from me and the anger seems far away. I consider relating the incident to her mom, but that's not what I'm here for. Instead, I ask the mom again about counseling for Jasmine.

"Yes, teacher," she says. "But Jasmine and Marta say they don't need it. They gave us the name of a place but Jasmine doesn't want to go."

"Who first sent them to counseling?" I ask.

"In court—after what happened."

I don't know what she's referring to, and I tell Juanita it might help if I did. She looks at Jasmine, who shrugs her shoulders and tells her mom it's OK to tell me.

"Well, it was after Jasmine was in fifth grade," Juanita begins. "Her and Marta were going to summer school. They would walk there with another girl. I didn't know that some guys—"

"How old?" I say, interrupting.

"Twenties," Jasmine says. "One was older, like in his thirties."

Juanita continues. "Well, these guys had offered Marta and this other girl money if they would go to their house to wash clothes."

At this point I start to feel sick and selfishly wish I had never asked.

"I didn't know, they didn't tell me anything," Jasmine's mom says emphatically. I nod that I am hearing her. "So Jasmine, Marta, and this other girl went to these guys' basement apartment on their way to school."

I look at Jasmine and she is staring into space. I wonder if she is seeing this play out in her head or if, in her mind, she is far away.

"Well, two guys took Marta and the other girl and they raped them," Juanita says. "They kept Jasmine in the main room with the older guy. He didn't rape her—he only touched her but he didn't rape her. But she could hear everything they were doing to Marta and the other girl."

I listen to her mom finish the story. For the first time since I've known Jasmine, I'm glad she is angry.

That first visit to Jasmine's apartment led to many more throughout that school year. Trying to get Jasmine counseling was a recurring theme in my conversations with her mother. Although she wasn't against her daughters going to counseling, she was also certain that with enough discipline and motivation they could get past what happened. "They don't need to let what happened to them ruin their lives," she would often say. "They aren't little kids anymore. They need to take responsibility." I was always careful not to sound like I was judging her but I kept insisting that what happened had long-term effects. The girls needed some help. However, short of driving Jasmine to counseling myself, I couldn't figure out how to make it happen.

In school I asked about the possibility of Jasmine seeing the social worker. I was relieved to discover that she had been referred previously, but my hopes were dashed when I received a memo that outlined Jasmine's new schedule with the social worker: she would be seen for twenty minutes per month.

I understood that, as a social worker for such a large system who split her time among three schools, Mrs. Hurtado was overwhelmed. But it was frustrating and disappointing to see how little she was able to help—and sometimes I felt she actually made things worse. Once, in a meeting with Jasmine, her mother, and me, Mrs. Hurtado suggested that what Jasmine really needed was medication since counseling obviously was not helping.

"Medication?" I practically shouted. "She hasn't received any consistent counseling since this began. You can't suggest medication if counseling hasn't been given a chance."

Mrs. Hurtado then turned to Jasmine. "A lot of girls go through what happened to you and they keep going," she said. "They don't start doing bad things. If you got hit by a car, you wouldn't let that stop you and use it as an excuse to be a failure."

I couldn't believe what I was hearing and I spoke up. "Jasmine, Mrs. Hurtado is right that many girls go through what you went through and heal from it. But they need help to do it. You need help and it needs to be consistent." I turned to her mom. "In my opinion, looking at medication doesn't make sense. We don't know that counseling hasn't worked because it hasn't been given a fair chance."

Jasmine's mom agreed. She told Mrs. Hurtado she wanted her to continue meeting with Jasmine. It was the smallest of victories.

My year with Jasmine was filled with moments where I felt powerless. I'm sure she did, too. So many situations were beyond my control. And finding the time to devote to Jasmine—with my other students, my own children, and a master's class also needing my attention—was extremely challenging. Still, I did what I could, though it always seemed insufficient. I knew that providing a safe place for Jasmine in my classroom was important. I also began picking her up once a week before school to have breakfast at a local coffee shop. Jasmine was intimidated by the menu at first, but she soon found her favorite combination: "Café mocha and a scone please," she would always say.

One morning toward the end of the summer, I asked her about a program she had been involved with the previous year.

"It's a lot of fun," she said. "They take us to the Botanic Gardens, and teach us about plants and stuff."

I wish everybody could see Jasmine like this, I thought. Happy. Carefree.

"Teacher, I don't want to go to eighth grade," she said suddenly. "It's going to be so hard."

"You won't be alone, Jasmine. I'll still be close by, just a couple of rooms down. And Mr. MacDonald is a great teacher. You'll like him." I had already begun arranging for her to be in his classroom, but with the end of the year approaching, I couldn't help wondering how much I had really helped her, how much of an impact I'd had.

Again I thought of my own journey. I knew that one of the most powerful lessons anyone had taught me was to remind me of my innate goodness. It's like the words of a poem I read recently: "Everything flowers, from within, though sometimes it is necessary to reteach a thing its loveliness." *Reteach a thing its loveliness.* Those words articulate so perfectly what I believe we as teachers are sometimes called to do. For Jasmine, and all the other students like her whose experiences have made it hard for them to see their goodness, we must be that constant reminder: you are lovely, you are lovely, you are lovely.

16

LESSONS FROM TEACHERS

Lisa Delpit

Lisa Delpit is a MacArthur "Genius Grant" awardee and executive director of the Florida International University Center for Urban Education and Innovation. A leading voice among urban educators, she is the author of the classic Other People's Children: Cultural Conflict in the Classroom, *and her many influential articles have been read and reprinted widely. In the following piece, she draws upon her extensive experience working with city schools to offer ten precepts for urban teachers.*

When I teach worn-out new teachers every Thursday at 5:30 in the evening, it breaks my heart to see the stress outlined around their eyes and the corners of their mouths. They seem so tired. On some days, some of them have been crying. I have come to know about their own children who make demands on their nonexistent time. I have come to know about their ailing parents for whom they are the sole caretakers, about their husbands who have had heart attacks, about their upcoming marriages or divorces, about the problematic pregnancies they are experiencing, or about the new babies who catch cold after cold.

And then, I hear about the parents of their students who don't care or about the children who are disrespectful, uninterested, cannot read, constantly talk, or always get into fights. And although my heart aches for the difficulties these hardworking teachers are facing, I find I must challenge their interpretations of the children and their parents and challenge them to look beyond what they think they see in parents and students to what they may see in themselves. I find I must add what must initially seem like more stress to their already stressful lives as I ask them to change their patterns of behavior and dig deep to become the teachers I know they can be—the teachers who can change the lives of the poor children of color that they teach and subsequently, the failing schools of this country's cities.

There is much talk about the problem of urban education, much research to study the problem, and many policies enacted to address the problem but little belief that anything will ever really change. After all, that little voice constantly asserts itself between the lines of the research reports, the policy documents, and the energetic beginning-of-school pep talks, saying we cannot change the community, we cannot change the parents, we cannot change the crime, the drugs, the violence. But despite mutterings to the contrary, I know that there are things that we can do, because I have seen them make a difference. I have seen children who, based on their socioeconomic status or their ethnicity, were expected to score at the bottom of their respective districts on standardized tests score, instead, they have scored in the top 10 percent of their state. Educators have proven this over and over again. For example, the Marcus Garvey School in Los Angeles, California; the Chick School in Kansas City, Missouri; Harmony-Leland in Cobb County, Georgia; and the Prescott School in Oakland, California, among many others, have all educated low-income African American children who have performed at higher levels on mandated standardized tests than schools serving the most affluent students in their respective districts (Hilliard, 2003).

Sankofa Shule, a public, African-centered, charter school in Michigan, has produced low-income African American students who are reading from two to four levels above grade level, who are doing algebra and calculus in grade school, and who outscored Lansing School District and the state of Michigan on the state-accountability test (MEAP) in 2000 in mathematics and writing. The school was called "an educational powerhouse" by *U.S. News and World Report* in its April 27, 1998, issue (Rivers, 2003).

When I share this information with my young teachers, I try to help them understand what needs to happen in schools to approach such results. They, like most others in the educational enterprise, tend to believe that there is some magic program out there that will solve their problems. My friend and colleague Martha Demientieff, a gifted Alaska Native teacher, says that we all seem to be waiting for some new program to ride in on a white horse and save us!

The reality is that we can actually save the children we teach and ourselves, regardless of which instructional program we adopt. With changes in attitudes and actions in classrooms, without the need for outside experts, we can change what happens in schools and we can change the lives of our students. I have tried to talk about these changes in ways teachers find not so overwhelming. The following is my attempt to codify the information gleaned from my own teaching, from my colleagues' or my own research, and most important, from what I have learned from watching and talking with extraordinary teachers who regularly perform magic. These teachers have taught me the following lessons.

SEE THEIR BRILLIANCE: DO NOT TEACH LESS CONTENT TO POOR, URBAN CHILDREN BUT INSTEAD, TEACH MORE!

So often in the belief that we are "being nice," we fail to realize the brilliance of our students and teach down to them, demanding little. In an insightful study titled "Racism Without Racists: Institutional Racism in Urban Schools," Massey, Scott, and Dornbusch (1975) found that under the pressures of teaching and with all intentions of being kind, teachers had essentially stopped attempting to teach black children. They showed how oppression could arise out of warmth, friendliness, and concern through a lack of challenging curricula and evaluation. Carter G. Woodson (1933/2000) wrote in his book *The Mis-Education of the Negro* that

> The teaching of arithmetic in the fifth grade in a backward county in Mississippi should mean one thing in the negro school and a decidedly different thing in the white school. The negro children as a rule come from the home of tenants and peons who have to migrate annually from plantation to plantation looking for light which they have never seen. The children

from the homes of white planters and merchants live permanently in the
midst of calculations, family budgets, and the like which enables them
sometimes to learn more through contact than a negro can acquire in
school. Instead of teaching such children less arithmetic, *we must teach them
more than white children.* (p. 4, italics added)

As in Woodson's world of 1933, today's middle-class children acquire a great deal of school knowledge at home. Those children who do
not come from middle-class families must be taught more to "catch
up." If children come to us knowing less, and we put them on a track of
slower paced, remedial learning, then where will they end up?

Teaching to state-mandated tests exacerbates this dilemma. By illus-
tration, when I visited a small, private school, the three- and four-year-
olds ran up to me eager to share what they had learned that week. They
showed me pictures and told me all about the structure of the middle
ear. One of them had a hearing loss, so they were all studying what that
meant. They could name all the parts of the ear and told me how the
brain processed sound. When I went up to the first- and second-grade
classroom, those children, too, were eager to share. They were studying
the constellations and had taken a trip to the planetarium so that they
could learn to identify them in the night sky. They were learning the
stories and myths that several cultures connected with various constellations. They were also writing their own myths about the star patterns
they saw at night.

When I go to inner-city schools, the children are just as excited to
share their work. However, they show me their handwriting papers,
their test-oriented workbook pages on subject-verb agreement, or their
multiple-choice responses to reading comprehension paragraphs.
These latter children may well improve their scores on the state-
mandated tests that ask them to prove they know such things, but which
children are receiving a better education? Which will have discovered
information that will give them the opportunity to become doctors, as-
tronomers, or writers? Which ones are likely to have the background
information college texts will demand?

ENSURE THAT ALL CHILDREN GAIN ACCESS TO "BASIC SKILLS"— THE CONVENTIONS AND STRATEGIES THAT ARE ESSENTIAL TO SUCCESS IN AMERICAN SOCIETY

What we call basic skills are typically the linguistic conventions of middle-class society and the strategies successful people use to access new information. For example, punctuation, grammar, specialized subject vocabulary, mathematical operations, five-paragraph essays, and so forth are all conventions. Using phonetic cues to read words, knowing how to solve word problems, determining an author's purpose, and finding meaning in context are all strategies. All children need to know these things. Some learn them being read to at home. Some learn them writing thank-you notes for their birthday presents under their parents' tutelage. Some learn them, as Woodson (1933/2000) suggested, just living in a middle-class home environment. Those who do not learn them before they come to school depend on school to teach them.

But this does not mean that we can do so by teaching decontextualized bits of material and expect children to learn how to function in the world. Answering fill-in-the-blank questions or focusing solely on the minutia of learning will not create educated people.

One evening when my daughter was in first grade, she had a homework assignment to write three sentences. She was a child who loved to write, so I did not anticipate any problems with the assignment. We discussed topics she could write about—her grandmother's upcoming visit, her recent birthday party, or the antics of her two new kittens. As she began to write, the telephone rang and I walked away to answer it. After finishing the phone call, I came back to see how she was doing. She informed me that she was finished and gave her notebook to read what she had written—"The dog can run. The boy is tall. The man is fat." I was puzzled by the lack of any personal significance in her words and finally responded, "That's really great, Maya, but what happened to writing about your grandmother or the party or the kittens?" My six-year-old looked patiently at me and said with great deliberateness, "But Mom, I'm supposed to write *sentences!*" Still trying to get a handle on her perspective, I asked, "Maya, what are sentences?" She responded quickly, "Oh, you know, Mom, stuff you write, but you never would say." "Ah so."

This teacher had, I am sure inadvertently, taught that sentences were meaningless, decontextualized statements you find in workbooks and on the blackboard that "you never would say." Written work in school was not connected to anything real, certainly not to real language. As all good, experienced teachers know, there are many ways to make school feel like it is a part of real life. Spelling words can be taken from stories children write in invented spelling. Grammar conventions can be taught as they arise in the letters children can write to their sports heroes or in the plays they might write to perform for the class. Strategies can be taught in the context of solving community problems, building model rockets, reading the directions for new board games, or learning to summarize and simplify a concept into a form appropriate for teaching it to a younger child. Strategies and conventions must be taught, but they must be taught within contexts that provide meaning.

WHATEVER METHODOLOGY OR INSTRUCTIONAL PROGRAM IS USED, DEMAND CRITICAL THINKING

There is evidence that a number of instructional approaches may "work" for children in urban settings who might not be expected to succeed. Whatever approach or methodology is implemented, however, one factor that is necessary for excellence is that children are demanded to think critically about what they are learning and about the world at large. A key word here is *demand*. Many times it will not initially feel comfortable for students who have previously been asked solely to complete workbook pages. Yet many children, especially African American children, need and expect the teacher to push them. "To," as one young African American man said, "*make* me learn."

Famed mathematics teacher Dr. Abdulahim Shabazz has successfully taught students who came to college with deficits in mathematics at three historically black universities. During the period from 1956 to 1963, while he was chair of the mathematics department at Atlanta University, 109 students graduated with master's degrees in math. More than one third of those went on to earn doctorates in mathematics or math education from some of the best universties in the United States. Many of the original 109 produced students who earned Ph.D.s in math. Nearly 50 percent of the African American Ph.D. mathematicians in 1990 in the United States (about 200) resulted in some way from the original 109 Shabazz master's students (Hilliard, 1991). Shabazz says that a significant percentage of the original 109 began with serious academic deficits in math and language arts. His slogan has always been, "Give me your worst ones and I will teach them." How has he done this?

In an interview with Dr. Asa Hilliard (1991), Shabazz made it clear that SAT and ACT scores have almost no meaning for him; instead, he has focused on a set of excellence-level goals that have shaped his approach to dealing with all students. His goals are

- To teach understanding rather than merely to teach mathematical operations;
- To teach mathematical language for the purpose of communicating in mathematics and not merely as a way to solve textbook problems;
- To teach his students that math is not at all a fixed body of knowledge but that it is an experimental enterprise in the truest sense of that word and that their approach to the solution of mathematical problems then and in the future should be to try a variety of strategies;
- To have students believe as he does that mathematics "is nothing more than a reflection of life and that life itself is mathematical." He wants them to know that the symbols used in mathematics approximate the reality of human experience and cosmic operations; and
- To give his students a sense of hope that they can become superior performers. (Hilliard, 1991, p. 23)

This is a testament to demanding critical thinking—not to accept anything as a given but to understand one's own agency in the process of education and connect teaching and learning to the students' own worlds. Other successful teachers have adopted various versions of this thinking strategy to their own subject areas and to varying ages of students. Carrie Secret, a phenomenal teacher of low-income African American elementary students in California, presents complex material to her charges by reading to them and having them listen to recordings of famous African American speakers. In one series of lessons, she has third graders re-create a sermon of famous minister Jeremiah Wright as a dramatic performance. The sermon is not written for children and is full of difficult vocabulary and complex metaphorical allusions. She and the children define the vocabulary together, delve into the metaphors, and explore the meaning of each line of the often-complicated text. The students write about how the text connects to their own lives and explore how the messages in the sermon connect to other literature they have studied. Only after exhaustive study do the children then "perform" the text for parents and for other adults. I have seen one of their performances and know firsthand why they routinely move their audiences to standing ovations, shouts of approval, and tears of pride. These children know what they are talking about, know what it means to them, and know how to make others believe it.

Although we sometimes seem to act to the contrary, there is no real dichotomy between teaching basic skills and insisting that children learn to think critically. As with Shabazz's and Secret's students, when we teach appropriate conventions and strategies within the context of critical thinking, we can produce the educated people we strive for. To quote my own previously published work,

> A "skilled" minority person who is not also capable of critical analysis becomes the trainable, low-level functionary of the dominant society, simply the grease that keeps the institutions which orchestrate his or her oppression running smoothly. On the other hand, a critical thinker who lacks the "skills" demanded by employers and institutions of higher learning can aspire to financial and social status only within the disenfranchised underworld. (Delpit, 1995, p. 19)

PROVIDE THE EMOTIONAL EGO STRENGTH TO CHALLENGE RACIST SOCIETAL VIEWS OF THE COMPETENCE AND WORTHINESS OF THE CHILDREN AND THEIR FAMILIES

Children are particularly susceptible to the media's assaults on the intelligence, morality, and motivation of people who look like them. The general notion in this country is that children who belong to stigmatized groups are "less than" their middle-class, lighter skinned classmates. Children readily internalize these beliefs about themselves. I was once working with a young girl who had failed to learn multiplication. When I announced my intention to work with her on the topic, she looked at me and said, "Ms. Lisa, why are you doing this? Black people don't multiply, they just add and subtract. White people multiply." Were it not for the poignancy of her statement, it would be funny. Here is a child who set severe limits on her potential based on a misguided notion of the limits of African Americans, a notion no doubt appropriated from general American culture. She had never been told that Africans created much of what we know as higher mathematics. She knew none of the great African American scientists and engineers.

It reminded me of my own nephew, who is only six years younger than I am—a difference great enough that I had experienced most of my early schooling in segregated schools, whereas he attended only schools that had officially been desegregated. When he was in high school and I was just out of college, I once berated him for making a D in chemistry. His response was, "What do you want from me? The white kids get Cs!" Although I had internalized the notion that we black kids had to be "twice as good as white kids to get half as far," as had been drilled into us by parents and teachers in all-black schools, he could not imagine that he could and should be equal to, if not better than, his white classmates.

Theresa Perry (2003), in *Young, Gifted and Black: Promoting High Achievement Among African-American Students*, pointed out that although there was no expectation of being rewarded for advanced education in the same ways as whites in the larger society, African Americans from slavery through the civil rights movement pursued educational achievement with a vengeance. In an attempt to develop a theory of black achievement, Perry offered an analysis of why education was such a clear goal for educational attainment in the past and why that goal has become so much murkier in today's society. Perry argued that because the country's dominant belief system has always denigrated the academic competence and capacity of African Americans—most overtly visible in Jim Crow and the pre–civil rights era—black institutions of the past, including segregated schools, organized themselves to counter this hegemonic belief:

> Most, if not all of the historically Black segregated schools that African-American children attended were intentionally organized in opposition to the ideology of Black inferiority. In other words, in addition to being sites of learning, they also instituted practices and expected behaviors and outcomes that not only promoted education—an act of insurgency in its own right—but also were designed to counter the ideology of African Americans' intellectual inferiority and ideologies that saw African Americans as not quite equal and as less than human. Everything about these institutions was supposed to affirm Black humanity, Black intelligence, and Black achievement. (p. 88)

In black schools, churches, clubs—indeed, all black community institutions—everything focused on this one goal. In all settings, there were intentional activities and belief systems designed to ensure achievement, including regularly practiced rituals that included uplifting songs, recitations, and performances; high expectations; extensive academic support in and out of school; and regular group meetings to express the expectations of adults that young people must work hard to be free in an oppressive society.

Today's schools, integrated or not, seldom develop the same kind of intentional communities. In the post–civil rights era, most public schools are de-ritualized institutions. Certainly, they are institutions that are not intentionally organized to counter inferiority myths—and the reality is, because of that kind of institutional space, black students today, as perhaps never before, are victims of the myths of inferiority and find much less support for countering these myths and embracing academic achievement outside of individual families.

When I spoke at Southern University a few years ago, a young African American woman who had been a student teacher the semester before told me that one of her students, a young African American teenager, came up to her after a social studies lesson and said, "So, Ms. Summer, they made us the slaves because we were dumb, right?" She had been so hurt by his words that she did not know how to respond.

To teach children who have internalized racist beliefs about themselves, one of the things that successful teachers must constantly say to them is, "You will learn! I know you will learn because you are brilliant." Jamie Escalante taught poor barrio children in California to pass advanced-placement calculus tests. As depicted in the movie *Stand and Deliver* (Menéndez & Musca, 1988), he would say to them, "You have to learn math. Math is in your blood. The Mayans discovered zero!" We have to be able to say to our children that we understand and they need to understand that this system is set up to guarantee their failure. To succeed in school is to cheat the system and we are going to spend our time cheating. Teachers have an important role to play here. They must not only make children aware of the brilliance "in their blood" but also help children turn any internalized negative societal view of their competence into a compelling drive to demand that any system attempting to relegate them to the bottom of society must, instead, recognize and celebrate their giftedness.

RECOGNIZE AND BUILD ON CHILDREN'S STRENGTHS

To do this requires knowledge of children's out-of-school lives. One of the teachers in Gloria Ladson-Billings's (1994) *The Dreamkeepers* speaks of having brought candy to school for a holiday party. She thought she brought enough candy for everyone, but all of the candy disappeared before half the children had been served. She was perplexed but then discovered that the children were putting some of the candy in their pockets. After some inquiries, she realized that they were doing so to take some home for their siblings. Many teachers might end any inquiries about the disappearing candy with the conclusion that the children were stealing. They might think, "I'm not going to bring candy into this classroom anymore because these children are selfish and untrustworthy." But this teacher understood that what was happening was a real strength that she could build on. After all, how many children from middle-class families would be so focused on making sure that siblings received the same treats as they had? These children were exhibiting a sense of caring for others and nurturing that could very well make instructional strategies such as peer tutoring or collaborative learning much easier to implement.

When I was a new teacher, Howard was a first-grader in my class. After several months of failing to get Howard to progress in mathematics, I was ready to take the advice I was given to refer him for special-education placement. Among other academic problems, Howard was having real difficulty with math worksheets, especially those concerning money where there are pictures of different configurations of coins and the child is supposed to indicate the total amount represented. It did not seem to matter how frequently we reviewed those worksheets, Howard just could not get it. Before I made any referrals, I had the opportunity to visit Howard's home and talk to his mother and his grandmother. I found out that Howard's mother was suffering with a substance addiction and that Howard was responsible for getting his four-year-old physically challenged sister up every morning and on the bus and to school. He also did the family's wash, which meant that he had to have a lot of knowledge about coins and money. He was very good at it because he knew he could not get cheated when he purchased laundry supplies from the corner store. What I found out through that experience was that I, without really knowing this child, almost made a terrible mistake. I assumed that because he could not do a task in my classroom that was de-contextualized and paperbound, he could not do the real-life task it represented. It is often very difficult for teachers, particularly those who may not be from the same cultural or class background as the children, to understand where strengths may lie. We must have means to discover what the children are able to do outside of school—in church, at community centers, as caretakers for younger siblings—or what skills they may be able to display on the playground with their peers. A lot of our youngsters in urban settings come to us with what we refer to as "street smarts," yet we seldom seem able to connect that kind of knowledge to school problem solving and advanced thinking.

USE FAMILIAR METAPHORS, ANALOGIES, AND EXPERIENCES FROM THE CHILDREN'S WORLD TO CONNECT WHAT CHILDREN ALREADY KNOW TO SCHOOL KNOWLEDGE

To connect students' out-of-school lives to academic content, another teacher described in Ladson-Billings (1994) taught about the governmental structure of the United States by connecting it to the black church structure. She had the children collect the articles of incorporation of their churches. She then made the connection to show how the minister could be compared to the president, how the deacons could be compared to the legislators, and how the board could be compared to the senators. The children not only learned about the Constitution in a way that they were able to apprehend with much greater clarity but also learned that institution building was not merely the purview of others but a part of their culture as well.

Yet another teacher, Amanda Branscombe (personal communication, 1990), who happens to be European American, had a class of ninth-graders who were considered special-education students. She had the children teach her the rules for writing a rap song. She told them, "No, no, you can't just tell me to write it, you have to tell me the rules. I know nothing about rap songs. I've never even heard one. What rules do I need to know to write one?" So the children really had to explore meter, verse, and the structure of a rap song. After they had done so—and that was a massive undertaking on its own—Branscombe compared their rules to those Shakespeare used to write his sonnets. Then they set about exploring Shakespeare's rules in the context of his writing.

One year my mother, who was a teacher, taught plane geometry by having the students make a quilt for a student who had dropped out of school to get married and have a baby. The students presented this quilt to this young woman as a present. There are several connections here. It is obvious that by making the quilt, the students were creating something for someone they cared about, but their teacher also taught them the theorems of geometry as they worked to piece the shapes of the quilt together. School knowledge was connected to a sense of community. Teachers really are cultural brokers who have the opportunity to connect the familiar to the unknown. We teachers have to work at learning to do that.

CREATE A SENSE OF FAMILY AND CARING IN THE SERVICE OF ACADEMIC ACHIEVEMENT

Jackie Irvine, a friend and colleague, told me about her interview with a teacher identified as an excellent teacher of African American children.

She asked Ms. Brandon (not her real name), "How do you view teaching? How do you ensure children's success?" The teacher answered, "Well, the first thing I have to do is make the children mine." She continued, saying that on the first day of school she would go down each row and say "Son, what is your name?" The little boy would say, "My name is Justin Williams." And she would say, "Sweetheart, that is a wonderful name, but in this class your name is going to be Justin Williams *Brandon*." She would ask the next child, "Darling, what's your name?" "My name is Mary Johnson." She would say, "And in this class, darling, your name is Mary Johnson *Brandon*." Ms. Brandon proceeded down each row to give each child her last name. She then said, "Now, you are all my children, and I have the smartest children in the entire world. So you are going to learn more this year than anybody every learned in one year. And we are going to get started right now."

In her dissertation research, Madge Willis (1995) looked at a very successful school in Atlanta serving low-income African American students and found an overwhelming sense of family, a sense of connectedness, and a sense of caring. I have discovered that children of color, particularly African American, seem especially sensitive to their relationship between themselves and their teacher. I have concluded that it appears that they not only learn from a teacher but also for a teacher. If they do not feel connected to a teacher on an emotional level, then they will not learn, they will not put out the effort.

Barbara Shade (1987) suggested that African American children value the social aspects of an environment to a greater extent than "mainstream" children and tend to put an emphasis on feelings, acceptance, and emotional closeness. Shade contended that the time and effort African American children will spend on academic tasks in a classroom depend on their interpretation of the emotional environment.

MONITOR AND ASSESS CHILDREN'S NEEDS AND THEN ADDRESS THEM WITH A WEALTH OF DIVERSE STRATEGIES

We do a lot of "monitoring" and "assessing," of course, but we are not very adept at addressing specific needs, especially in diverse cultures.

Assessment in these contexts is not as straightforward as it may seem on the surface. In her studies of the narrative styles of young children, Sarah Michaels (1981) found that black and white first-graders tended to tell "sharing time" stories differently. White children tended to tell "topic-centered" stories, focused on a single object or event, whereas black children tended to tell "episodic" stories, usually longer and always including shifting scenes related to a series of events. In a subsequent study, Courtney Cazden (1988) and Michaels created a tape of a white adult reading the oral narratives of black and white first-graders with all dialectical markers removed. They then played the tape for a racially mixed group of educators and asked each educator to comment about the children's likelihood of success in school. The researchers were surprised by the differential responses of African American and European American educators to an African American child's story.

The white adults' comments included statements such as

"Terrible story, incoherent."

"Not a story at all in the sense of describing something that happened."

"This child might have trouble reading."

"This child exhibits language problems that will affect school achievement; family problems or emotional problems might hamper academic progress." (p. 18)

By contrast, the African American adults found the story "well-formed, easy to understand, and interesting with lots of detail and description" (Cazden, 1988, p. 18). All five of the African American adults mentioned the "shifts" and "associations" or "nonlinear" qualities of the story, but they did not find this distracting. Three of the five African American adults selected this story as the best of the five they heard. All but one judged the child as exceptionally bright, highly verbal, and/or potentially successful.

This is not a story about racism. Again, there was no way that the adults knew the race of the child who told the story, because all the stories were read by a white researcher. The point here is that when a teacher is familiar with aspects of a child's culture, then the teacher may be better able to assess the child's competence. Many teachers, unfamiliar with the language, the metaphors, or the environments of the children they teach, may easily underestimate the children's competence.

I have also discovered that to effectively monitor and assess the needs of children who may come from a different cultural background, the notion of basic skills often needs to be turned on its head. We must constantly be aware that children come to school with different kinds of knowledge. Our instruction must be geared toward understanding that knowledge, building on it, and teaching that which children do not already know. To offer appropriate instruction, we need to understand that because what we typically think of as basic skills are those skills that middle-class children learn before they come to school—knowledge of letter names and sounds, color names, and counting; recognition of numerals; familiarity with storybooks and with the particular kinds of language found in them; and so forth. Those skills may not be "basic" to children from nonmainstream or non–middle-class backgrounds. We also need to rethink the general belief that critical and creative thinking, the ability to analyze, and the ability to make comparisons and judgments are higher-order skills. It is often the case that for children who are from poor communities, critical-thinking skills are basic. Those are the skills they come to us with. They are accustomed to being more independent. Often they are familiar with real-life problems and how to solve them.

So those children who appear to learn the basic skills presented in school quickly typically learn most of them during their five or six *years* at home. Low-income children who did not learn these skills at home, and who do not learn them in the first five or six *months* of school are often labeled remedial at best or special-education material at worst. Even more problematic, the knowledge that these children do come to school with is often viewed as a deficit rather than an advantage. I have seen far too many children labeled as "too streetwise" by adults who see their ability to solve problems with near-adult sophistication as violating some preconceived notion of childhood innocence.

An Anglo teacher I worked with in Alaska successfully taught low-income Alaska Native children in rural villages. When she came to teach in the city, she was appalled at how dependent the middle-class children were. "They don't even know how to tie their shoes," she said of her kindergarten class. The village kindergartners could not only tie their shoes but also fix meals for their siblings, clean up, and help their parents with all sorts of tasks. The village kindergartners, members of an ethnic group typically stigmatized by the larger society, took on the responsibility of keeping areas of the classroom in order with little adult supervision, which freed their teacher to work on academic tasks with small groups. The teacher found the city kids unprepared for such responsibilities. When paint spilled on the floor, most of the middle-class children stood around waiting for someone to clean it up. In the village, the children would take care of the problem without the teacher ever knowing a problem had occurred.

What I am suggesting is that we teach traditional school knowledge to those children for whom basic skills are not so basic and appreciate and make use of the higher-order knowledge that they bring from home. On the other hand, I suggest that we appreciate the school knowledge middle-class children bring and teach them the problem solving and independence that they sometimes lack.

We must also be very aware that we need to use a variety of strategies to teach. Although it is important for children to have the opportunity to "discover" new knowledge, we must not fool ourselves that children need only, for example, a "literacy-rich" environment to discover literacy. What we seldom realize is that middle-class parents are masters at "direct teaching" long before their children ever enter school.

I recently visited a child-care center where I saw children pounding nails into a tree trunk and having a great time. When a father arrived to pick up his daughter, she called out to him, "Come see what I'm doing!" The father joined her at the tree trunk to admire her work. The father inquired, "Do you remember what we said those rings in the tree trunk were for? Yes, to tell how old the tree is. Let's count the rings and see how old this tree is." The point here is that if that child were later put into a "tree trunk–rich" environment, it might appear that she discovered the meaning of tree rings on her own. We have to know when to teach information directly and when to provide opportunities for children to explore and discover—and we have to realize the difference between teaching and merely allowing children to display what they have already learned at home.

We have to have a variety of methodologies, we have to be able to assess broadly, and we have to be able to pull out of our teaching hats the appropriate method for the children who are sitting before us at any given moment.

HONOR AND RESPECT THE CHILDREN'S HOME CULTURE

When educators hear this precept, they frequently interpret it to mean that they are being directed to create an all–African American or all–Latino or all–Native American curriculum. This is not what is being asked of them. Most parents do want their children to learn about their own culture, but they also want them to learn about the rest of the world. I have described what I want for my child as an academic house built on a strong foundation of self-knowledge but with many windows and doors that look out onto the rest of the world. A problem, however, is that the cultures of marginalized groups in our society tend to be either ignored, misrepresented, viewed from an outsider perspective, or even denigrated. Aside from a yearly trek through the units on Martin Luther King Jr. and perhaps, Rosa Parks, the historical, cultural, and scientific contributions of African Americans are usually ignored or rendered trivial.

Even when they have the desire to do so, educators are often unable to connect to the cultures of their students because our universities are so limited in what is taught about other cultures. I sometimes ask my students to make a list of the names of an explorer, a philosopher, a scientist, a poet, and a mathematician. After they have completed their lists, I then ask that they write the names of a Chinese explorer, a Latino philosopher, a South American scientist, a Native American poet, and an African mathematician. Obviously, the first list is much easier for them and is usually populated with names of European males. The second list is impossible for them to complete. I point out the "cultural deficits" with which we in this country are typically saddled as a result of our limited education!

Teachers who wish to learn the culture of their students usually have to pursue the study on their own. One excellent example of a teacher who has done so is Stephanie Terry of Baltimore, Maryland. When I visited her classroom, Stephanie taught first grade in an all–African American school. Although she considered herself an "Afrocentric" teacher, she taught the curriculum mandated by the Baltimore school system. However, she always added material about the children's cultural heritage as well. When she taught the mandated unit on libraries, for example, she taught about the first major libraries in Africa. When she taught about health, she taught Imhotep, the famous African physician, philosopher, and scientist. She ensured that the children would find people who looked like them in the curriculum. Stephanie's students always scored near the top of any standardized tests administered, yet she never spent a moment "teaching to the test."

On a cautionary note, however, I should mention my observation of the teacher next door to Stephanie's classroom. That teacher also tried to use African American culture in her curriculum, but her manner of talking to the children seemed to militate against their getting any benefits from the enriched curriculum. Although she had done a lot of research to create her curriculum, she said things to the children such as "You see the way you're acting; you could never be Gwendolyn Brooks! You just don't know how to act. You all act like you don't have any sense at all!" and "You all don't even care about all the work I put into this. You don't have any respect. You just need to sit down and stop acting like idiots. I don't even know why I try anything nice with this class! You'll never be anything!"

I happened to be at an assembly later in the week where the children were watching the presidential inauguration and the principal asked, "How many of you think you could be president?" It is interesting that all of Stephanie's kids raised their hands. When I looked at the class from the teacher next door, I saw only one or two hands raised. It struck hard that it is not just the curriculum but also the attitudes toward the children that affect what the children believe about themselves. One cannot "honor and respect" the culture without honoring and respecting the children themselves.

To get teachers to consider the wealth and strength of African

American cultural contributions to this country, Ladson-Billings (1994) has asked teachers to consider what the United States might look like today if African Americans had arrived only recently. There were many thoughtful responses: if African Americans had just immigrated, this country would not have the rich musical heritage provided by blues, jazz, and gospel. Other teachers suggested that the moral conscience of the nation might not have been heightened without the experience of the civil rights movement. Another teacher suggested that the country would be unrecognizable because we may have failed to grow beyond the thirteen original colonies without the labor of enslaved Africans. The point of the exercise was to help teachers keep in mind the value and the contributions of a particular people to this country when we teach their children.

FOSTER A SENSE OF CHILDREN'S CONNECTION TO COMMUNITY—TO SOMETHING GREATER THAN THEMSELVES

The role of community in education has changed considerably during the years since the desegregation of schools. Prior to desegregation, the black community played an especially significant role in schools, providing many of the resources the local districts refused to provide (see Walker, 1996). The children of the community were told in no uncertain terms by their parents and their teachers that their role was to excel in school because so many had suffered so that they might be in the position to receive an education. We students were admonished that we must excel for those who had come before us, for our communities, for our descendants, in short, for all to whom we were connected by kinship or affiliation.

Perry (2003) pointed out that prior to the civil rights movement, although there was no expectation of being rewarded for advanced education in the same ways as whites in the larger society, African Americans pursued educational achievement:

> For African Americans, from slavery to the modern Civil Rights movement, . . . you pursued learning because this is how you asserted yourself as a free person; how you claimed your humanity. You pursued learning so you

could work for social uplift, for the liberation of your people. You pursued education so you could prepare yourself to lead your people. (p. 11)

Today's students receive a different message. We tell them that they must do well in school for only one purpose—to get a good job. This incentive to succeed is meager, indeed, when compared to the incentive derived from disappointing one's community, prior and future generations, and in truth, the entire race! It would behoove us to rethink how we talk to children about education and its purposes. The connection to community, to something greater than our individual selves, can be the force that propels our children to be their best.

In *Urban Sanctuaries*, McLaughlin, Irby, and Langman (2001) studied urban children who were and those who were not involved in community organizations. What they found is that children who were a part of some community-based group that valued educational achievement tended to be more successful in school. Whether the group was Boy Scouts, a sports team, or a church group, when the children regularly heard adults important to them outside of school and home discuss the importance of school achievement, they pushed themselves harder to excel. It seems that such groups can create a culture of achievement in which children are wont to disappoint their fellow members. Again, the children were able to benefit by identifying with something greater than themselves.

My young Thursday-night teachers have no idea of the power they actually hold. Despite their feeling of inadequacy, of being overwhelmed and undervalued, what they fail to understand is that they have the potential to change the lives of so many children. When I have asked adults who, based on their childhood demographics, should not have but did achieve significant success—those who came from low-income communities, from single-parent families, from the foster-care system, or who spent many years in special-education classrooms—they have all identified one common factor to explain their accomplishments. Each of these adults attributed his or her success to one or more teachers. All talked about a teacher who was especially encouraging, or who demanded their best, or who convinced them they were more than the larger world believed. Teachers changed their lives, even when the teachers themselves did not realize they were doing so.

And so, when teachers express feeling ineffectual, I remind them of the significant role they can choose to play. The above ten precepts are offered to assist them in that role. By knowing their students and their students' intellectual heritage and using that knowledge in their instruction, by always demanding students' best, by fighting against societal stereotypes, and by helping students understand the important role they can play in changing their communities and the world, teachers truly can revolutionize the education system and save this country, one classroom at a time.

REFERENCES

Cazden, C.B. (1988). *Classroom discourse: The language of teaching and learning.* Portsmouth, NH: Heinemann.

Delpit, L. (1995). *Other people's children: Cultural conflict in the classroom.* New York: New Press.

Hilliard, A.G., III. (1991). Do we have the will to educate all children? *Educational Leadership, 49*(1) 31–36.

Hilliard, A.G., III. (2003). No mystery: Closing the achievement gap. In T. Perry, C. Steele, & A.G. Hilliard III (Eds.), *Young, gifted and black: Promoting high achievement among African-American students* (pp. 131–65). Boston: Beacon.

Ladson-Billings, G. (1994). *The dreamkeepers.* San Francisco: Jossey-Bass.

Massey, G.C., Scott, M.V., & Dornbusch, S.M. (1975). Racism without racists: Institutional racism in urban schools. *Black Scholar, 7*(3) 2–11.

McLaughlin, M.W., Irby, M.A., & Langman, J. (2001). *Urban sanctuaries: Neighborhood organizations in the lives and futures of inner-city youth.* San Francisco: Jossey-Bass.

Menéndez, R. (Director/Writer) & Musca, T. (Writer). (1988). *Stand and deliver* [Motion picture]. United States: Warner Bros.

Michaels, S. (1981). "Sharing time": Children's narrative styles and differential access of literacy. *Language in Society, 10*, 423–42.

Perry, T. (2003). Up from the parched earth. Toward a theory of African-American achievement. In T. Perry, C. Steele, & A.G. Hilliard III (Eds.), *Young, gifted and black: Promoting high achievement among African-American students* (pp. 1–108). Boston: Beacon.

Rivers, F. (2003). [Unpublished proposal draft]. Baton Rouge, LA: Author.

Shade, B. (1987). Ecological correlates of educative style of African American children. *Journal of Negro Education, 60*, 291–301.

Walker, E.V.S. (1996). *Their highest potential: An African American school community in the segregated south*. Chapel Hill: University of North Carolina Press.

Willis, M. (1995). *"We're family": Creating success in a public African American elementary school*. Unpublished doctoral dissertation, Georgia State University, Atlanta.

Woodson, C.G. (2000). *The mis-education of the Negro*. Chicago: African American Images. (Original work published 1933.)

▪ PART III ▪

CITY CLASSROOMS, CITY SCHOOLS

INTRODUCTION

Pedro A. Noguera

America expects a lot from its frequently maligned urban public schools, but it does relatively little to make it possible for such schools to succeed. Our urban public schools are responsible for educating our neediest children, students whose most basic needs for housing, nutrition, and health care are often not met. Remarkably, schools in cities such as Newark, Detroit, St. Louis, and Los Angeles, are subjected to stinging criticism and humiliation when, predictably, test scores are low and students do not do as well academically as students in more privileged communities. Why should we expect students whose lives are so difficult to do as well as children who have everything they need and much more?

Our politicians claim that our schools should insure that the United States will maintain its economic and technological dominance in the world, but they are unwilling to provide any of the services and supports that are typically available to children and families in the nations we compare ourselves to. In such countries, access to health care and preschool are universal, and the level of desperation caused by poverty is nothing like that found in the United States. Arizona State University professor David Berliner has referred to this state of affairs and unrealistic expectations as "our impoverished view of education."

For several years our politicians have claimed that education is a top priority, yet they refuse to address the wide disparities in funding between urban and suburban schools. Consistently, we spend the most to educate the most privileged children and the least to educate the children with the greatest needs. We pay teachers salaries that make it difficult to attract the top college students into the profession, and we celebrate those who join programs such as Teach for America, as though teaching in urban schools were like working for the Peace Corps or some form of missionary work.

Finally, we frequently hear that "education is the cornerstone of democracy" and we expect schools to provide students with the knowledge, understanding, and frame of mind to participate intelligently in civic life. Yet, increasingly, the curriculum is so focused on preparing students for state-mandated exams that there is little time for critical thinking. At a time when our nation is at war, when our leaders are oblivious to threats such as global warming, and our civil liberties are under attack, the need to use education to provide students with a critical perspective on society and America's place in the world has never been greater.

Given our unrealistic and unfair expectations, it is hardly surprising that urban schools, more often than not, disappoint and fall short of the goals that have been set. Such disappointments have become even more common since the adoption of the federal No Child Left Behind (NCLB) Act. Under NCLB public schools are required to produce evidence that *all children are learning*. As simple and reasonable as this goal might seem, it actually represents a radical departure from generations of past practice. American schools have never been expected to educate *all children*, especially in communities where poverty is concentrated and the poor are isolated. More important, they have never been expected to eliminate racial disparities in achievement.

For the first time in American history, closing the racial achievement gap has been embraced as a national priority. New York City Chancellor of Public Education, Joel Klein, refers to this effort as the "unfulfilled legacy of the civil rights movement." The profound significance of such a crusade can only be appreciated if one considers that for most of America's history, racial differences in achievement were presumed to be natural (i.e., rooted in innate ability), unalterable, and, therefore, acceptable.

For those seeking to understand what it might take to accomplish such lofty goals—to raise student achievement, to close the racial achievement gap, and improve urban schools, the critical question that must be answered is: why is it that failure has been accepted for so long? When one considers that in most American cities 50 percent of students will drop out before graduation, that in many schools concerns about safety and discipline take precedence over efforts to ensure student learning, and that alienation and disengagement among students are so common, is it possible to take our politicians and the goals they assert seriously?

The most common explanation for the problems that beset urban schools is that they have too many lazy students and uncaring parents. Self-serving unions and a lack of professionalism among teachers are also cited as underlying causes of school failure. Missing from the analysis and much of the discourse on urban education is a clear understanding of the ways in which poverty and racism contribute to widespread failure and institutional dysfunction. The mere fact that failure among urban public schools is so pervasive throughout the United States, that in every major city and most minor cities as well, public schools generally do not meet the academic needs of the children they serve, should serve as an indication that something more is going on than laziness and a lack of motivation.

The fact that more than fifty years after the *Brown* decision our urban schools remain largely segregated and that this is no longer regarded as a policy matter that warrants a serious response is perhaps the clearest indication that improving education for children in urban areas is not really a national priority. Throughout the country we typically concentrate the poorest and neediest students in schools without sufficient resources. Even in New Orleans, where politicians pledged to rebuild one of America's poorest cities following the devastation of Hurricane Katrina, public schools remain in total disarray more than two years later. In contrast, the resources needed to restore the Saints (a professional football team) and to rebuild the stadium where they play were readily available. Despite the lofty rhetoric that frames education policies like NCLB, it is clear that there is very little willingness to address the basic problems confronting urban public schools. Instead, we pretend that schools can be improved through pressure and humiliation, by raising standards, and by merely adopting more stringent measures of accountability.

I spend a great deal of time working with schools throughout the country on efforts to improve the quality of education they provide to students and "close the achievement gap." I am often impressed by the sincerity of those who lead these efforts, inspired by the teachers who work under difficult circumstances to find ways to motivate and stimulate the children they serve, and find hope among children who typically haven't given up—even though so many others have. Through my experiences I have come to understand that in many ways urban schools have been set up to fail by the impossible combination of inadequate resources and high student needs. Yet, I have also learned that the reason why a small number of schools do better than others and succeed at engaging their students, cultivating a desire to learn and finding a way to respond to their basic needs, has less to do with *skill* than with *will*. Schools like Edison Elementary in Port Chester, New York, Benjamin Bannaker High School in Brooklyn, or Fenway High School in Boston, serve as proof that it is indeed possible to educate poor black and Latino children. The striking deviation of such schools from the failure and mediocrity that characterizes so much of urban education cannot be explained by their use of a special curriculum, their possession of extra resources, or the presence of a single charismatic leader. Rather, what sets such schools apart and makes them unique is the dedication, commitment, and focus of the educators who work there, the respect and care they show toward the children and families they serve, and the culture they have created in the schools themselves.

Of course, there is more to it than that. In the best schools where all children are achieving regardless of race or class, there are typically several strategies in place, including:

1. a commitment to engage parents as partners in education with explicit roles and responsibilities for parents and educators;

2. a clear and focused commitment to quality instruction that provides teachers with the support and guidance needed to be effective in the classroom;

3. strong leadership that provides the vision needed to sustain the educational mission and a tough-mindedness to evaluate interventions and reforms to insure quality.

4. a recognition that discipline practices must be linked to educational goals and must always aim at reconnecting troubled students to learning, and employing consequences that help children to learn from their mistakes.

5. a commitment to finding ways to meet the nonacademic needs of poor students.

With the exception of item five on the list it could be argued that such conditions are necessary in all schools. While this may be true, it is important to recognize that in most urban areas it is uncommon to find this combination of characteristics in more than a handful of schools. How can it be that practices that seem so obvious and rooted in common sense are not more widely embraced? The simple answer to this question is that many schools simply do not know what it takes to educate the children they serve.

To help schools figure out how best to meet the learning needs of their students, a growing number of researchers have focused upon the need for educators to acquire a degree of cultural competence when teaching poor black and Latino children in the inner city. For many, this consists largely of the need for educators to know and value the cultural heritage of their students. Yet, while such information may provide teachers with important background information, it rarely provides the insights they will need to actually be successful in the classroom. In contrast, teachers who take time to know their students are compelled to engage in an ongoing process of learning and inquiry, because the children they serve are not static or "knowable" in an anthropological sense. Educators who acknowledge their inability to ever completely know their students see teaching as an ongoing process of learning. In so doing, they are able to see beyond the stereotypes that frequently malign and limit their ability to work with the children, and to recognize the assets, knowledge, and experiences that their students bring with them. As they search to understand who their students are as individuals and as social beings, they also find ways to make education meaningful to them.

As a teacher, my experiences have mostly been with students who have been written off as incorrigible and unteachable. From my experience teaching inner-city youth I have learned that by taking time to listen without judgment one can begin to understand that there are legitimate reasons for the anger they so often exhibit, an anger that occasionally contributes to bad choices and behavior that is self-destructive and injurious to the communities where they live. For me, understanding the source of their anger is not the same as justifying or condoning how that anger may be manifest or expressed. However, without an understanding of its source it may be impossible to figure out how to help young people channel feelings of anger and alienation in more positive and constructive ways, or how to intervene so that some of the more destructive tendencies among inner-city youth can be prevented. I have also come to understand that there is logic behind the choices they make, one that grows out of a sensibility and sometimes even a critical awareness of the forces stacked against them in American society and in their local environment. I have also come to see that understanding the logic that guides the behavior of inner-city youth is the first step to engaging young people in an educational process aimed at changing the way they respond to the forms of hardship and the forces of oppression that shape and constrain their lives.

Engaging inner-city youth in a critical analysis of their lives must begin from an awareness of what their lives are like and how they have come to perceive and interpret their social reality. In order to gain this understanding educators must be willing to open themselves to learning about the lives of the students they teach. It is important to recognize that such pedagogical practice must include an openness to hearing young people share their perceptions of the social reality they inhabit, and a willingness to engage in acts of solidarity in the fight against the oppression they face.

For me, this is more than an academic exercise. The conditions facing many inner-city youth are extreme—homicide rates remain high (and rising in cities like Oakland, Detroit, Baltimore, and Washington, D.C.) and incarceration rates for juveniles show no signs of being reduced in the near future. Given the dire circumstances confronting inner-city youth, I have found it helpful to draw upon the ideas of Paulo Freire, education theorist and author of *Pedagogy of the Oppressed*, for a "theory of change" that can guide our work. Freire understood that it is not possible for educators to "save" the oppressed, but through acts of compassion and solidarity it is possible to work with them to find ways to transform the circumstances under which they live.

17

FROM *THE SHAME OF THE NATION*

Jonathon Kozol

With bestselling books, such as Death at an Early Age *and* Savage Inequalities, *National Book Award–winner Jonathon Kozol has been one of the most persistent and eloquent critics of the inequities faced by children in poor urban schools. In this selection from* The Shame of the Nation, *published in 2005, Kozol once again visits public-school classrooms and finds that, fifty years after* Brown vs. Board of Education, *city schools are, to an alarming degree, still separate and still unequal: resegregated, underfunded, and too often serving up mind-numbing scripted curricula to their low-income students.*

———————

Many Americans who live far from our major cities and who have no firsthand knowledge of the realities to be found in urban public schools seem to have the rather vague and general impression that the great extremes of racial isolation that were matters of grave national significance some thirty-five or forty years ago have gradually but steadily diminished in more recent years. The truth, unhappily, is that the trend, for well over a decade now, has been precisely the reverse. Schools that were already deeply segregated twenty-five or thirty years ago are no less segregated now, while thousands of other schools around the country that had been integrated either voluntarily or by the force of law have since been rapidly resegregating.

In Chicago, by the academic year 2002–2003, 87 percent of public-school enrollment was black or Hispanic; less than 10 percent of children in the schools were white. In Washington, D.C., 94 percent of children were black or Hispanic; less than 5 percent were white. In St. Louis, 82 percent of the student population were black or Hispanic; in Philadelphia and Cleveland, 79 percent; in Los Angeles, 84 percent; in Detroit, 96 percent; in Baltimore, 89 percent. In New York City, nearly three-quarters of the students were black or Hispanic.

Even these statistics, as stark as they are, cannot begin to convey how deeply isolated children in the poorest and most segregated sections of these cities have become. In the typically colossal high schools of the Bronx, for instance, more than 90 percent of students (in most cases, more than 95 percent) are black or Hispanic. At John F. Kennedy High School in 2003, 93 percent of the enrollment of more than 4,000 students were black and Hispanic; only 3.5 percent of students at the school were white. At Harry S. Truman High School, black and Hispanic students represented 96 percent of the enrollment of 2,700 students; 2 percent were white. At Adlai Stevenson High School, which enrolls 3,400 students, blacks and Hispanics made up 97 percent of the student population; a mere eight-tenths of 1 percent were white.

A teacher at P.S. 65 in the South Bronx once pointed out to me one of the two white children I had ever seen there. His presence in her class was something of a wonderment to the teacher and to the other pupils. I asked how many white kids she had taught in the South Bronx in her career. "I've been at this school for eighteen years," she said. "This is the first white student I have ever taught."

Perhaps most damaging to any serious effort to address racial segregation openly is the refusal of most of the major arbiters of culture in our northern cities to confront or even clearly name an obvious reality they would have castigated with a passionate determination in another section of the nation fifty years before—and which, moreover, they still castigate today in retrospective writings that assign it to a comfortably distant and allegedly concluded era of the past. There is, indeed, a seemingly agreed-upon convention in much of the media today not even to use an accurate descriptor like "racial segregation" in a narrative description of a segregated school. Linguistic sweeteners, semantic somersaults, and surrogate vocabularies are repeatedly employed.

Schools in which as few as 3 or 4 percent of students may be white or Southeast Asian or of Middle Eastern origin, for instance—and where *every other child* in the building is black or Hispanic—are referred to as "diverse." Visitors to schools like these discover quickly the eviscerated meaning of the word, which is no longer a proper adjective but a euphemism for a plainer word that has apparently become unspeakable.

School systems themselves repeatedly employ this euphemism in describing the composition of their student populations. In a school I visited in the fall of 2004 in Kansas City, Missouri, for example, a document distributed to visitors reports that the school's curriculum "addresses the needs of children from diverse backgrounds." But as I went from class to class, I did not encounter any children who were white or Asian—or Hispanic, for that matter—and when I was later provided with precise statistics for the demographics of the school, I learned that 99.6 percent of students there were African American. In a similar document, the school board of another district, this one in New York State, referred to "the diversity" of its student population and "the rich variations of ethnic backgrounds." But when I looked at the racial numbers that the district had reported to the state, I learned that there were 2,800 black and Hispanic children in the system, 1 Asian child, and 3 whites. Words, in these cases, cease to have real meaning; or, rather, they mean the opposite of what they say.

High school students whom I talk with in deeply segregated neighborhoods and public schools seem far less circumspect than their elders and far more open in their willingness to confront these issues. "It's more like being hidden," said a fifteen-year-old girl named Isabel[1] I met some years ago in Harlem, in attempting to explain to me the ways in which she and her classmates understood the racial segregation of their neighborhoods and schools. "It's as if you have been put in a garage where, if they don't have room for something but aren't sure if they should throw it out, they put it there where they don't need to think of it again."

I asked her if she thought America truly did not "have room" for her or other children of her race. "Think of it this way," said a sixteen-year-old girl sitting beside her. "If people in New York woke up one day and

---

[1] The names of children mentioned in this piece have been changed to protect their privacy.

learned that we were gone, that we had simply died or left for somewhere else, how would they feel?"

"How do you think they'd feel?" I asked.

"I think they'd be relieved," this very solemn girl replied.

Dear Mr. Kozol," wrote the eight-year-old, "we do not have the things you have. You have Clean things. We do not have. You have a clean bathroom. We do not have that. You have Parks and we do not have Parks. You have all the things and we do not have all the things. Can you help us?"

The letter, from a child named Alliyah, came in a fat envelope of twenty-seven letters from a class of third-grade children in the Bronx. Other letters that the students in Alliyah's classroom sent me registered some of the same complaints. "We don't have no gardens," "no Music or Art," and "no fun places to play," one child said. "Is there a way to fix this Problem?" Another noted a concern one hears from many children in such overcrowded schools: "We have a gym but it is for lining up. I think it is not fair." Yet another of Alliyah's classmates asked me, with a sweet misspelling, if I knew the way to make her school into a "good" school— "like the other kings have"—and ended with the hope that I would do my best to make it possible for "all the kings" to have good schools.

The letter that affected me the most, however, had been written by a child named Elizabeth. "It is not fair that other kids have a garden and new things. But we don't have that," said Elizabeth. "I wish that this school was the most beautiful school in the whole why world."

"The whole why world" stayed in my thoughts for days. When I later met Elizabeth, I brought her letter with me, thinking I might see whether, in reading it aloud, she'd change the "why" to "wide" or leave it as it was. My visit to her class, however, proved to be so pleasant, and the children seemed so eager to bombard me with their questions about where I lived, and why I lived there rather than in New York, and who I lived with, and how many dogs I had, and other interesting questions of that sort, that I decided not to interrupt the nice reception they had given me with questions about usages and spelling. I left "the whole why world" to float around unedited and unrevised in my mind. The letter itself soon found a resting place on the wall above my desk.

In the years before I met Elizabeth, I had visited many other schools in the South Bronx and in one northern district of the Bronx as well. I had made repeated visits to a high school where a stream of water flowed down one of the main stairwells on a rainy afternoon and where green fungus molds were growing in the office where the students went for counseling. A large blue barrel was positioned to collect rainwater coming through the ceiling. In one makeshift elementary school housed in a former skating rink next to a funeral establishment in yet another nearly all-black-and-Hispanic section of the Bronx, class size rose to thirty-four and more; four kindergarten classes and a sixth-grade class were packed into a single room that had no windows. The air was stifling in many rooms, and the children had no place for recess because there was no outdoor playground and no indoor gym.

In another elementary school, which had been built to hold 1,000 children but was packed to bursting with some 1,500, the principal poured out his feelings to me in a room in which a plastic garbage bag had been attached somehow to cover part of the collapsing ceiling. "This," he told me, pointing to the garbage bag, then gesturing around him at the other indications of decay and disrepair one sees in ghetto schools much like it elsewhere, "would not happen to white children."

Libraries, once one of the glories of the New York City school system, were either nonexistent or, at best, vestigial in large numbers of the elementary schools. Art and music programs had also for the most part disappeared. "When I began to teach in 1969," the principal of an elementary school in the South Bronx reported to me, "every school had a full-time licensed art and music teacher and librarian." During the subsequent decades, he recalled, "I saw all of that destroyed."

School physicians also were removed from elementary schools during these years. In 1970, when substantial numbers of white children still attended New York City's public schools, 400 doctors had been present to address the health needs of the children. By 1993, the number of doctors had been cut to 23, most of them part-time—a cutback that affected most severely children in the city's poorest neighborhoods, where medical facilities were most deficient and health problems faced by children most extreme. Teachers told me of asthmatic children who came into class with chronic wheezing and who at any moment of the day might undergo more serious attacks, but in the schools I visited there were no doctors to attend to them.

In explaining these steep declines in services, political leaders in New York tended to point to shifting economic factors, like a serious budget crisis in the middle 1970s, rather than to the changing racial demographics of the student population. But the fact of economic ups and downs from year to year, or from one decade to the next, could not convincingly explain the permanent shortchanging of the city's students, which took place routinely in good economic times and bad. The bad times were seized upon politically to justify the cuts, and the money was never restored once the crisis years were past.

"If you close your eyes to the changing racial composition of the schools and look only at budget actions and political events," says Noreen Connell, the director of the nonprofit Educational Priorities Panel in New York, "you're missing the assumptions that are underlying these decisions." When minority parents ask for something better for their kids, she says, "the assumption is that these are parents who can be discounted. These are kids who just don't count—children we don't value."

This, then, is the accusation that Alliyah and her classmates send our way: "You have. . . . We do not have." Are they right or are they wrong? Is this a case of naive and simplistic juvenile exaggeration? What does a third-grader know about these big-time questions of fairness and justice? Physical appearances apart, how in any case do you begin to measure something so diffuse and vast and seemingly abstract as having more, or having less, or not having at all?

Around the time I met Alliyah in the school year 1997–98, New York's Board of Education spent about $8,000 yearly on the education of a third-grade child in a New York City public school. If you could have scooped Alliyah up out of the neighborhood where she was born and plunked her down in a fairly typical white suburb of New York, she would have received a public education worth about $12,000 a year. If you were to lift her up once more and set her down in one of the wealthiest white suburbs of New York, she would have received as much as $18,000 worth of public education every year and would likely have had a third-grade teacher paid approximately $30,000 more than her teacher in the Bronx was paid.

The dollars on both sides of the equation have increased since then, but the discrepancies between them have remained. The present per-pupil spending level in the New York City schools is $11,700, which may be compared with a per-pupil spending level in excess of $22,000 in the well-to-do suburban district of Manhasset, Long Island. The present New York City level is, indeed, almost exactly what Manhasset spent per pupil eighteen years ago, in 1987, when that sum of money bought a great deal more in services and salaries than it can buy today. In dollars adjusted for inflation, New York City has not yet caught up to where its wealthiest suburbs were a quarter century ago.

Gross discrepancies in teacher salaries between the city and its affluent white suburbs have remained persistent as well. In 1997 the median salary for teachers in Alliyah's neighborhood was $43,000, as compared with $74,000 in suburban Rye, $77,000 in Manhasset, and $81,000 in the town of Scarsdale, which is only about eleven miles from Alliyah's school. Five years later, in 2002, salary scales for New York City's teachers rose to levels that approximated those within the lower-spending districts in the suburbs, but salary scales do not reflect the actual salaries that teachers typically receive, which are dependent upon years of service and advanced degrees. Salaries for first-year teachers in the city were higher than they'd been four years before, but the differences in median pay between the city and its upper-middle-income suburbs had remained extreme. The overall figure for New York City in 2002–2003 was $53,000, while it had climbed to $87,000 in Manhasset and exceeded $95,000 in Scarsdale.

Many people, even while they do not doubt the benefit of making very large investments in the education of their own children, somehow— paradoxical as it may seem—appear to be attracted to the argument that money may not really matter that much at all. No matter with what regularity such doubts about the worth of spending money on a child's education are advanced, it is obvious that those who have the money, and who spend it lavishly to benefit their own kids, do not do it for no reason. Yet shockingly large numbers of well-educated and sophisticated people whom I talk with nowadays dismiss such challenges with a surprising ease. "Is the answer really to throw money into these dysfunctional and failing schools?" I'm often asked. "Don't we have some better ways to make them 'work'?" The question is posed in a variety of forms. "Yes, of course, it's not a perfectly fair system as it stands. But money alone is surely not the sole response. The values of the parents and the kids themselves must have a role in this as well—you know, housing, health conditions, social factors." "Other factors"—a term of overall reprieve one often hears—"have got to be considered, too." These latter points are obviously true but always seem to have the odd effect of substituting things we know we cannot change in the short run for obvious solutions like cutting class size and constructing new school buildings or providing universal preschool that we actually could put in place right now if we were so inclined.

Frequently these arguments are posed as questions that do not invite an answer because the answer seems to be decided in advance. "Can you really buy your way to better education for these children?" "Do we know enough to be quite sure that we will see an actual return on the investment that we make?" "Is it even clear that this is the right starting point to get to where we'd like to go? It doesn't always seem to work, as I am sure that you already know," or similar questions that somehow assume I will agree with those who ask them.

Some people who ask these questions, although they live in wealthy districts where the schools are funded at high levels, don't even send their children to these public schools but choose instead to send them to expensive private day schools. At some of the well-known private prep schools in the New York City area, tuition and associated costs are typically more than $20,000 a year. During their children's teenage years, they sometimes send them off to very fine New England schools like Andover or Exeter or Groton, where tuition, boarding, and additional expenses rise to more than $30,000. Often a family has two teenage children in these schools at the same time, so they may be spending more than $60,000 on their children's education every year. Yet here I am one night, a guest within their home, and dinner has been served and we are having coffee now; and this entirely likable, and generally sensible, and beautifully refined and thoughtful person looks me in the eyes and asks me whether you can really buy your way to better education for the children of the poor.

■ ■ ■

As racial isolation deepens and the inequalities of education finance remain unabated and take on new and more innovative forms, the principals of many inner-city schools are making choices that few principals in public schools that serve white children in the mainstream of the nation ever need to contemplate. Many have been dedicating vast amounts of time and effort to create an architecture of adaptive strategies that promise incremental gains within the limits inequality allows.

New vocabularies of stentorian determination, new systems of incentive, and new modes of castigation, which are termed "rewards and sanctions," have emerged. Curriculum materials that are alleged to be aligned with governmentally established goals and standards and particularly suited to what are regarded as "the special needs and learning styles" of low-income urban children have been introduced. Relentless emphasis on raising test scores, rigid policies of nonpromotion and nongraduation, a new empiricism and the imposition of unusually detailed lists of named and numbered "outcomes" for each isolated parcel of instruction, an oftentimes fanatical insistence upon uniformity of teachers in their management of time, an openly conceded emulation of the rigorous approaches of the military and a frequent use of terminology that comes out of the world of industry and commerce—these are just a few of the familiar aspects of these new adaptive strategies.

Although generically described as "school reform," most of these practices and policies are targeted primarily at poor children of color; and although most educators speak of these agendas in broad language that sounds applicable to all, it is understood that they are valued chiefly as responses to perceived catastrophe in deeply segregated and unequal schools.

"If you do what I tell you to do, how I tell you to do it, when I tell you to do it, you'll get it right," said a determined South Bronx principal observed by a reporter for the *New York Times*. She was laying out a memorizing rule for math to an assembly of her students. "If you don't, you'll get it wrong." This is the voice, this is the tone, this is the rhythm and didactic certitude one hears today in inner-city schools that have embraced a pedagogy of direct command and absolute control. "Taking

their inspiration from the ideas of B.F. Skinner..." says the *Times*, proponents of scripted rote-and-drill curricula articulate their aim as the
establishment of "faultless communication" between "the teacher, who
is the stimulus," and "the students, who respond."

The introduction of Skinnerian approaches (which are commonly
employed in penal institutions and drug-rehabilitation programs), as a
way of altering the attitudes and learning styles of black and Hispanic
children, is provocative, and it has stirred some outcries from respected
scholars. To actually go into a school where you know some of the children very, very well and see the way that these approaches can affect
their daily lives and thinking processes is even more provocative.

On a chilly November day four years ago in the South Bronx, I entered P.S. 65, a school I had been visiting since 1993. There had been
major changes since I'd been there last. Silent lunches had been insti-
tuted in the cafeteria, and on days when children misbehaved, silent recess had been introduced as well. On those days the students were
obliged to sit in rows and maintain perfect silence on the floor of a
small indoor room instead of going out to play. The words SUCCESS FOR
ALL, the brand name of a scripted curriculum—better known by its
acronym, SFA—were prominently posted at the top of the main stair-
way and, as I would later find, in almost every room. Also frequently
displayed within the halls and classrooms were a number of administrative memos that were worded with unusual didactic absoluteness. "Authentic Writing," read a document called "Principles of Learning" that
was posted in the corridor close to the principal's office, "is driven by
curriculum and instruction." I didn't know what this expression meant.
Like many other undefined and arbitrary phrases posted in the school,
it seemed to be a dictum that invited no interrogation.

I entered the fourth grade of a teacher I will call Mr. Endicott, a
man in his mid-thirties who had arrived here without training as a
teacher, one of about a dozen teachers in the building who were sent
into this school after a single summer of short-order preparation. Now
in his second year, he had developed a considerable sense of confidence
and held the class under a tight control.

As I found a place to sit in a far corner of the room, the teacher
and his young assistant, who was in her first year as a teacher, were

beginning a math lesson about building airport runways, a lesson that provided children with an opportunity for measuring perimeters. On the wall behind the teacher, in large letters, was written: "Portfolio Protocols: 1. You are responsible for the selection of [your] work that enters your portfolio. 2. As your skills become more sophisticated this year, you will want to revise, amend, supplement, and possibly replace items in your portfolio to reflect your intellectual growth." On the left side of the room: "Performance Standards Mathematics Curriculum: M-5 Problem Solving and Reasoning. M-6 Mathematical Skills and Tools . . ."

My attention was distracted by some whispering among the children sitting to the right of me. The teacher's response to this distraction was immediate: his arm shot out and up in a diagonal in front of him, his hand straight up, his fingers flat. The young co-teacher did this, too. When they saw their teachers do this, all the children in the classroom did it, too.

"Zero noise," the teacher said, but this instruction proved to be unneeded. The strange salute the class and teachers gave each other, which turned out to be one of a number of such silent signals teachers in the school were trained to use, and children to obey, had done the job of silencing the class.

"Active listening!" said Mr. Endicott. "Heads up! Tractor beams!" which meant, "Every eye on me."

On the front wall of the classroom, in hand-written words that must have taken Mr. Endicott long hours to transcribe, was a list of terms that could be used to praise or criticize a student's work in mathematics. At Level Four, the highest of four levels of success, a child's "problem-solving strategies" could be described, according to this list, as "systematic, complete, efficient, and possibly elegant," while the student's capability to draw conclusions from the work she had completed could be termed "insightful" or "comprehensive." At Level Two, the child's capability to draw conclusions was to be described as "logically unsound," at Level One, "not present." Approximately fifty separate categories of proficiency, or lack of such, were detailed in this wall-sized tabulation.

A well-educated man, Mr. Endicott later spoke to me about the form of classroom management that he was using as an adaptation from a model of industrial efficiency. "It's a kind of 'Taylorism' in the classroom," he explained, referring to a set of theories about the management of factory employees introduced by Frederick Taylor in the early 1900s. "Primitive utilitarianism" is another term he used when we met some months later to discuss these management techniques with other teachers from the school. His reservations were, however, not apparent in the classroom. Within the terms of what he had been asked to do, he had, indeed, become a master of control. It is one of the few classrooms I had visited up to that time in which almost nothing even hinting at spontaneous emotion in the children or the teacher surfaced while I was there.

The teacher gave the "zero noise" salute again when someone whispered to another child at his table. "In two minutes you will have a chance to talk and share this with your partner." Communication between children in the class was not prohibited but was afforded time slots and, remarkably enough, was formalized in an expression that I found included in a memo that was posted on the wall beside the door: "An opportunity . . . to engage in Accountable Talk."

Even the teacher's words of praise were framed in terms consistent with the lists that had been posted on the wall. "That's a Level Four suggestion," said the teacher when a child made an observation other teachers might have praised as simply "pretty good" or "interesting" or "mature."

There was, it seemed, a formal name for every cognitive event within this school: "Authentic Writing," "Active Listening," "Accountable Talk." The ardor to assign all items of instruction or behavior a specific name was unsettling me. The adjectives had the odd effect of hyping every item of endeavor. "Authentic Writing" was, it seemed, a more important act than what the children in a writing class in any ordinary school might try to do. "Accountable Talk" was something more self-conscious and significant than merely useful conversation.

"There's something crystal clear about a number," says a top adviser to the U.S. Senate committee that has jurisdiction over public education, a point of view that is reinforced repeatedly in statements coming from the office of the U.S. education secretary and the White House. "I want to change the face of reading instruction across the United States from an art to a science," said an assistant to Rod Paige, the former education secretary, in the winter of 2002. This is a popular position among advocates for rigidly sequential systems of instruction, but the longing to turn art into science doesn't stop with reading methodologies alone. In many schools it now extends to almost every aspect of the operation of the school and of the lives that children lead within it. In some schools even such ordinary acts as children filing to lunch or recess in the hallways or the stairwells are subjected to the same determined emphasis upon empirical precision.

"Rubric For Filing" is the printed heading of a lengthy list of numbered categories by which teachers are supposed to grade their students on the way they march along the corridors in another inner-city district I have visited. Someone, in this instance, did a lot of work to fit the filing proficiencies of children into no more and no less than thirty-two specific slots:

"Line leader confidently leads the class. . . . Line is straight. . . . Spacing is tight. . . . The class is stepping together. . . . Everyone shows pride, their shoulders high . . . no slumping," according to the strict criteria for filing at Level Four.

"Line is straight, but one or two people [are] not quite in line," according to the box for Level Three. "Line leader leads the class," and "almost everyone shows pride."

"Several are slumping. . . . Little pride is showing," says the box for Level Two. "Spacing is uneven. . . . Some are talking and whispering."

"Line leader is paying no attention," says the box for Level One. "Heads are turning every way. . . . Hands are touching. . . . The line is not straight. . . . There is no pride."

The teacher who handed me this document believed at first that it was written as a joke by someone who had simply come to be fed up with all the numbers and accounting rituals that clutter up the day in many overregulated schools. Alas, it turned out that it was no joke but had been printed in a handbook of instructions for the teachers in the city where she taught.

There is no misery index for the children of apartheid education. There ought to be; we measure almost everything else that happens to them in their schools. Do kids who go to schools like these enjoy the days they spend in them? Is school, for most of them, a happy place to be? You do not find the answers to these questions in reports about achievement levels, scientific methods of accountability, or structural revisions in the modes of governance. Documents like these don't speak of happiness. You have to go back to the schools themselves to find an answer to these questions. You have to sit down in the little chairs in first and second grade, or on the reading rug with kindergarten kids, and listen to the things they actually say to one another and the dialogue between them and their teachers. You have to go down to the basement with the children when it's time for lunch and to the playground with them, if they have a playground, when it's time for recess, if they still have recess at their school. You have to walk into the children's bathrooms in these buildings. You have to do what children do and breathe the air the children breathe. I don't think that there is any other way to find out what the lives that children lead in school are really like.

High school students, when I first meet them, are often more reluctant than the younger children to open up and express their personal concerns; but hesitation on the part of students did not prove to be a problem when I visited a tenth-grade class at Fremont High School in Los Angeles. The students were told that I was a writer, and they took no time in getting down to matters that were on their minds.

"Can we talk about the bathrooms?" asked a soft-spoken student named Mireya.

In almost any classroom there are certain students who, by the force of their directness or the unusual sophistication of their way of speaking, tend to capture your attention from the start. Mireya later spoke insightfully about some of the serious academic problems that were common in the school, but her observations on the physical and personal embarrassments she and her schoolmates had to undergo cut to the heart of questions of essential dignity that kids in squalid schools like this one have to deal with all over the nation.

Fremont High School, as court papers filed in a lawsuit against the state of California document, has fifteen fewer bathrooms than the law requires. Of the limited number of bathrooms that are working in the school, "only one or two . . . are open and unlocked for girls to use."

Long lines of girls are "waiting to use the bathrooms," which are generally "unclean" and "lack basic supplies," including toilet paper. Some of the classrooms, as court papers also document, "do not have air-conditioning," so that students, who attend school on a three-track schedule that runs year-round, "become red-faced and unable to concentrate" during "the extreme heat of summer." The school's maintenance records report that rats were found in eleven classrooms. Rat droppings were found "in the bins and drawers" of the high school's kitchen, and school records note that "hamburger buns" were being "eaten off [the] bread-delivery rack."

No matter how many tawdry details like these I've read in legal briefs or depositions through the years, I'm always shocked again to learn how often these unsanitary physical conditions are permitted to continue in the schools that serve our poorest students—even after they have been vividly described in the media. But hearing of these conditions in Mireya's words was even more unsettling, in part because this student seemed so fragile and because the need even to speak of these indignities in front of me and all the other students was an additional indignity.

"The problem is this," she carefully explained. "You're not allowed to use the bathroom during lunch, which is a thirty-minute period. The only time that you're allowed to use it is between your classes." But "this is a huge building," she went on. "It has long corridors. If you have one class at one end of the building and your next class happens to be way down at the other end, you don't have time to use the bathroom and still get to class before it starts. So you go to your class and then you ask permission from your teacher to go to the bathroom and the teacher tells you, 'No. You had your chance between the periods. . . .'

"I feel embarrassed when I have to stand there and explain it to a teacher."

"This is the question," said a wiry-looking boy named Edward, leaning forward in his chair. "Students are not animals, but even animals need to relieve themselves sometimes. We're here for eight hours. What do they think we're supposed to do?"

"It humiliates you," said Mireya, who went on to make the interesting statement that "the school provides solutions that don't actually work," and this idea was taken up by several other students in describing course requirements within the school. A tall black student, for example, told me that she hoped to be a social worker or a doctor but was programmed into "Sewing Class" this year. She also had to take another course, called "Life Skills," which she told me was a very basic course—"a retarded class," to use her words—that "teaches things like the six continents," which she said she'd learned in elementary school.

When I asked her why she had to take these courses, she replied that she'd been told they were required, which as I later learned was not exactly so. What was required was that high school students take two courses in an area of study called "The Technical Arts," and which the Los Angeles Board of Education terms "Applied Technology." At schools that served the middle class or upper-middle class, this requirement was likely to be met by courses that had academic substance and, perhaps, some relevance to college preparation. At Beverly Hills High School, for example, the technical-arts requirement could be fulfilled by taking subjects like residential architecture, the designing of commercial structures, broadcast journalism, advanced computer graphics, a sophisticated course in furniture design, carving and sculpture, or an honors course in engineering research and design. At Fremont High, in contrast, this requirement was far more often met by courses that were basically vocational and also obviously keyed to low-paying levels of employment.

Mireya, for example, who had plans to go to college, told me that she had to take a sewing class last year and now was told she'd been assigned to take a class in hairdressing, as well. When I asked her teacher why Mireya could not skip these subjects and enroll in classes that would help her to pursue her college aspirations, she replied, "It isn't a question of what students want. It's what the school may have available. If all the other elective classes that a student wants to take are full, she has to take one of these classes if she wants to graduate."

A very small girl named Obie, who had big blue-tinted glasses tilted up across her hair, interrupted then to tell me with a kind of wild gusto that she'd taken hairdressing *twice*! When I expressed surprise that this was possible, she said there were two levels of hairdressing offered here at Fremont High. "One is in hairstyling," she said. "The other is in braiding."

Mireya stared hard at this student for a moment and then suddenly began to cry. "I don't *want* to take hairdressing. I did not need sewing, either. I knew how to sew. My mother is a seamstress in a factory. I'm trying to go to college. I don't need to sew to go to college. My mother sews. I hoped for something else."

"What would you rather take?" I asked.

"I wanted to take an AP class," she answered.

Mireya's sudden tears elicited a strong reaction from one of the boys who had been silent up till now: a thin, dark-eyed student named Fortino, who had long hair down to his shoulders. He suddenly turned directly to Mireya and spoke into the silence that followed her last words.

"Listen to me," he said. "The owners of the sewing factories need laborers. Correct?"

"I guess they do," Mireya said.

"It's not going to be their own kids. Right?"

"Why not?" another student said.

"So they can grow beyond themselves," Mireya answered quietly. "But we remain the same."

"You're ghetto," said Fortino, "so we send you to the factory." He sat low in his desk chair, leaning on one elbow, his voice and dark eyes loaded with a cynical intelligence. "You're ghetto—so you sew!"

"There are higher positions than these," said a student named Samantha.

"You're ghetto," said Fortino unrelentingly. "So sew!"

18

"YES, BUT HOW DO WE DO IT?": PRACTICING CULTURALLY RELEVANT PEDAGOGY

Gloria Ladson-Billings

In her groundbreaking book The Dreamkeepers *and in numerous scholarly publications, University of Wisconsin professor Gloria Ladson-Billings has portrayed and analyzed the practice of successful teachers of African American students—teachers who embody what Ladson-Billings calls "culturally relevant teaching." Her work is used widely in teacher-preparation programs and has influenced a generation of educators. In the following essay, Ladson-Billings explains the elements of culturally relevant pedagogy, while arguing that improving the education of poor students of color is as much a matter of how we think as of "what to do."*

In 1989, when I began documenting the practice of teachers who achieved success with African American students, I had no idea that it would create a kind of cottage industry of exemplary teachers. I began the project with the assumption that there were indeed teachers who could and did teach poor students of color to achieve high levels of academic success (Ladson-Billings, 1994). Other scholars (Foster, 1997; Mathews, 1988) verified this aspect of my work. Unfortunately, much of the work that addresses successful teaching of poor students of color is linked to the notion of the teacher as heroic isolate. Thus, stories such as those of Marva Collins (Collins & Tamarkin, 1990), Jaime Escalante (Mathews, 1988), Vivian Paley (2000), and Louanne Johnson (1992) inadvertently transmit a message of the teacher as savior and charismatic maverick without exploring the complexities of teaching and nuanced intellectual work that undergirds pedagogical practices.

In this chapter, I discuss the components of culturally relevant teaching (Ladson-Billings, 1995) and provide practical examples of how teachers might implement these components in their classrooms. I choose to provide practice-based examples to remove some of the mystery and mythology tied to theory that keep teachers from doing the work designed to support high levels of achievement for poor students of color.

BUT HOW DO WE DO IT?

Almost every teacher-educator devoted to issues of diversity and social justice finds himself or herself confronted by prospective and in-service teachers who quickly reject teaching for social justice by insisting that there are no practical exemplars that make such teaching possible. A semester or staff development session typically ends with teachers unsure of what they can or should do and eventually defaulting to regular routines and practices. Nothing changes in the classroom and poor students of color are no closer to experiencing the kind of education to which they are entitled.

I argue that the first problem teachers confront is believing that successful teaching for poor students of color is primarily about "what to do." Instead, I suggest that the problem is rooted in how we think—about the social contexts, about the students, about the curriculum, and about instruction. Instead of the specific lessons and activities that we select to fill the day, we must begin to understand the ways our theories and philosophies are made to manifest in the pedagogical practices and rationales we exhibit in the classroom. The following sections briefly describe the salient elements of teacher thinking that contribute to what I have termed "culturally relevant teaching."

Social Contexts

Teaching takes place not only in classrooms. It takes place in schools and communities. It takes place in local, state, national, and global contexts that impact students regardless of whether teachers acknowledge them or not. How teachers think about those contexts creates an environment for thinking about teaching. Teachers who believe that society is fair and just believe that their students are participating on a level playing field and simply have to learn to be better competitors than other students. They also believe in a kind of social Darwinism that supports the survival of the fittest. Teachers with this outlook accept that some students will necessarily fall by the wayside and experience academic failure.

Teachers who I term "culturally relevant" assume that an asymmetrical (even antagonistic) relationship exists between poor students of color and society. Thus, their vision of their work is one of preparing students to combat inequity by being highly competent and critically conscious. While the teachers are concerned with the students who sit in their classrooms each day, they see them in relation to a continuum of struggle—past, present, and future. Thus, the AIDS crisis in black and brown communities, immigration laws, and affordable health care are not merely "adult" issues, but also are a part of the social context in which teachers attempt to do their work.

Being aware of the social context is not an excuse for neglecting the classroom tasks associated with helping students to learn literacy, numeracy, scientific, and social skills. Rather, it reminds teachers of the larger social purposes of their work.

The Students

Of course, teachers think about their students. But *how* they think about their students is a central concern of successful teaching. In my work as a teacher educator, I regularly see prospective teachers who approach teaching with romantic notions about students. They believe that the goodwill and energy they bring to the classroom will be rewarded by enthusiastic, appreciative students, who will comply with their requests and return the love they purport to give their students. Unfortunately, real life rarely matches that ideal. Poor students of color, like all children, live complex lives that challenge teachers' best intentions. Whether teachers think of their students as needy and deficient or capable and resilient can spell the difference between pedagogy grounded in compensatory perspectives and those grounded in critical and liberatory ones.

My best examples of the first perspective come from years of observing prospective teachers enter classrooms where students fail to comply with their wishes and directives. Quickly the students are constructed as problems—"at risk," behavior problems, savages—and those constructions become self-fulfilling prophecies (Rist, 1970). Before long, the classroom is no longer a place where students are taught and expected to learn. Rather, it becomes a place where bodies are managed and maintaining order becomes the primary task. Unfortunately, many urban schools reinforce and reward this type of pedagogical response (Haberman, 1991).

Culturally relevant teachers envision their students as being filled with possibilities. They imagine that somewhere in the classroom is the next Nobel laureate (a Toni Morrison), the next neurosurgeon (a Benjamin Carson), or the next pioneer for social justice (a Fannie Lou Hamer).[1] This perspective moves the teachers from a position of sympathy ("you poor dear")[2] to one of informed empathy. This informed empathy requires the teacher to feel with the students rather than feel for them. Feeling with the students builds a sense of solidarity between the teacher and the students but does not excuse students from working hard in pursuit of excellence.

Culturally relevant teachers recognize that their students are "school dependent."[3] I use this term to suggest that some students are successful in spite of their schooling, as a result of material resources and cultural capital. If they have incompetent or uncaring teachers, their parents and families have the resources to supplement and enhance the schooling experience. However, most poor students of color look to schools as the vehicle for social advancement and equity. They are totally dependent on the school to help them achieve a variety of goals. When the school fails to provide for those needs, these students are locked out of social and cultural benefits. For example, a number of poor students of color find themselves in classrooms with teachers who are unqualified or underqualified to teach (Ladson-Billings, 2005). More striking is that some of these children find themselves in classrooms where there is no regularly assigned teacher. Instead, the students spend entire school years with a series of substitute teachers who have no responsibility for supporting their academic success.

The Curriculum

Typically, teachers are expected to follow a prescribed curriculum that state and local administrators have approved. In many large school districts, that approved curriculum may merely be a textbook. In several poorly performing districts, that curriculum may be a script that teachers are required to recite and follow. I argue that teachers engaged in culturally relevant pedagogy must be able to deconstruct, construct, and reconstruct (Shujaa, 1994) the curriculum. "Deconstruction" refers to the ability to take apart the "official knowledge" (Apple, 2000) to expose its weaknesses, myths, distortions, and omissions. "Construction" refers to the ability to build curriculum. Similar to the work that John Dewey (1997) advocated, construction relies on the experiences and knowledge that teachers and their students bring to the classroom. "Reconstruction" requires the work of rebuilding the curriculum that was previously taken apart and examined. It is never enough to tear down. Teachers must be prepared to build up and fill in the holes that emerge when students begin to use critical analysis as they attempt to make sense of the curriculum.

The perspective of culturally relevant teachers is that the curriculum is a cultural artifact and as such is not an ideologically neutral document. Whereas the highly ideological nature of the curriculum is evident in high-profile communities where there are fights over evolution versus creation or sex education curricula that advocate safe sex versus abstinence, it is more subtle and pernicious in other curriculum documents. For example, the history curriculum reflects ethnocentric and sometimes xenophobic attitudes and regularly minimizes the faults of the United States and some European nations. Even an area such as mathematics is susceptible to ideology that leaves poor children of color receiving mathematics curricula that focus on rote memorization and algorithms whereas middle-class students have early access to algebraic thinking and more conceptually grounded approaches.

Instruction

No curriculum can teach itself. It does not matter if teachers have access to exceptional curriculum if they do not have the instructional skills to teach all students. College and university professors have the means to provide students with intellectually challenging and critical knowledge, but few professors are able to teach the wide variety of students who show up in K–12 classrooms. Precollegiate teachers must have a wide repertoire of teaching strategies and techniques to ensure that all students can access the curriculum. Unlike postsecondary teachers, K–12 teachers teach students who may or may not wish to be students. That means that their teaching must engage, cajole, convict, and perhaps even fool students into participation. Culturally relevant teachers understand that some of the pedagogical strategies that make teaching easier or more convenient for them may be exactly the kind of instruction they should avoid. For example, placing students in ability groups or tracks may serve to alienate struggling students further. Lecturing, no matter how efficient, may do nothing more than create greater gaps between successful students and those who are not. Even those strategies that progressive educators see as more democratic may fail to create the equal access teachers desire. In this instance, I refer to the almost unanimous belief that cooperative learning is a preferred teaching strategy. Many teacher preparation programs emphasize cooperative and other group strategies as preferable to more traditional classroom arrangements. However, when poorly managed, cooperative learning creates unequal workloads and instances in which students exclude other students from the process. High achievers sometimes resent being placed with struggling students and struggling students can be embarrassed by their inability to be full participants in the group setting.

Thus, if teachers must consider the ways that the social contexts of schooling impact their work and that their context may not be supportive, what, if anything, can they do? I argue that teachers must engage in a culturally relevant pedagogy that is designed to attend to the context while simultaneously preparing students for the traditional societal demands (i.e., high school completion, postsecondary education, workplace requirements, active and participatory citizenship). I next address the elements of culturally relevant pedagogy that teachers must attend to in order to achieve success with students who have been underserved by our schools.

ACADEMIC ACHIEVEMENT

When I wrote the words "academic achievement" almost ten years ago, I never dreamed that I would regret using this term. What I had in mind has nothing to do with the oppressive atmosphere of standardized tests; the wholesale retention of groups of students; scripted curricula; and the intimidation of students, teachers, and parents. Rather, what I envisioned is more accurately described as "student learning"— what it is that students actually know and are able to do as a result of pedagogical interactions with skilled teachers. However, because I started with the term "academic achievement," I will stay with it for consistency's sake.

The teachers who focus on academic achievement (i.e., student learning) understand that this is their primary function. They are not attempting to get students to "feel good about themselves" or learn how to exercise self-control. Rather, they are most interested in the cultivation of students' minds and supporting their intellectual lives. They understand that through engaged learning students will develop self-esteem and self-control. They recognize that the outbursts and off-task behaviors are symptoms, not causes, and as teachers the one thing they have at their disposal are pedagogical tools to draw students into the learning in meaningful ways.

Culturally relevant teachers think deeply about what they teach and ask themselves why students should learn particular aspects of the curriculum. In these classrooms, teachers are vetting everything in the curriculum and often supplement the curriculum. For example, in a culturally relevant high school English class the teacher may understand that he or she has to teach *Romeo and Juliet* but would couch that book in the context of students' own struggles with parents over dating. There may even be a detailed discussion of suicide and the level of desperation that adolescents may experience when they cannot communicate with adults. Finally, the teacher may include some films, popular music, or other stories that take up the theme of young, forbidden love. The point here is that a culturally relevant teacher does not take the book as a given. Rather, the teacher asks himself or herself specific questions about what reading this book is supposed to accomplish. This same teacher might be quite explicit about the place of the text in the literary canon and the cachet and clout students acquire when they can speak intelligently about such texts. One of the major academic activities in the classroom of culturally relevant teachers is engaging in critique of texts and activities. Over and over students ask and are asked, "Why are we doing this?" "Why is this important?" and "How does this enrich my life and/or the life of others?"

For tasks that seem mundane, teachers may use a very pragmatic skill (e.g., changing a tire) to help students understand how simple component parts of a task (e.g., blocking and braking the car), are necessary prerequisites to the larger task. The chemistry teacher may spend time helping students learn the precise way to light and use a Bunsen burner, not because lighting a Bunsen burner is a marketable skill, but because having a lit Bunsen burner will be important for many of the subsequent labs.

Repeatedly, culturally relevant teachers speak in terms of long-term academic goals for students. They rarely focus on "What should I do on Monday?" and spend a considerable amount of their planning trying to figure out what the semester or yearlong goals are. They share those goals with students and provide them with insights into their teaching so that students know why they are doing what they are doing. These teachers use many real-life and familiar examples that help the classroom come alive. They may use metaphors to paint word pictures. One teacher refers to the classroom experience as a trip and uses many travel metaphors. "We're still in San Jose and you know we've got to get to L.A." is what she might say when the class is falling behind where she thinks it should be. Or, she can be heard to say, "Hey, Lamar, why are you in Petaluma?" when referring to a student who is off task and doing the exact opposite of what she wishes to accomplish.

Interestingly, Foster (1989) describes a community college teacher who structured her classroom as an economy. Even with adult learners, this teacher understood that the metaphorical language helped her students visualize their objectives. The students who were "on welfare" wanted to get jobs in "the bank." The symbolism and imagery resonated with the students and the teacher used it as a way to get the very best out of her students.

CULTURAL COMPETENCE

Of the three terms ("academic achievement," "cultural competence," "sociopolitical consciousness") that I use to describe the components of culturally relevant pedagogy, I find the notion of cultural competence the most difficult to convey to teachers who wish to develop their own practice in this way. One of the problems is that like academic achievement, the term "cultural competence" has another set of meanings. Currently, many of the helping professions—such as medicine, nursing, counseling, social work—refer to something called "cultural competence." However, in these professions the notion of cultural competence refers to helping dominant group members become more skillful in reading the cultural messages of their clients. As a consequence, novice practitioners in these fields practice aspects of their work in ways that represent culturally sensitive behaviors—not pointing; speaking in direct, declarative sentences; directing questions and statements to an elder. Unfortunately, these practices reflect a static and essentialized view of culture and tend to reinforce stereotypes, rather than dispel them.

My sense of cultural competence refers to helping students to recognize and honor their own cultural beliefs and practices while acquiring access to the wider culture, where they are likely to have a chance of improving their socioeconomic status and making informed decisions about the lives they wish to lead. The point of my work is to maintain teachers' focus on what improves the lives of the students, families, and communities they serve—not to make teachers feel better about themselves. I presume that teachers who do learn more about their students' backgrounds, cultures, and experiences feel more capable and efficacious in their work as teachers, but the teachers are not my primary objective. In the most instrumental way, I think of the teachers as a vehicle for improving students' lives.

Teachers who foster cultural competence understand that they must work back and forth between the lives of their students and the life of school. Teachers have an obligation to expose their students to the very culture that oppresses them. That may seem paradoxical, but without the skills and knowledge of the dominant culture, students are unlikely to be able to engage that culture to effect meaningful change.

I visited two middle school teachers who created an etiquette unit in which they introduced students to information about manners. However, it was not a unit merely focused on what to do; it included historical, cultural, and sociological information about why these practices are as they are. At the end of the unit, the teachers took the students in small groups out to dinner at a quality restaurant. For many of the students, this was the first time they had attended a restaurant with linen napkins and multicourse dinners. The idea of this activity was not to attempt to make the students middle class but, rather, to have the students experience and critique middle-class ways. A surprising response to the dining experience was that of one female student, who said, "Now that I know what this is like I'm not going to let a guy take me to McDonald's and call that taking me out to dinner."

In one of the most powerful and striking instances of cultural competence, MacArthur Award winner,[4] teacher, and forensics coach Tommie Lindsey of James Logan High School in Union City, California, uses culturally specific speeches and dialogues to help his largely black and brown forensics team win local, state, and national competitions. The students use pieces from African American and Latina/Latino writers in the midst of a venue that can only be described as upper middle class and mainstream. Lindsey has successfully merged the students' cultural strengths with the forensics form. The students have exposure to a wider world without compromising aspects of their own culture.

SOCIOPOLITICAL CONSCIOUSNESS

I can typically convince teachers (both preservice and in-service) that it is important to focus on student learning as well as make use of students' culture. However, the idea that developing sociopolitical consciousness is important is a much harder sell. One of the reasons that this aspect of the theory is difficult is that most of the teachers I encounter have not developed a sociopolitical consciousness of their own. True, most hold strong opinions about the sociopolitical issues they know about, but many do not know much about sociopolitical issues. When I talk to teachers about economic disparities, they rarely link these disparities with issues of race, class, and gender. Thus, the first thing teachers must do is educate themselves about both the local sociopolitical issues of their school community (e.g., school board policy, community events) and the larger sociopolitical issues (e.g., unemployment, health care, housing) that impinge upon their students' lives.

The second thing teachers need to do is incorporate those issues into their ongoing teaching. I am not talking about teachers pushing their own agendas to the detriment of student learning. Rather, the task here is to help students use the various skills they learn to better understand and critique their social position and context. For example, in my original study of cultural competence and sociopolitical awareness, a student complained about the deterioration of the community and expressed strong emotions about how unhappy he was living in a place that had lots of crime, drugs, and little in the way of commerce and recreational facilities. The teacher used the student's emotion to develop a community study. Although it is typical for students to study their community, this study involved a detailed examination of the reality of the community, not a superficial look at "community helpers." The teacher retrieved information from the historical society's archives so that the students could compare the community's present condition with that of the past and raise questions about how the decline had occurred. Ultimately, the students developed a land-use plan that they presented to the city council.

THE CULPABILITY OF TEACHER EDUCATION

Most discussions of what teachers fail to do give teacher education a pass. We presume that teachers are doing something separate and apart from their preparation. However, I argue that teacher preparation plays a large role in maintaining the status quo. Teacher educators are overwhelmingly white, middle-aged, and monolingual English speakers. Although more women are entering the academy as teacher educators, the cultural makeup of the teacher-education profession is embarrassingly homogeneous. This cultural homogeneity of the teacher-education profession makes it difficult to persuade convincingly preservice teachers that they should know and do anything different in their classrooms.

In addition to the overwhelming cultural homogeneity of the teacher-education profession, we organize our profession in ways that suggest that issues of diversity and social justice are tangential to the enterprise. Most preservice teachers enter a program that ghettoizes issues of diversity. Somewhere in a separate course or workshop, students are given "multicultural information." It is here that students often are confused, angry, and frustrated because they do not know what to do with this information. Regularly preservice teachers report feelings of guilt and outrage because they receive information about inequity, racism, and social injustice in ways that destabilize their sense of themselves and make them feel responsible for the condition of poor children of color in our schools.

In some instances, preservice teachers participate in a teacher-education program that requires them to have at least one field experience in a diverse classroom and/or community setting. When such field experiences are poorly done, this requirement becomes just another hoop through which students jump to earn a credential. Students in these circumstances regularly speak of "getting over" their diversity requirement. Rarely do such students want to do their most significant field experience—student teaching—in diverse classrooms. When these field experiences are well conceived, they allow preservice teachers to be placed in classrooms with skillful teachers and be supervised by careful teacher educators who can help them make sense of what they are experiencing and create useful applications for the multicultural knowledge they are learning.

Although the National Council for the Accreditation of Teacher Education includes a diversity standard in its accreditation process, most programs struggle to equip novice teachers fully to work with children who are poor, linguistically diverse, and/or from racial or ethnic minority groups. Teacher candidates may resist the lessons of diversity and social justice, but that resistance may be intimately tied to the lack of credibility their professors and teacher-education instructors possess. Why should preservice students believe that teacher educators who spend much of their lives in the comforts of the academy can understand the challenges today's classrooms present? Why should tenuous 1960s civil rights credentials be made proxies for twenty-first-century problems? I am not suggesting that participation in the civil rights struggle is an unimportant part of one's biography—it is a part of my own biography. Rather, I am suggesting that in this new time and space, that aspect of one's biography may not prove adequate for helping students navigate the multiple ways that race, class, gender, and language identities complicate the pedagogical project. Teacher education has much to answer for concerning its role in preparing teachers who fail to serve classrooms of poor children of color well.

WHAT IS A TEACHER TO DO?

As I noted earlier, many well-meaning teachers lament the fact that they do not know what to do when it comes to meeting the educational needs of all students. Indeed, a group of soon-to-be teachers recently said to me, "Everybody keeps telling us about multicultural education, but nobody is telling us how to do it!" I responded, "Even if we could tell you how to do it, I would not want us to tell you how to do it." They looked at me with very confused expressions on their faces. I went on to say, "The reason I would not tell you what to do is that you would probably do it!" Now, the confused expressions became more pronounced. "In other words," I continued, "you would probably do exactly what I told you to do without any deep thought or critical analysis. You would do what I said regardless of the students in the classroom, their ages, their abilities, and their need for whatever it is I proposed." I concluded by asking the students who had taught them to "do democracy." They acknowledged that no one had taught them to do democracy, and I rejoined that doing democracy is one of their responsibilities. Slowly, the conversation moved to a discussion of how democracy is a goal for which we are all striving and although there are a few cases such as voting and public debate during which we participate in democracy, for the most part democracy is unevenly and episodically attended to. As teachers they have the responsibility to work toward educating citizens so that they are capable of participating in a democracy and nobody (and no teacher-education program) is going to tell them how to do it. They are going to have to commit to democracy as a central principle of their pedagogy.

Eventually, the preservice teachers began to see multicultural education and teaching for social justice as less a thing and more an ethical
position they need to take in order to ensure that students are getting
the education to which they are entitled. As a teacher educator, I have
worked hard to motivate preservice teachers to become reflective practitioners who care about the educational futures of their students. Often we are naive enough to think that all teachers care about the
educational futures of their students. The truth is that most teachers
care about what happens to their students only while they have responsibility for them. To that end, they take on a tutorial role for some students, making sure they learn and advance. They take on a custodial
role for some students, taking care of them in whatever state they are in
but not advancing them educationally. They take on a referral agent
role for others, shipping them off to someone else (e.g., a special educator, a parent volunteer, a student teacher) and expecting others to take
responsibility for them educationally. But, how many teachers look at
the students in their classrooms and envision them three, five, ten years
down the road? Our responsibility to students is not merely for the nine
months from September to June. It is a long-term commitment, not
just to the students but also to society. Although we may have only a
yearlong interaction with students, we ultimately have a lifelong impact
on who they become and the kind of society in which we all will ultimately live.

An analogy I will use to illustrate this point is my experience with
healthcare professionals. I do this with full knowledge that many people
have not benefited from our current healthcare arrangements. Thus,
this analogy uses an N of 1. Currently, I see four different physicians—
an internist, an allergist, a gynecologist, and an oncologist. My internist
is like my "homeroom" teacher. He tracks my schedule and makes sure
I get to my other classes (i.e., the other physicians) on a regular basis.
All of my physicians take responsibility not just for the aspect of my
health in which he or she is expert but also for my total health. They all
want my weight to be within a certain range. They all monitor my
blood pressure. They all look at the various medications I am taking so
that they can make intelligent decisions about what they should or
should not prescribe. I am not so naive to believe that the physicians are

merely invested in me. I am arguing that my physicians are invested in the health of the community as well as my personal health. It does not benefit the community to have me be unhealthy within it. Similarly, it does not benefit our democracy to have uneducated and undereducated people within it. Our responsibility to the students who sit before us extends well into the future, both theirs and ours.

CONCLUSION

This chapter asks the question Yes, but how do we do it? I have laid out an argument for why "doing" is less important than "being." I have argued that practicing culturally relevant pedagogy is one of the ways of "being" that will inform ways of "doing." I have suggested that our responsibility extends beyond the classroom and beyond the time students are assigned to us. It extends throughout their education because we contribute to (or detract from) that education. In a very real sense, the question is not how we do it but, rather, How can we not do it?

REFERENCES

Apple, M.W. (2000). *Official knowledge: Democratic education in a conservative age.* New York: Routledge.

Collins, M., & Tamarkin, C. (1990). *Marva Collins' way.* New York: Penguin.

Dewey, J. (1997). *Experience and education.* New York: Simon & Schuster.

Foster, M. (1989). "It's cookin' now": A performance analysis of the speech events of a black teacher in an urban community college. *Language in Society, 18*(1) 1–29.

Foster, M. (1997). *Black teachers on teaching.* New York: New Press.

Haberman, M. (1991). The pedagogy of poverty versus good teaching. *Phi Delta Kappan, 73,* 290–94.

Johnson, L. (1992). *My posse don't do homework.* New York: St. Martin's Press.

Ladson-Billings, G. (1994). *The Dreamkeepers: Successful teachers of African American children.* San Francisco: Jossey Bass.

Ladson-Billings, G. (1995). Toward a theory of culturally relevant pedagogy. *American Educational Research Journal, 31,* 465–69.

Ladson-Billings, G. (2005). No teacher left behind: Issues of equity and teacher quality. In C.A. Dwyer (Ed.), *Measurement and Research in Accountability Era.* Mahwah, NJ: Lawrence Erlbaum, 141–62.

Mathews, J. (1988). *Escalante: The best teacher in America*. New York: Henry Holt.

Paley, V. (2000). *White teacher*. Cambridge, MA: Harvard University Press.

Rist, R. (1970). Student social class and teacher expectations: The self-fulfilling prophecy in ghetto education. *Harvard Educational Review, 40*(3) 411–51.

Shujaa, M.W. (Ed.) (1994). *Too much schooling, too little education: A paradox of black life in white societies*. Trenton, NJ: Africa World Press.

NOTES

1. I purposely chose examples that represent people who came from working-class and poor backgrounds.
2. I borrowed this term from Professor Pat Campbell, University of Maryland.
3. I first used this term in a school-funding equity case against the State of South Carolina.
4. The MacArthur Award is also referred to as a "genius" award.

19

DESDE ENTONCES, SOY CHICANA: A MEXICAN IMMIGRANT STUDENT RESISTS SUBTRACTIVE SCHOOLING

Angela Valenzuela

Angela Valenzuela is an associate professor in the Department of Curriculum and Instruction and the Center for Mexican American Studies at the University of Texas at Austin. In her book Subtractive Schooling: U.S.-Mexican Youth and the Politics of Caring, *Valenzuela examines how attempts to "Americanize" Mexican immigrant students at a Houston high school often end up stripping away, or at least muting, students' linguistic and cultural identities. Yet a few immigrant students—sometimes with the support of their teachers, many times on their own—figure out ways to become truly bicultural, holding on to and valuing their cultural assets, while also navigating the expectations of the U.S. mainstream. Valenzuela profiles one such student in the following selection.*

In a three-year study of immigrant and nonimmigrant youth attending Seguín High School (a pseudonym), an overcrowded, segregated, inner-city school in Houston, Texas, I observed the existence of powerful pressures for immigrants to rapidly assimilate, or "Americanize." I explore this pattern in my book, *Subtractive Schooling: U.S.-Mexican Youth and the Politics of Caring.*[1] There I argue that the Americanization of immigrant students' identities results from the way the curriculum at Seguín High School is organized—and not organized. Specifically, the educational process fails to promote bilingualism, biculturalism, and biliteracy. Instead, schooling is more about subtracting than adding these competencies, and in so doing compromises the achievement of immigrant and nonimmigrant youth alike.

Most of the youth I interviewed for the study were members of the "1.5 generation," those who had immigrated from Mexico at an early age but who, for the major part of their young lives, had a U.S. schooling experience and were thus similar in many respects to their more acculturated, U.S.-born Mexican American peers. I conclude that recent immigrants' rush to claim a new identity renders them marginal not only with respect to the academic mainstream, but also with respect to their families' social identities.

The rapid assimilation of first-generation immigrant youth is often a sign of maladjustment, because identity "choices" are based on a disaffirmation of the self and of the family's social identity. While I observed this pattern, however, I also observed that some students are able both to assimilate *and* to learn to value the cultural assets that they bring to the schooling context. Nelda was one such student from whom we can learn a great deal.

NELDA

I first encountered Nelda, an eleventh-grader, through her English teacher, an Anglo female, who insisted that I meet her. The teacher found Nelda to be a phenomenal student because she had arrived in the United States only three years earlier (in eighth grade) and was already a high achiever. Nelda was virtually fluent in English and blended in well socially with the other students in the class. The teacher was most impressed with the fact that, except for a "very mild" accent, Nelda seemed little different from "the others" (i.e., U.S.-born youth) in the way she carried herself. Explaining to Nelda my interest as a researcher, the teacher prepared her for my morning visit to her class.

When I arrived, the students were busy working at their desks. Nelda saw me and, after a nod from the teacher, stepped out into the hall with me, where we talked for the greater part of the fifty-minute period. Our conversation began with questions about her background. The entire conversation took place in English, with Nelda occasionally asking me to translate certain words for her.

Nelda said that she was from the interior of Mexico but had lived for several years in Matamoros, Tamaulipas, which is adjacent to the city of Brownsville at Texas's southernmost border. She explained that her family was lured to the U.S.-Mexican border by the availability of industrial jobs. The pay was still low, however, and to make ends meet her mother crossed the border daily into Brownsville, where she worked as a cleaning woman in various homes. Nelda's family lived in Matamoros for five years, where Nelda and her younger sister had the opportunity to attend *secundaria* (middle school). An English-language course was offered at the school one year, but the instruction was very poor. Nevertheless, Nelda appreciated the opportunity to plow through the assigned book for the course. The family's continuing economic struggles ultimately drove her father to seek better-paying construction jobs in Houston. Her mother still works cleaning homes.

I next asked Nelda which subjects she liked the most in school. This question sparked an immediate intellectual exchange. Nelda began by saying that she has always been interested in history, but especially Mexican and Mexican American history. She said that she had always wondered if the relationship between Mexico and the United States parallels that between Anglos and Mexicans in Texas. "Well, what do you think?" I asked. "I think it is very similar," she said. She went on to explain very articulately that Mexico is a poor country compared to the United States and that Mexican Americans are poor compared to Anglos, "though they are richer here than they are in Mexico." Already the budding scholar, Nelda said that she wanted to read and study more to find out why this parallel exists. Nelda also said that she would love to attend college and continue with her interest in history.

I then asked Nelda whether her parents were educated, where her interest in history came from, and how she acquired nativelike fluency in English in such a short period of time. She told me that her father had attained a *secundaria* level of schooling, while her mother had received no more than a primary education: "They both had to work to support their families. Life is very hard in Mexico."

Regarding her interest in history and her facility with English, Nelda explained that living on the border and having a lot of exposure to Chicanas/os, hearing the English language, and reading books in

English influenced both her thinking and her language fluency. Her mother's experiences as a cleaning woman were pivotal. She explained that in Brownsville her mother worked for many years for a middle-class Mexican American woman. The woman frequently gave Nelda's mother books in English as gifts, which were soon passed on to Nelda. Nelda said she welcomed the opportunity, dictionary in hand, to improve her literacy in English. She recalled reading such authors as Isabel Allende and Laura Esquivel in English. Most important, however, was her discovery of Rodolfo Acuña's book, *Occupied America*, which provides a historical perspective on the taking of the southwestern lands formerly owned by the Mexican government.[2] "*Desde entonces, soy Chicana,*" she said. ("Since then, I am Chicana.") Interestingly, this was the only complete sentence she said in Spanish during any of our interviews.*

Given the vexed relationship between immigrants and Mexican Americans, her comment about being Chicana stunned me at the time. The actual terms *Chicana* and *Chicano* were rarely used as self-identifiers by Mexican American students at Seguín, much less by immigrant females. U.S.-born students prefer to refer to themselves as Mexican Americans, Mexicans, or Hispanics. Our hallway discussion was thus more enlightening for me than for her, though I did jot down on a piece of paper some additional readings that I thought she could locate in the public library.

Nelda said she often talked with her parents at home about how possible it was for Mexican Americans to become middle class. Although she was exposed to a lot of criticism about Chicanas/os, even in her own family, Nelda felt that through reading history she had come to see their struggles as her own. Nelda further explained that while she will always consider herself Mexican, she sees herself as different from other Mexicans who "look down" on Chicanos. Thus, she manages the dual identities of Mexican and Chicana without seeing any conflict between the two.

---

*In her use of the term *Chicana*, Nelda identifies herself not only with her own biculturalism (which began with her experience living along the U.S.-Mexico border), but also with the Chicano movement ideology of seeking social justice and a right to self-determination for Mexican Americans.

THE EXCEPTION OR THE RULE?

Nelda's case strongly suggests the role that ideology can play in mediating the assimilation of adolescents. Armed with excellent literacy skills and empowering historical knowledge, Nelda demonstrated the capacity both to achieve and to blend in within her social milieu. I later wondered why she was not placed in the honors or magnet level of the curriculum. I speculated that, like the vast majority of immigrant students, she had been tracked into regular-level courses during her first year in middle school.

While living on the border and being exposed to Chicanas/os were contributing factors, these are arguably not sufficient for any immigrant to assimilate as rapidly as Nelda seems to have done. Such contexts abound wherever Mexicans and Mexican Americans are concentrated, yet rapid assimilation within a three-year period is nevertheless exceptional. Clearly, Nelda's passion for history and her desire to understand more fully the sources of both Mexicans' and Chicanas/os' oppression was gripping. The fact that she bore at least some of the emblems of Americanized speech, dress, and interpersonal skills is a side note to a more central awakening within her that helps explain her rapid transformation into a Chicana against the historical and institutional odds of her doing so.

While it is impressive that Nelda was able to arrive at an in-depth understanding of the Mexican American experience, it is unfortunate that she represents the exception rather than the rule. Indirectly, her case embodies an implicit critique of the more general pattern of subtractive schooling, wherein a child's opportunity to develop her or his existing knowledge base is virtually nonexistent. Most significantly, Nelda's case reveals how schools can support a positive sense of identity for immigrant students in ways that are "additive" and empowering. When immigrant youth, and indeed all Mexican American youth, are allowed to maintain their cultural identities—even if that means deliberately exploring the distinct challenges they can expect to face as bicultural people—they can develop an enhanced sense of efficacy and personal control over their futures and reap immense psychic, social, emotional, and academic benefits.

NOTES

1. Angela Valenzuela, *Subtractive Schooling: U.S.-Mexican Youth and the Politics of Caring* (Albany: State University of New York Press, 1999).

2. Rodolfo Acuña, *Occupied America: A History of Chicanos*, 3rd ed. (New York: HarperCollins, 1988).

20

WHAT TEACHERS NEED TO KNOW ABOUT POVERTY

Sue Books

In many urban school districts, between 70 and 90 percent of students come from low-income families. But professional development for city teachers rarely includes efforts to help them understand poverty and its consequences for students. In the following chapter, Sue Books, professor of education at the State University of New York at New Paltz, argues that in order to teach poor children effectively, teachers first need to make concerted efforts to educate themselves about the social causes of poverty and its day-to-day impact on poor families.

Poor children bear the brunt of almost every imaginable social ill. In disproportionate numbers, they suffer hunger and homelessness; untreated sickness and chronic conditions such as asthma, ear infections, and tooth decay; lead poisoning and other forms of environmental pollution; and a sometimes debilitating level of distress created by crowded, run-down living spaces, family incomes that fall far short of family needs, and ongoing threats of street violence and family dissolution. These same children are assigned, again in skewed numbers, to the nation's worst public schools—schools in the worst states of disrepair and with the lowest levels of per-pupil funding. Not surprisingly, therefore, poor children as a group lag far behind others in educational achievement.

I start with these facts because the social horror of poverty and injustice, two sides of the same coin, is so often overlooked or discounted, as if it doesn't really matter. Yes, I can imagine someone saying, some do get more than others, but whoever said life was fair? And what about the significance of personal initiative and the courage to "go for one's dreams"? Certainly, luck, talent, and determination figure into the winding path any person's life takes. This chapter is not about that, however, but rather about the social, and especially the educational, significance of poverty. Many children who grow up in poverty thrive despite tremendous hardships. This testifies to the amazing strength of their young spirits, but cannot, or ought not, be used as a reason to deny the profound significance of poverty in young lives. That some children flourish despite the poverty they suffer is a credit to them, not a justification for nonchalance in the face of socially induced hardship. Blake's (1789/2003) young chimney sweep of the eighteenth century spoke prophetically to one of the horrors of our time, too:

> And because I am happy and dance and sing,
> They think they have done me no injury.
> And are gone to praise God and his Priest and King
> Who make up a heaven of our misery.

That many poor children "dance and sing" does not make child poverty not so bad after all. Rather, it underscores how much is destroyed when a growing "social toxicity" (Vorrasi & Garbarino, 2000) suffused by poverty is either rationalized as inevitable or ignored because it is regarded as unimportant.

Teachers obviously cannot eliminate poverty single-handedly. They cannot reconfigure the nation's political economy or redraw its social landscape. They cannot reshape the job market or change social policies governing housing and health care. At the same time, teachers can—and inevitably do—*respond* to the injustice to which poor children bear such painful witness. Consider, for example, the compassion and understanding Polakow (1993) observed in a kindergarten classroom, taught by Ms. Juno. Six-year-old Carrie often came to school distraught. Quick to pick fights with classmates, she was slow to join group activities. On this day:

> The children sit on the rug and listen to the story *The Very Hungry Caterpillar*. All are in the circle except Carrie, who sits at the arts and crafts table

cutting paper. "Ms. Juno, Carrie's not in the circle," says one little girl. "I know," replies Ms. Juno, "she'll come when she's ready." When the story is over, Ms. Juno announces she has a surprise. She goes into the closet and emerges with a large tank filled with sand. "Guess what I have in here." "A caterpillar," says Travis. "Right," replies Ms. Juno, "all sorts of worms and caterpillars." In twos the children take turns at the tank and fish out worms and caterpillars. Carrie, after watching from her vantage point at the table, slowly edges closer until she is in the circle. Ms. Juno calls her up together with Annie, a child who sometimes plays with Carrie. After the hands-on caterpillar activity, the children are given a choice of painting, drawing, or writing a story about caterpillars. Carrie chooses painting and goes straight to the easel; with deep concentration she spends almost fifteen minutes painting a picture of a "caterpillar family" and then counting all their legs. (Polakow, 1993, pp. 135–36)

Later:

During small group time, when Carrie is sitting next to Pat, she takes his colored marker and pokes him. Pat moves away, saying, "I wish I didn't have sat next to you." Carrie tries to write on his shirt with the marker. Pat shouts, "Quit it," and calls, "Ms. Juno, Ms. Juno, Carrie's writing on my shirt." Ms. Juno comes over and moves Carrie, saying, "Carrie, you cannot write on people's shirts, that really makes Pat feel bad—now come over here with me by my table." Carrie goes to Ms. Juno and pleads with her tearfully, "Don't tell my mother, she got sick again in the hospital." "Your mother will be real pleased to hear how well you've been doing, Carrie. Yesterday you were real helpful, and today's been hard for you, but we'll work on it." (Polakow, 1993, p. 136)

Carrie and her two siblings live in a subsidized apartment with their mother, who has been hospitalized twice with a serious illness. Since Carrie's mother lost a part-time job due to illness, the family has lived in "constant crisis," her teacher said, and has struggled to survive on public assistance through periods of eviction and a temporary cutoff of Medicaid insurance. When Carrie becomes aggressive with classmates, Ms. Juno pulls her away from the situation, gives her time to calm down, then works with all the children to help them understand each other's feelings. "Carrie is worried about her mommy and sometimes she feels sad or mad because she's going through a hard time, and we all need to help her," she told the children in the class (Polakow, 1993, p. 137). Some of Carrie's classmates avoid her, but others seek her out and try to make her feel better.

Like all classroom interactions, this one is complex. Yet it suggests the role of basic understanding in shaping teacher–student relationships. Carrie's teacher, Ms. Juno, knows something about the enormous stress in Carrie's life and responds with warmth, compassion, and the flexibility she believes Carrie needs to find a place for herself in the classroom. Over the course of her observations, Polakow (1993) saw some progress—no miracles, but signs of growing confidence and participation. "I can read real books now," Carrie told a friend enthusiastically. "Ms. Juno said I get to read my book I made to the whole class in circle time" (p. 138).[1]

After many years of observing "star teachers of children in poverty," Haberman (1995) concluded that these teachers' judgments and actions in the classroom reflect deep-seated beliefs about teaching, learning, and children. Consequently, Haberman (1995) offers not "10 easy steps" to becoming a star teacher, but rather a discussion of some of the commitments and beliefs evident in classrooms in which poor children flourish. One such belief is recognition that challenges come with the territory of teaching. "Star" teachers

> begin each semester knowing they will teach some youngsters who are affected by handicapping conditions. They anticipate that horrendous home, poverty, and environmental conditions will impinge on their students. They know that inadequate health care and nutrition, and various forms of substance and physical abuse, typify the daily existence of many of their students. In short, stars assume that the reason youngsters need teachers is

---

[1] Polakow (1993) observed Carrie during the course of a broader research project that documents the classroom worlds of poor children. As Section III of her book *Lives on the Edge: Single Mothers and Their Children in the Other America* shows, Carrie's experience of compassion and understanding contrasts sharply with the demeaning treatment many other poor children receive.

because there will be all manner of serious interferences with their teaching and with students' learning. (Haberman, 1995, p. 3)

"Because they do not regard their students as animals to be shaped," star teachers are not preoccupied with rewards and punishments (Haberman, 1995, p. 7). Because they do not regard poor families as scapegoats, they use what they know about their students and their families as a basis for helping students learn, never as fodder for parent bashing. Star teachers recognize that "most parents care a great deal and, if approached in terms of what they can do, will be active, cooperative partners" (Haberman, 1995, p. 12).

These teachers see their fundamental task as engaging students in educationally worthwhile activities and consequently "evaluate themselves whenever they assess student performance" (Haberman, 1995, p. 12). If students seem disengaged, star teachers wonder what they might do differently, and try something new—again and again, if necessary. These teachers *persist*, not because of an irrational faith in their students, not because they regard themselves as heroes, and not because they are determined to have their way. Rather, their persistence "reveals the deep and abiding beliefs that stars hold about the nature of children in poverty and their potential; the nature of stars' roles as teachers; and the reasons stars believe they and the children are in school"—namely, for children to learn about themselves and their world (Haberman, 1995, p. 21).

All teachers need the kind of understanding evident in Ms. Juno's response to Carrie as well as the commitment and persistence Haberman (1995) praises. Such a foundation cannot be reduced to the acquisition of information. At the same time, although knowing more does not guarantee better practice, knowing something about poverty gives teachers a place to start.

Such a foundation would include the recognition that poverty is a function of political economy, not of scarcity and not of personality. In wealthy nations such as the United States where there is no absolute scarcity of food, shelter, health care, or opportunity, poverty results from the politics of distribution. Although statistics justify the popular observation that "the rich get richer and the poor get poorer," politics drives this distributive trend, not natural law and not personal traits. Laziness, promiscuity, poor judgment, devaluation of education—none of these popular assumptions about the poor are either unique to any socioeconomic group or a cause of poverty in any demonstrable sense. Poor people do not cause poverty any more than enslaved human beings caused a system of institutionalized slavery to thrive in this country (Chamberlin, 1999), and just as studying the behavior or beliefs of slaves will not provide insight into institutionalized slavery, scrutinizing the behavior or beliefs of impoverished people will not lead to an understanding of how and why poverty persists in the United States.

Second, teachers need to recognize that poverty is not a black problem, an immigrant problem, a single-mother problem, or a "don't want to work" problem. Statistics do not back up this picture of poverty and its causes. Most people living in poverty are white, most live outside central cities (many in isolated rural areas), and about half of all poor families are headed by two parents or by single fathers. It is also the case that people of color, people living in central cities, and single-mother families are poor in disproportionate numbers. Both realities are important. Recognizing the scope of poverty and its prevalence among people of all racial and ethnic groups, in all family configurations, and in all geographic areas mediates against notions of the poor as "them"—those "others" who in some essential way, many people imagine, are not at all like themselves (Katz, 1989). At the same time, recognizing how widely (disproportionately) poverty is suffered by people of color, especially by young children in single-mother families in central cities, leads, or ought to lead, to questions about the role of racism and sexism in perpetuating destitution.

An emotionally charged public discourse props up a host of theories about the causes of poverty: single motherhood, lack of a work ethic, failure to accept personal responsibility or to "find" a job, and "dependency," the alleged personality flaw behind the need for public assistance. None of this stands up under the light of serious inquiry. As just one example, consider a comparative study of child poverty in twenty-three wealthy nations by the United Nations Children's Fund Innocenti Research Centre (2000a). The study found that neither the percentage of children living in single-parent families nor a nation's rate of joblessness correlated very closely with its rate of child poverty.[2] The percentage of children living in single-parent families varies greatly across the nations, from less than 1 percent in Turkey to more than 20 percent in Sweden, but these percentages bear little relationship to rates of child poverty. Proportionally, more children live in single-parent families in Sweden than in the United States, yet the child poverty rate in Sweden is one-tenth the rate of child poverty in this country. Almost the same percentage of children live in single-parent families in Canada as in Finland, but the child poverty rate in Canada is more than three times as high as the rate in Finland. Although children in single-parent families are much more likely to grow up in poverty than children in two-parent families, at least in the United States, this cross-nation comparison suggests the need to look beyond single motherhood as a *cause* of poverty. When strong social supports for families and decent job opportunities are available, single-mother families are far less likely to live in poverty.

The Innocenti researchers also found no clear-cut relationship between rates of unemployment and of child poverty across the twenty-three nations. Spain and Japan have widely differing rates of joblessness but about the same level of child poverty. The United States and Mexico have relatively low levels of unemployment, but relatively high levels of child poverty. In Finland, the reverse is true. Critical factors, of course, are wages and the distribution of job opportunities. If wages are too low, jobs do not lift families out of poverty, and if jobs that pay a living wage go primarily to members of households already living comfortably, they do little to alter a nation's child poverty rate.

Welfare reformers in the United States trumpeted the 1996 repeal of the sixty-year-old federal guarantee of support for poor families as a much-needed crackdown on the alleged problem of "dependency," to which poor mothers presumably had fallen victim. Faced with the choice of finding a job or accepting a "handout," the story went, poor mothers in droves opted not to work. In fact, welfare benefits had been

---

[2] The study, based largely on analysis of the household data sets in the Luxembourg Income Study, used a relative measure of child poverty: a family income below half the median in the nation. Poverty rates, depending on the country, refer to the years 1990 through 1997.

dropping for decades prior to the passage of the Personal Responsibility and Work Opportunity Act of 1996 and never brought families up even to the official poverty line. Far from enabling poor families to live comfortably, the maligned Aid to Families with Dependent Children (AFDC) program never enabled poor mothers even to meet basic family needs. Furthermore, a corresponding drop in the rate of child poverty has not accompanied the precipitous drop in the welfare rolls of almost 60 percent between 1996 and 2002.

With very few exceptions, work is now the law of the land, but this has not changed the lot of millions of children still living in poverty and in many cases has made it worse. The Economic Policy Institute (Boushey, Brocht, Gundersen, & Bernstein, 2001) estimates that almost 30 percent of families with one to three children under twelve have incomes too small to meet basic family needs, and that half of these families include an adult who works. In 1999, most poor children (78 percent) lived in a family in which someone worked at least part of the year (Children's Defense Fund, 2001a).

In addition to gaining some understanding of the causes and consequences of poverty, teachers need to recognize that almost all parents and caregivers, regardless of family income, want the best for their children and care about their education. Without the respect grounded in this recognition, teachers and school administrators cannot develop constructive relationships with families and communities. It has been said so often it now seems accepted as truth that parents in poor communities "don't care" about education. Neither research nor the experience of school leaders supports this presumption (Haberman, 1995; Lareau, 1989). "All parents want the best for their children. I've had crack-addicted mothers in my office demanding the best for their children," the principal of a high-poverty elementary school in Yonkers, New York, told me. "Parents want their kids to do well in school. With whatever they can bring to this world to make that happen, they're doing it," another Yonkers principal observed."[3]

---

[3] During the summer of 1999, I interviewed nine principals and assistant principals in seven high-poverty schools in upstate New York about how poverty affects schooling, in general as well as in their own work. In all but one of the schools, most of the students were eligible to receive subsidized lunches, a commonly used index of poverty. For a fuller analysis, see Books (2001).

Finally, teachers need to recognize that in schooling, as in society, poverty matters. Paul Houston, executive director of the American Association of School Administrators, makes the point well: "I don't think there's an educator who wouldn't stand up and say, 'Poor kids have more problems when they come to school than kids who come from homes where they're not poor'" (quoted in Hayden & Cauthen, 1998). Study after study, at least since the Coleman (1966) report, has confirmed the significance of poverty in schooling.

At the same time, although poverty matters in schooling, it is not all that matters. In the words of New York State Supreme Court Justice Leland DeGrasse, who overturned New York's highly inequitable system of funding public schools in 2001, "Demography is not destiny" (*Campaign for Fiscal Equity v. State of New York*, 2001). Poverty does not render children uneducable. Yet the school experience of many poor children hinders them more than it helps. This is what needs to change.

In 2001, more than 16 percent of all children in the United States lived in poverty, according to official calculations. The poverty rate for children of color is almost three times as high as the rate for white children. In many of our major cities and rural areas, entire communities are completely impoverished (Chatterley & Rouveral, 2000; Jargowsky, 1997; Kozol, 1995; Shirk, Bennett, & Aber, 1999). In such a society, teachers and teacher educators need to understand something about why poverty persists and how it affects young people. On one hand, this seems like an obvious point, hardly worth making: teachers need to know something about their students' lives and about the broader social-cultural context of those lives. On the other hand, however, few teacher-education programs require any systematic study of poverty or its consequences for children.

As a foundation of compassion, caring, and empathy, understanding is a prerequisite for good teaching (Martin, 1992; Noddings, 1992; Valenzuela, 1999)—a necessary condition, if nevertheless insufficient in and of itself. And understanding comes, of course, not from affirmation of preexisting prejudices (prejudgments) or of media-hyped stereotypes, but rather, at least in part, from a concerted effort to learn, undertaken with openness to the possibility of being challenged and changed. As Greene (1988) argues passionately, insight can make claims on one's life. Coming to understand something in a new way can leave us with no choice but to change our lives, including our professional lives, in response.

What any of us do with that knowledge is up to us. What we cannot do, however, is pull ourselves out of the equation. Poverty walks into the classroom in the minds and bodies of children, and we respond— with ignorance or understanding, with hostility or affection, by refusing to acknowledge the toll poverty takes or by throwing our weight into the long struggle for social justice and for the equality in educational opportunity that that struggle has promised but not yet delivered.

REFERENCES

Blake, W. (2003). *Songs of innocence and songs of experience.* (Original work published 1789.) Retrieved from The William Blake Archive, http://www.blakearchive .org. *Board of Education of Oklahoma City v. Dowell*, 498 U.S. 237 (1991).

Boushey, H., Brocht, C., Gundersen, B., & Bernstein, J. (2001). *Hardships in America: The real story of working families.* Washington, DC: Economic Policy Institute.

Campagin for Fiscal Equity v. State of New York, 719 N.Y.S. 2d 475 (2001). Can be retrieved from http://www.cfequity.org/decision/html.

Chamberlin, J.G. (1999). *Upon whom we depend: The American poverty system.* New York: Peter Lang.

Chatterley, C.N., & Rouveral, A.J. (2000). *"I was content and not content": The story of Linda Lord and the closing of Penobscot Poultry.* Carbondale: Southern Illinois University Press.

Children's Defense Fund. (2001a). *State of America's children: Yearbook 2001.* Washington, DC: Author.

Coleman, J. (1966). *Equality of educational opportunity.* Washington, DC: U.S. Government Printing Office.

Greene, M. (1998). *The dialectic of freedom.* New York: Teachers College Press.

Haberman, M. (1995). *Star teachers of children in poverty.* West Lafayette, IN: Kappa Delta Pi.

Hayden, J., & Cauthen, K. (Producers). (1998). *Children in America's schools*, Film. Columbia, SC: South Carolina ETV.

Jargowsky, P.A. (1997). *Poverty and place: ghettos, barrios, and the American City.* New York: Russell Sage Foundation.

Katz, M.B. (1989). *The undeserving poor: From the war on poverty to the war on welfare.* New York: Pantheon.

Kozol, J. (1995). *Amazing grace: The lives of children and the conscience of a nation.* New York: Crown.

Lareau, A. (1989). *Home advantage: Social class and parental intervention in elementary education.* New York: Falmer.

Martin, J.R. (1992). *The schoolhome: Rethinking schools for changing families.* Cambridge: Harvard University Press.

Noddings, N. (1992). *The challenge to care in schools: An alternative approach to education.* New York: Teachers College Press.

Polakow, V. (1993). *Lives on the edge: Single mothers and their children in the other America.* Chicago: University of Chicago Press.

Shirk, M., Bennett, N.G., & Aber, J.L. (1999). *Lives on the line: American families and the struggle to make ends meet.* Boulder, CO: Westview Press.

United Nations Children's Fund. (June 2000a). *A league table of child poverty in rich nations.* Innocenti Report Card No. 1. Florence, Italy: Innocenti Research Centre.

Valenzuela, A. (1999). *Subtractive schooling: U.S.-Mexican youth and the politics of caring.* Albany, NY: SUNY Press.

Vorrasi, J.A., & Garbarino, J. (2000). In V. Polakow (Ed.), *The public assault on America's children: Poverty, violence, and juvenile injustice* (pp. 59–77). New York: Teachers College Press.

21

DISCONNECT: 1984 & THE FAILURE OF
EDUCATION OR CPS GETS AN F U

Kevin Coval

One of the most frequently voiced critiques of urban schools is that the standard curriculum has little relevance to the lives of kids growing up in the city. In this piece from his book Slingshots: A Hip-hop Poetica, *Chicago-based poet Kevin Coval observes that part of the problem may lie in teachers' squandered opportunities to connect classic literature to students' lived experiences.*

---

what you readin, joe

> *this book sucks, dog*

two boys banter on the orange line west
vocational high school english teachers assigned Orwell's classic

> *i gotta write about this dude bein watched*

for real?

salesmen head back to new england via Midway
hold laptop leather bags closer on creased khakis

the boys exit at Pulaski
55 yrs after the book first dropped

what you gonna write about

> *i don't even know*

blue light box video recorders hover
over street lamp corners like spaceships

aliens in the hood
big brother in blue

is white, always
watching

22

"COMIN' FROM THE SCHOOL OF HARD KNOCKS": HIP-HOP AND THE REVOLUTION OF ENGLISH CLASSROOMS IN CITY SCHOOLS

Ernest Morrell and Jeff Duncan-Andrade

Creating curriculum that resonates with kids in city schools means taking their questions, concerns, and interests seriously. It also means validating the forms of cultural expression—TV shows, films, Web sites, graphic novels, music— that students find meaningful. In the article that follows, Ernest Morrell and Jeff Duncan-Andrade, who both taught at an urban high school in Northern California, reflect on their experiences incorporating a study of hip-hop music into a "traditional" English poetry unit.

Morrell is now associate professor in the Urban Schooling division of the Graduate School of Education and Information Studies at UCLA; and Duncan-Andrade is an assistant professor of Raza Studies and Education Administration and Interdisciplinary Studies and Co-Director of the Educational Equity Initiative at San Francisco State University's César Chávez Institute.

———————

As classrooms across the country become increasingly diverse, and as the stakes of acquiring academic literacy continue to rise, determining how to connect in significant ways across multiple lines of difference may be the greatest challenge facing teachers today (Ladson-Billings, 1994). Teachers in twenty-first-century city schools must meet this challenge and find ways to forge meaningful relationships with students who come from different worlds, while also helping these students to develop academic skills and the skills needed to become critical citizens in a multicultural democracy. This challenge, therefore, also presents a tremendous opportunity for progressive, critical educators who wish to promote curricula and pedagogies that value and affirm the cultural practices of urban students and members of urban communities.

As English teachers at an urban high school in Northern California, we witnessed the impact of hip-hop music and culture on all of our students. We saw at the same time that the culture's influence seemed to transcend race, as students from a variety of ethnic backgrounds were strongly influenced by the culture (Mahiri, 1998). We also noticed that students were developing sophisticated literacy skills through their involvement with hip-hop; literacy skills that we could draw upon to make connections to academic content. We ultimately decided that we could utilize hip-hop music and culture to forge a common and critical discourse that was centered upon the lives of the students, transcended the racial divide, and allowed us to tap into students' lives in ways that promoted academic literacy and critical consciousness.

Baker (1993), Farley (1999), and George (1998) all argue that the creative people who are talking about youth culture in a way that makes sense happen to be rappers, and the youth are responding in many ways. Hip-hop artists sold more than 81 million CDs, tapes and albums in 1998, more than in any other genre of music. Although hip-hop got its start in black America, more than 70 percent of albums are purchased by whites. Taking their cue from the music industry, other major corporations are creating advertising schemes that cater to the "hip-hop generation." Even mainstream Hollywood is consistently dealing with issues related to hip-hop. Although the music is largely criticized by politicians, religious groups, and some women's groups, its proponents claim that it is here to stay as it represents a resistant voice of urban youth through its articulation of problems that this generation and all Americans face on a daily basis.

We do not mean to minimize the serious critiques levied against hip-hop music, especially those critiques that emanate from concerned members of inner-city communities. Particularly, critics have expressed concern over the glorification of violence and drug use, the celebration of material wealth, and the dehumanization of women of color in lyrics and in hip-hop videos. Hip-hop's proponents argue that certain elements of the music and culture foster ethnic and community pride, a sense of history, and a commitment to social justice. We agree with both sides; however, it is not our purpose to either celebrate or denigrate hip-hop music. Hip-hop music's relevance to city youth requires it to be relevant to city teachers. Nobel Laureate Toni Morrison (1993) reminds us that national literatures reflect what is on the national mind. Hip-hop music, for better and for worse, provides valuable insights into the social and cultural worlds of city youth. Rose (1994) and Tabb-Powell (1991) argue strongly that hip-hop music is the representative voice of urban youth as the genre was created by and for them. Tabb-Powell states:

> [Rap] emerged from the streets of inner-city neighborhoods as a genuine reflection of the hopes, concerns, and aspirations of urban Black youth in this, the last quarter of the twentieth century. Rap is essentially a homemade, street-level musical genre . . . Rap lyrics concentrate primarily on the contemporary African American experience . . . Every issue within the Black community is subject to exposition in the rap arena. Hit rap tunes have broached touchy subjects such as sex, sexism, racism, and crime . . . Rap artists, they contend, "don't talk that love stuff, but [rather] educate the listeners."(p. 245)

Many rappers consider themselves educators and see at least a portion of their mission as promoting consciousness within their communities (Spady, Alim, and Meghelli, 2006; Lipsitz, 1994; Rose, 1994). The influence of rap as a voice of resistance and liberation for urban youth proliferates through such artists as Lauryn Hill, Pras, and Wyclef Jean of the Refugee Camp, Public Enemy, Nas, and Mos Def who endeavor to bring an accurate, yet critical depiction of the urban situation to a hip-hop generation.

Giroux (1996) takes a much less celebratory view of the impact of hip-hop culture on working-class urban youth but, nevertheless, agrees that it is a worthy topic of study in urban schools. His work addresses the crisis confronting youth, whom he labels a generation under siege, where they are enmeshed in a culture of violence coded by race and class. He speaks to the negative connotations of youth culture promoted in popular media that propel youth toward mistrust, alienation, misogyny, violence, apathy, and the development of fugitive cultures. This same media, he contends, has commercialized the working-class body and criminalized black youth. Critical educators, he argues, must consider elements of popular culture such as hip-hop music as a serious site for social knowledge to be discussed, interrogated, and critiqued. Whether the power in its messages can be used for good or ill, few can dispute the impact of hip-hop culture in the lives of working-class, urban youth.

Hip-hop texts are powerful manifestations of urban languages and literacies (Alim, 2006; Fisher, 2007); they are rich in imagery and metaphor and can be used to teach irony, tone, diction, and point of view. Also, hip-hop texts can be analyzed for theme, motif, plot, and character development. It is very possible to perform feminist, Marxist, structuralist, psychoanalytic, or postmodernist critiques of particular hip-hop texts, the genre as a whole, or subgenres such as gangsta rap. Once learned, these analytic and interpretative tools developed through engagement with popular cultural texts can be applied to canonical texts as well (Lee, 1993). If one goal of critical educators is to empower urban students to analyze complex literary texts, hip-hop texts can be used as a bridge linking the seemingly vast span between the streets and the world of academics.

Hip-hop texts, given their thematic nature, can be equally valuable as springboards for critical discussions about contemporary issues facing urban youth. Provocative rap texts can be brought into the classrooms and discussion topics may be produced from a listening/reading of the text. These discussions may lead to more thoughtful analyses, which could translate into expository writing, the production of poetic texts, or a commitment to social action for community empowerment. Additionally, critical discussions stemming from hip-hop texts can challenge city youth to think differently about their personal actions and attitudes.

Teaching hip-hop as a music and culture of resistance can facilitate the development of critical consciousness in urban youth. Analyzing the social commentary produced by the old school and contemporary artists can lead to consciousness-raising discussions, essays, and research projects attempting to locate an explanation for the current state of affairs for urban youngsters. The knowledge reflected in these lyrics could engender discussions of gender relationships, race, self-esteem, urban economics, and police brutality; further, the study of hip-hop can encourage students to expand their own knowledge of history, urban sociology, and politics (Dagbovie, 2005). In this way, hip-hop music should stand on its own merit in the academy and be a worthy subject of study in its own right rather than necessarily leading to something more "acceptable" like a Shakespeare text. It can, however, serve as a bridge between urban cultures and the literary canon.

Given the social, cultural, and academic relevance of hip-hop music and culture, we designed a classroom unit with three objectives:

1. To draw upon students' analytic and literacy skills developed as a result of their involvement with hip-hop culture.
2. To provide students with the awareness and confidence they need to transfer these skills into/onto the literary texts from the canon and the production of their own expository and poetic texts.
3. To enable students to critique the messages sent to them through the popular cultural media that permeate their everyday lives.

The unit was designed to incorporate hip-hop music into a "traditional" senior English poetry unit. Our desires were to increase motivation and participation in discussions and assignments, and to teach critical-essay writing and literary terminology in the context of, among other types of poetry, rap music. We also wanted our students to understand hip-hop in its historical context as a music and cultural practice that represented young people's rage and frustration at the social and economic conditions they faced in America's urban centers. Further, we wished to encourage youth to view elements of popular culture through a critical lens and to critique messages sent to them through popular media, and to help students understand the intellectual integrity, literary merit, and social critique contained within elements of their own youth culture.

There were several goals and objectives for this unit that combined our simultaneous agendas of tapping into popular culture and facilitating academic and critical literacy development. To accomplish this, we needed to cover the poetry of the Elizabethan Age, the Puritan Revolution, and the Romantics that were a part of the district-mandated curriculum for 12th grade English and that students would be expected to have knowledge of for the advanced-placement exam and college English courses. It was also important to learn about the poets in the context of the literary and historical periods in which they wrote to gain a greater understanding of the role poetry plays as a critique of its contemporary society.

In addition to a critical exposure to the literary canon, we felt it important to concentrate on the development of issues and ideas presented in poetry and song as a vehicle to expository writing. Our objectives were:

1. To develop oral and written debate skills,
2. To facilitate the ability to work in groups,
3. To help students to deliver formal public presentations,
4. To teach students how to critique a poem/song in a critical essay,
5. To help students to develop note-taking skills in lectures and presentations; and
6. To help students to become comfortable writing in different poetic forms such as the sonnet, elegy, and ballad.

We began the unit with an overview of poetry in general, attempting to redefine poetry and the role of a poet in society. We emphasized the importance of understanding the historical period in which a poem was written to come to a deep interpretation of the poem. In the introductory lecture, we outlined all of the historical/literary periods that would be covered in the unit (Elizabethan, Puritan Revolution, Romantics, and Metaphysical Poets from England, and the Civil War, Harlem Renaissance, civil rights movement, and Post–Industrial Revolution in the United States). It was our intention to place hip-hop music—as a postindustrial art form—right alongside these other historical periods and poems so that the students would be able to use a period and genre of poetry they were familiar with as a lens with which to examine the other literary works and also to encourage the students to reevaluate the manner in which they view elements of their popular culture.

The second major portion of the unit involved a group presentation of a canonical poem along with a hip-hop text. The groups were commissioned to prepare a justifiable interpretation of their texts, situating each within its specific historical and literary period while also analyzing the linkages between the two. There were eight groups for this portion who were, after a week of preparation, each given a day to present to the class and have their arguments critiqued by their peers. The groups were assigned as follows:

GROUP	POEM	SONG
1	"Kubla Khan," Coleridge	"If I Ruled the World," Nas
2	"Love Song of J. Alfred Prufrock," Eliot	"The Message," Grand Master Flash
3	"O Me! O Life!" Whitman	"Don't Believe the Hype," Public Enemy
4	"Immigrants In Our Own Land," Baca	"The World Is a Ghetto," Geto Boys
5	"Sonnet 29," Shakespeare	"Affirmative Action," Nas
6	"The Canonization," Donne	"Manifest," Refugee Camp
7	"Repulse Bay," Chin	"Good Day," Ice Cube
8	"Still I Rise," Angelou	"Cell Therapy," Goodie Mob

Note: Other poems used for this unit were "Let America Be America Again" by Langston Hughes and "Elegy Written in a Country Churchyard" by Thomas Gray.

In addition to the group presentations, students were asked to complete an anthology of ten poems that contained an elegy, a ballad, a sonnet, and a poem that described a place with which they were familiar. Also, the students were asked to write a poem that conveyed a mood, a poem that dealt with a political, social, or economic problem that was important to them (i.e. racism, teen pregnancy, drug abuse, police brutality, poverty, homelessness, etc.), a love poem, a poem that celebrated a particular facet of life (first date, summertime, graduation, etc.), and two open poems that dealt with whatever subject students chose and written in any style they desired. Following the group presentations, we held a poetry reading where each student selected five of his/her original poems to read for the class, giving brief comments on each poem such as the context or a special meaning. For the outside-of-class assignment, students were allowed to pick any song of their choice and write a five-to-seven-page critical essay of that song. They were also required to submit a transcription of that song.

The unit held consistent with the original goals of being culturally and socially relevant, critically exposing students to the literary canon, and facilitating the development of college-level expository writing. The positioning of hip-hop as a genre of poetry written largely in response to postindustrialism was a concept with which the students were able to relate. The issues of joblessness, poverty, rage, racism, and alienation all had resonance to the urban youth culture of which the students were a part. The forefronting of hip-hop as a genre of poetry also helped to facilitate the transition to understanding the role individual poets may have played in their own societies.

The students were able to generate some excellent interpretations as well as make interesting linkages between the canonical poems and the rap texts. For instance, one group articulated that both Grand Master Flash and T.S. Eliot gazed out into their rapidly deteriorating societies and saw a "wasteland." Both poets were essentially apocalyptic in nature as they witnessed death, disease, and decay. Also, both poems talk about a message, indicating the role of a poet in society as a messenger or prophet. Another group discussed the role of allegory in their two texts, where both John Donne and the artists from the Refugee Camp utilize relationships with lovers to symbolize the love and agony poets can feel for their societies.

The unit was consistent with the basic tenets of critical pedagogy in that it was situated in the experiences of the students (as opposed to those of the teacher), called for critical dialogue and a critical engagement of the text, and related the texts to larger social and political issues. The students were also able to have fun learning about a culture and a genre of music with which they had great familiarity. Ultimately, our experiences introducing hip-hop and other elements of popular culture into traditional curricula lead us to believe that there are countless possibilities for urban educators who wish to jump outside of the box and tap into the worlds of their students. In doing so, they can make more powerful connections with traditional academic texts and affirm, in meaningful ways, the everyday lives of their students.

REFERENCES

Alim, H.S., (2006). *Roc the mic: The language of hip-hop*. New York: Routledge.

Baker, H.A., (1993). *Black studies, rap, and the academy*. Chicago: University of Chicago Press.

Barton, D., & Hamilton, M. (2000). Literary practices. In D. Barton, M. Hamilton, & R. Ivanic (Eds.), Situated literacus: Reading and writing in context (pp. 7–15). New York: Routledge.

Dagbovie, P. (2005). Of all our studies, history is best qualified to reward our research: Black history's relevance to the hip-hop generation. *Journal of African-American History*, *90*(3) 299–323.

Farley, C. (1999). Hip-hop nation: There's more to rap than just rhythms and rhymes. After two decades, it has transformed the culture of America. *Time*, *153*(5) 55–65.

Ferdman, B. (1990). Literacy and cultural identity. *Harvard Educational Review*, *60*(2) 181–204.

Fisher, M. (2007). *Writing in rhythm: Spoken word poetry in urban classrooms*. New York: Teachers College Press.

Freire, P. (1970). *Pedagogy of the oppressed*. New York: Continuum.

George, N. (1998). *Hiphopamerica*. New York: Penguin.

Giroux, H.A. (1996). *Fugitive cultures: Race, violence, and youth*. New York: Routledge.

Kellner, D. (1995). *Media culture: Cultural studies, identity and politics between the modern and the postmodern*. New York: Routledge.

Ladson-Billings, G. (1994). *The dreamkeepers: Successful reachers of African-American children*. San Francisco: Jossey Bass.

Lee, C.D. (1993). *Signifying as a scaffold for literary interpretation: The pedagogical implications of an African-American discourse genre*. Urbana, IL: NCTE.

Lipsitz, G. (1994). History, hip-hop, and the post-colonial politics of sound. *Dangerous crossroads: Popular music, postmodernism, and the poetics of place* (pp. 23–48). New York: Verso.

Mahiri, J. (1998). *Shooting for excellence: African American and youth culture in new century schools*. New York: Teachers College Press.

Morrison, T. (1993). *Playing in the dark: Whiteness and the literary imagination*. New York: Vintage.

Nas. (1996). *It was written*. New York: Columbia Records.

National Center for Education Statistics. (1998). *Digest of education statistics*. Washington, DC.

The Refugee Camp. (1996). *The score*. New York: Columbia Records.

Rose, T. (1994). *Black noise: Rap music and black culture in contemporary America*. Wesleyan University Press.

Spady, J., Alim, S., & Meghelli, S. (2006). *The global cipha: Hip-hop culture and consciousness*. Black History Museum Press.

Tabb-Powell, C. (1991). Rap music: An education with a beat from the street. *Journal of Negro Education, 60*(3) 245–59.

23

PARENTS AS WRITERS: TRANSFORMING THE ROLE OF PARENTS IN URBAN SCHOOLS

Janise Hurtig

Involving parents in meaningful ways is essential for schools in poor urban neighborhoods. But parent involvement programs in city schools often place adults—usually mothers—in subservient roles rather than encouraging them to be decisionmakers and leaders. In the next piece, Janise Hurtig decribes her work as co-director of the Community Writing and Research Projects at the PRAIRIE Group, an adult writing program at the University of Illinois at Chicago, which aims to involve Chicago parents in their neighborhood schools "in ways that recognize and respect their experiences and wisdom, and that draw on their intellectual, artistic, moral, and critical insights."

PARENTS AS TEACHERS?

Six of us—five parent writers and myself, the writing workshop teacher—are sitting together in the library of the North/South High School.[1] North/South is a campus of four small high schools that serves two adjacent city neighborhoods, one primarily Latino, the other primarily African American. We are all mothers; some are also grandmothers. We are African American, Latin American, and European American women. Some of us came up through urban school districts in the United States; others went to rural or urban schools in Mexico or Guatemala. It is March and the period of standardized testing is on the horizon for our school-aged kids. We are talking about how much formal teaching and educational decision making is expected of us as parents. We debate whether or not it is appropriate for schools to expect

---

[1] All school and parent names are pseudonyms, except when citing excerpts of parent writing.

parents to be responsible for making sure their children learn to read or do arithmetic.

"Isn't that what the *schools* are supposed to do?" asks Debra, provocatively and rhetorically, in English.

As soon as I translate the question into Spanish, Flor's eyes open widely: "At my children's school they tell us that our children aren't learning to read because we don't read to them in English. But how can I do that? I only speak a little English."

Angie chimes in: "Maybe they're just telling you that because they can't figure out how to teach everyone the basics—I mean, with thirty-five kids in the classroom and no aide, and a school day that's about half what it was when I was a kid. You know, just blame it on the parents."

"So why is it suddenly our job to be the schoolteachers?" Angie asks.

"The *volunteer* schoolteachers," Irma adds, and the group laughs—perhaps recalling our conversation the previous week about being "volunteered to death," as one mom had put it.

Flor, who has been listening as though riveted to every comment, speaks up: "I've been blaming myself for how my kids are doing in school—because I don't speak much English, because I don't know enough math to help my son in seventh grade with his homework, because I don't have time to keep my home in order and stay on top of all my kids' homework. I have just accepted that the people at the school know what they are talking about when they tell me I'm not supporting my children as a parent. And why should I question them? I can't compare it to what school was like for me. This is nothing like it was in Mexico, at least the small town I come from. Parents don't teach their children at home. They respect the teachers and expect their children to respect the teachers. But we have a saying: school is for *enseñanza* (academic learning); home is for *educación* (moral education; manners)."

"Well, that's all well and fine," Denise notes, "as long as that academic learning means something.

"Mhmm," Angie agrees. "They're so busy making sure our kids get those test scores up, they aren't learning anything about the real world."

"Well, I guess that's our job as volunteer teachers," Maria says and cracks a smile. "To teach them how to live in the world."

"So are we or aren't we teachers?" Irma asks provocatively.

Denise, one of two seasoned writers assisting me in leading the North/South group, says, "Now *that* would be a great writing topic: 'Are we teachers or are we parents?'" The group agrees that it is a great topic, and we set about to write. Here is an excerpt from that session's writing:

> Why am I letting you cause friction in my home? You're asking me to be a teacher at home, but I haven't asked you to be a parent at school and even if I did, your legal staff wouldn't allow it to happen. You're putting this idea of perfection in our heads but I know no human is perfect. I also know we all have strengths and weaknesses. I, as a parent, go home to my child to listen, learn, cook, wash, protect, pay rent, and so on and now you want me to teach math. . . . Do you? Is that my job? Or yours?[2]

In the book *Rethinking Family-School Relations*, the Brazilian educator Maria Eulina P. de Carvalho[3] presents a social and cultural critique of the institutionalization of parent involvement as educational policy in the United States. Carvalho identifies many of the same issues raised by parents in the North/South High School writing group: the narrow emphasis on educational accountability that "limits schooling to economic purposes and outcomes" (p. 20); the tendency of teachers— themselves made vulnerable by arbitrary extremes of educational accountability—to blame the underachievement of students on parents, further enhancing parents' sense of vulnerability (pp. 21–22); and the invasive attempts by the educational system to dictate family life in conformity with the narrow educational needs of the school—an ironically homogenizing impulse toward family life, Carvalho points out, at a time when "diversity is celebrated in the school curriculum" (p. 20). In analyzing this tendency Carvalho goes beyond critique to issue a warning about the "totalitarian movement in educational policy" (p. 10) that this kind of institutionalized homogeneity represents. This totalitarian impulse should be troubling to all of us as we watch the tentacles of

---

[2] Lilnora Foster, "Friction at Home," 2006.
[3] Maria Eulina P. de Carvalho, *Rethinking Family-School Relations: A Critique of Parental Involvement in Schooling*. Mahwah, NJ: Lawrence Erlbaum, 2001.

standardization work their way beyond the walls of the school and into our homes.

The institutionalization and standardization of parent involvement is particularly troubling in the way it affects families in socially and economically marginalized communities. To begin with, these are communities whose cultural traditions and historical knowledge tend to be discounted, denigrated, feared, or ignored by the educational institutions of our society. Because parent-involvement programs are focused narrowly on the academic aims and needs of the school, they rarely take into account the culturally specific roles, strengths, needs, and values of parents and other adult caretakers in poor, minority, and immigrant households and communities.[4] There are myriad ways in which parents from different backgrounds consider themselves to be meaningfully supporting the formal and informal education of their children, like the demonstration of the "value of hard work" that Gerardo Lopez documents in his ethnographic account of how rural immigrant parents choose to educate their children and prepare them for the world.[5] But this kind of parental support and modeling simply do not count in the eyes of the educational system. Moreover, parent-involvement programs often ask the participants—most of them mothers and grandmothers already overburdened with the responsibilities of maintaining a home life under conditions of economic poverty and social marginalization— to take on additional child-raising responsibilities, whether as home educators or school volunteers. Rather than offering these women opportunities to engage in meaningful and creative activity, most school programs for parents tend to reinforce women's subservient roles in the family and wider society.[6]

One of the aims of the Community Writing Project, the adult writing and publishing program through which I teach the writing workshop at North/South and other city schools, is to involve parents and other adult residents in their neighborhood schools in ways that recog-

[4] M. David, *Parents, Gender, and Educational Reform.* Oxford: Blackwell Publishers, 1993.
[5] Gerardo Lopez, "The Value of Hard Work: Lessons on Parent Involvement from an (Im)migrant Household." *Harvard Educational Review* 71(3): 416–29, 2001.
[6] Wendy Glasgow Winters, *African American Mothers and Urban Schools: The Power of Participation.* New York: Lexington Books, 1993; Wendy Luttrell, "Taking Care of Literacy: One Feminist's Critique." *Educational Policy* 10(3): 342–65, 1995.

nize and respect their experiences and wisdom, and that draw on their intellectual, artistic, moral, and critical insights in order to broaden and enrich the education of urban youth. The Community Writing Project offers adult writing workshops to residents of poor and immigrant neighborhoods and publishes selections of their writings in the magazine *Real Conditions*, which is distributed for free to the writers, their families and friends, and to other interested individuals, schools, and community groups. Our intention is to provide a forum for creative expression in which ordinary people—many of whom have not previously thought of themselves as writers—can share writings based in their experiences, draw on their work to examine their lives, develop the art of writing, and become recognized within and beyond their communities as writers, thinkers, and leaders.[7]

The Community Writing Project has been offering writing workshops in neighborhood schools since before the tyranny of parent involvement as educational policy was institutionalized as a handmaiden to high-stakes testing. And while the Community Writing Project has always aimed to counter the deficit-based mind-set framing many adult education programs in poor communities, this effort takes on particular urgency in the context of the increasingly scripted, formulaic, and homogenizing approach to parent involvement in schools. Here, I am referring to the narrow and rigid codification of parent involvement according to roles that are meant to impact students' academic achievement—whether directly through classes in homework assistance, test preparation for their children, "family" literacy programs aimed at raising students' reading performance, or indirectly through programs that seek to change the culture of family life in ways that are meant to reinforce the culture of the school. Rather than letting parents shine as thinkers and leaders in the eyes of their children and letting parents act as models and inspirations to their children, these programs place parents in demeaning or subservient roles within the school and aim to script the practices and culture of family life in ways that conform narrowly with the academic ambitions of the school—whether those

---

[7] Hal Adams and Janise Hurtig, "Creative Acts, Critical Insights: Adult Writing Workshops in Two Chicago Neighborhoods." In *Case Studies in Community Partnerships*, Elsa Auerbach, ed. TESOL, 2001.

ambitions are internally generated or imposed by federal mandates such as the No Child Left Behind Act. By contrast, small writing workshops offer parents the opportunity to engage in the creative, personally rewarding, and publicly recognized activity of sharing their experiences and insights, writing and publishing stories based on their lives and wisdom, and offering critiques of society. Moreover, children come to respect the adults of their communities as artists, thinkers, and leaders when they are exposed to their elders' stories and wisdom in the context of their schools.

COURAGE AND DETERMINATION

My colleague Hal Adams and I are working with five parents around a table in the parent room (a glorified storage area) of Chapman School. The parent room is really a basement storage room located next to the pre-K classrooms. Chapman School is a magnet elementary school that serves a mixture of neighborhood children and children from all around the city who were selected by lottery to attend this school. The students come primarily from Latino, African American, and East Asian families. The majority of families are working class or working poor. Most of the Euro American students are from working-class families recently displaced from this north-side neighborhood as it gentrifies and their homes become unaffordable.

The women who attend the morning writing group are all settlers in this city: two are from Mexico, one from El Salvador, and another from Michigan. Two of the women regularly bring their preschool-aged children to the writing group. The youngsters play with cars and dolls as we write, talk, sip coffee, and snack on donuts. Occasionally a child crawls up onto her mother's legs or squeezes in beside her onto the chair. We begin this session as we do most sessions—by reading and discussing the previous week's writings. The topic is "coming north."

Manuela, a Mexican immigrant woman whose two oldest children attend Chapman School, reads the account she had written the week before about the voyage she took as a young adult to come to this country seeking better opportunities. The story begins in her mother's bedroom as she bids her mother good-bye in the middle of the night:

With a knot in your throat and with a broken heart, you enter your mother's little room where she waits, nervous, about to cry because of the moment that is approaching, the farewell. She gets up and opens her arms to you like when you were a baby, to tell you, "Take care of yourself and hopefully you will cross soon. . . . You, without being able to talk, get on your knees so that she can bless you, the blessing of a mother who is like a treasure to you. . . . [8]

Manuela recounts the fears and humiliations she experienced on her journey across the border, and ends on a hopeful note with her safe settlement in the city. Holding back tears with tissues and the sympathetic encouragement of the other writers, Manuela reads from her paper and the others follow along with the typed version. Manuela is a sure and seemingly fearless woman, not comfortable with her demonstration of emotion, and she quickly composes herself as she waits for the group's responses. Gloria, another immigrant mother, expresses her admiration for Manuela's courage and determination. Rachel, a U.S.-born Anglo mother, fights back her own tears as she praises Manuela for the power of her story: "It really tells the truth about how unjustly people are treated just for wanting to make something of their lives."

There is the briefest moment of silence as the group awaits Manuela's response to their comments. She looks up from her paper, which she has been contemplating during the discussion. "I have never told this story to my children," she confesses. She explains to the group that she doesn't want her children to think that she suffered to come here, that she had to sacrifice her dignity for them. She doesn't want them to see her as having been weak or humiliated.

For the first time that day, María, a parent writer who came to the United States from El Salvador during the Salvadoran Revolution, speaks up. At previous meetings María had shared stories about her inability to attend school because of fears that either the army or the guerrilla would kidnap her on the way to school and make her and her brothers serve in the war. "For me, when I hear your story, I think it is a story of courage and determination. You can't give in to the people who

[8] Maribel Arias, "A New Opportunity." *Real Conditions* 2(2), 2001. (Translated from the Spanish by Janise Hurtig.)

tried to humiliate you when you crossed the border. You can't give in to the ideas some people have here about immigrants. I think you should be proud of your courage."

Rachel says to Manuela, "You should be proud of your story and how beautifully you tell it." The others agree. Manuela listens but doesn't respond.

The group moves on to listen to and comment on the other writings: Gloria's story about the suitcase full of dollar-store knickknacks her father brought back with him the first time he returned to Mexico after working two years as a field hand in California; María's story about the differences between the fears she faced in her Salvadoran home town and the fears she faced in her new neighborhood. Each story provokes lengthy group discussions that range from the challenges families face when they are divided by immigration, to the global economics that could send the foreman of a construction company to California to pick vegetables in order to support his family. The preschool children, still playing on the perimeter of the group, seem oblivious to their mothers' work. But once in a while, when the discussion becomes animated, one or two turn to watch their mothers engaged in what is obviously important work.

After each writer has read and discussed her story with the group, they begin to consider a theme they will write about for the last fifteen or twenty minutes of the meeting. The group decides to write about "new beginnings"—"the positive side to all these sad stories," Gloria suggests. The class's dynamic shifts as each writer turns her focus away from the entire group, downward toward the blank sheet of paper in front of her, and inward toward her own thoughts, memories, and experiences. Gloria's three-year-old daughter, Ana, climbs up onto the chair beside her mother and asks if she can write, too; the group responds by providing her with paper and pencil, and she begins to scribble alongside her mother.

As four of the women write, Manuela looks up from her still blank paper and makes an announcement: "I think I will finish writing my story about coming north. I would like to put it in the magazine. I would like to read my story to my children, and talk to them about it." The group applauds Manuela's announcement, and returns to the task of writing.

PARENTS WRITING FOR CHANGE

The primary purpose of the writing groups is to give ordinary people the opportunity to write about their experiences, have their stories published, and become part of a community of writers. As parents often note, the reason they write and publish their stories is to document their lives and struggles on their own terms—to set the story straight, as some writers have put it—and to counsel others in their community about raising children, making a living, and organizing for a better world. While there is a tendency among adult educators and organizers to emphasize visible changes that result from ordinary people's work together, it is just as important for people living in poverty to have the chance to be writers and to develop their craft—an opportunity that people with privilege take for granted—as it is for them to organize for change.

There are certainly occasions in which the writing workshop has been a catalyst for parent writers to take action within and beyond their children's schools. In these instances, activism and writing come together. For instance, several parent writers at one school that serves residents of public-housing units under siege by the city's housing authority and local developers have become active in local activist groups that are working to preserve the rights of people currently living in the public-housing complex. They have used current issues of the magazine we publish to introduce themselves to the activist organizations. Parent writers at a small school in a predominantly Mexican community have similarly used their published stories as the basis for confronting local officials around their demands for better sanitation services and improved park facilities for their children.

Most recently parent writers from several schools have decided to use the magazine as a means of confronting a facet of school reform that is deeply troubling to them: namely, the messages about families living in poverty that are contained in the work of the teacher educator Ruby Payne, in particular, in her book *A Framework for Understanding Poverty*.[9] In this training manual—which is meant to accompany a teacher training process for teachers to use "when dealing with children

---

[9] Ruby Payne, *A Framework for Understanding Poverty* (Third Revised Edition). Highlands, TX: aha! Process, Inc., 1996.

from poverty"—Payne proposes that the low educational achievement of students in poor communities can be attributed to two things. The first is their lack of certain resources that she attributes to the condition of poverty. These lacks are not only economic, claims Dr. Payne, but social, moral, mental, spiritual, and physical. She also claims that people who live in "generational" poverty (which she distinguishes from "situational" poverty) have adopted "hidden rules" for their "class," which further keep them from getting out of poverty. According to Dr. Payne, people who live in poverty value education in the abstract but not as a reality; they have ineffective disciplining methods involving physical punishment and then forgiveness; they treat others as objects; they are afraid of leaving their communities. Poor youth, she proposes (despite abundant research and local knowledge to the contrary), are not taught appropriate linguistic skills, the ability organize their time, and do not have adequate role models. These are among the stereotypes she attributes to people living in conditions of "generational poverty."

The parent writers who have read Payne's book disagree with just about every facet of her argument. Based on their own experiences and realities, they disagree with her characterizations of people who live in conditions of poverty, as well as her "cultural" argument for why people may remain poor. They also reject the notion that youth from poor families should be obligated to leave their communities to have successful lives. Finally, they reject Payne's reduction of schooling to its instrumental value as a means of climbing the economic ladder—a perspective several parents have described as "impoverished." Engaging critically and experientially with Payne's discourse, one writer pointed out that Payne opposes aspects of life that in reality are not opposed: "Poverty is a condition, not a state of mind or a culture." Another writer illustrated this point by describing her own life: "Here in this city I live in a poor neighborhood, but I am well educated in many ways, as are my children. I have a job to address my family's basic needs, but I am also interested in academic issues and in abstract ideas. I work in a low-paying job, but I continue to learn and to teach my children."

In order to challenge Payne's work, a group of parent writers from several schools have decided to prepare a *Real Conditions* magazine that contains stories they have written based on their own experiences and realities that respond to and contest passages in *A Framework for Understanding Poverty*. They have prepared these writings so that educators can hear the voices and read of the experiences of those people Dr. Payne seeks to stereotype, denigrate, and silence. On two occasions parent writers have organized public readings in educational settings that take on Ruby Payne's framework; and it is their hope that the issue of *Real Conditions* that contests Ruby Payne's bigoted framework will be used as a companion/counter text in teacher education so that teachers can be encouraged to think about their students' families and communities in humane and respectful ways. The title of this special issue of *Real Conditions* the parents have proposed is "Rich Lives, Real Struggles: Our Stories about Living in Poverty."

GOOD EXAMPLES, GOOD AUTHORS

There are many ways to tell a story—many points to make, many stances to take. The version we choose to write and share is based on a certain amount of deliberation over the message we hope to convey and the audience we hope to reach. I have chosen to tell stories from the writing groups that are optimistic, hopeful, and illustrative of the value the writing groups have for parents, their children, and their children's school. My intention is to encourage readers to think about these and other ways in which schools can support the meaningful participation of parents in the school's educational community. But my stories would be misleading if I didn't include the caveat that introducing and sustaining innovative parent programs in urban schools is not an easy matter; for every school in which the writing project has thrived, there are schools in which it has been met with indifference or resistance. The current climate of high-stakes accountability, standardization, and homogeneity further discourages schools to risk investment in programs like the writing project.

Nonetheless, when parents are afforded the opportunity to write together they will use that opportunity, as the writers themselves have put it, to "spread and share our stories," to "use the magazine [as] a tool of communication that allows us to make known and understood—to those within and outside this group of writers—the experiences, desires, dreams, and travels we have had, from childhood until the present day."[10] The writers' children will learn important truths from those stories and acquire new respect for their parents. As these parents have written and discussed, they are the ones best able to "instill the value of writing and reading in our children" and to "tell about our customs our values, and our dreams."[11] And they are best able to instill that insight and inspiration by showing their children how they do it. The parent writers from one school put it this way in their introduction to a magazine:

> We think that by spending time at the school writing, we are doing something we couldn't do when we were of school age, and we spend time in school instead of being at home. For us, it is very important that we set good examples for our children because they want to be like us. If our children see us writing, they will feel proud and will be more motivated in their studies. It is not necessary to have a formal education to show that we can be good authors. We all have something to share.[12]

---

[10] Sandra Carasco and Rebeca Nieto in collaboration with the Telpochealli Writing Group, Introduction, *Real Conditions* 4(3), 2003.
[11] Abel Angeles in collaboration with the Parents as Writers Group, Introduction, *Real Conditions* 4(2), 2003.
[12] Ibid.

24

NCLB'S SELECTIVE VISION OF EQUALITY: SOME GAPS COUNT MORE THAN OTHERS

Stan Karp

High-stakes accountability measures mandated by the No Child Left Behind Act (NCLB) have altered the landscape of schools across the country, but perhaps nowhere has their impact been more severe than in city schools. Often lost in the debate over NCLB, however, is an analysis of how educational inequities are linked to equality gaps in the broader society. In the following essay, Rethinking Schools *editor and Paterson, N. J. high school teacher Stan Karp argues that if we really want to leave no child behind, a broader, deeper commitment to equity is needed—both inside and outside schools.*

———————

Thanks to No Child Left Behind, AYPs have been replacing the ABCs as the most important letters in many schools.

AYP, or "adequate yearly progress," refers to the formulas that the No Child Left Behind Act (NCLB) uses to evaluate schools on the basis of standardized test scores. Under NCLB, all schools receiving federal funds are required to reach 100 percent passing rates for all student groups on state tests by the 2013–14 school year. The declared goal is to have all students meet state standards and to eliminate academic achievement gaps.

This inappropriate, and ultimately fanciful, federal mandate has become the main preoccupation of districts and schools across the country. NCLB sets up an elaborate system of test score targets and any school that misses even one of these targets for two consecutive years faces an escalating series of sanctions, from the loss of federal funds to the imposition of private management on public schools or even possible closure.

Yet the goal of equality in test scores for all student groups, including special-education and bilingual students, contrasts sharply with the widespread inequality that is tolerated, or even promoted, by federal policy in many other areas. NCLB imposes a mandate on schools that is put on no other institution in society: wipe out inequalities while the factors that help produce them remain in place. A closer look at this contradiction sheds light on why critics see NCLB as part of a calculated political campaign to use achievement gaps to label schools as failures, without providing the resources and strategies needed to overcome them.

To "make" AYP, schools must meet separate test score targets for up to ten different student categories. Multiply this by the number of federally mandated tests, currently math and language arts with others on the horizon, and you have a dizzying obstacle course of hoops that schools must jump through. A diverse K–8 school can fail in more than 240 ways.

Schools that miss any target for two consecutive years get put on the "needs-improvement" list and face sanctions. After two years, they must use federal funds to support student transfers. Three years brings "corrective action" and voucherlike fund transfers for supplemental tutorial services; four years brings "reconstitution," including replacement of school staff; five years brings "restructuring," which can mean anything from state takeover to imposing private management on public schools.

Supporters of NCLB claim that the tests and sanctions are the keys to bringing improvement and accountability to all schools. But the AYP system is a narrow and arbitrary assessment scheme that does not provide an accurate picture of how schools are serving their students. It grossly overstates the number of "failing schools" by measuring them against unrealistic and unhelpful criteria, and the sanctions it imposes for low test scores have no record of success as school improvement strategies. In fact they are not educational strategies at all, but political strategies designed to bring a kind of "market reform" to public education.

Under AYP, the only thing that counts is the number of students who score above the passing level on the state test. So on a test like New Jersey's High School Proficiency Assessment, where a passing score is 200, helping a bilingual, special-education student from a low-income household raise his/her test score from, say, 50 to 199 counts for nothing. In fact, such a score counts as a failure in four different subgroups. Moving a student from 199 to 200 is success.

More than 25 percent of the nation's ninety thousand schools missed their AYP targets for the 2005–2006 school year and estimates indicate that ultimately over 80 percent of all public schools will be labeled "in need of improvement."[1] The main effect has not been to promote school improvement or accountability, but to create a widespread public perception of systemic failure that erodes the common ground a universal system of public education needs to survive.

As this new federal testing scheme begins to document an inability to reach its unrealistic and underfunded goals, it will provide new ammunition for a push to fundamentally overhaul and reshape public schooling. Conservative pundits will press their critique of public education as a failed monopoly that must be reformed through market measures, vouchers, and other steps toward privatization.

Many educators are understandably reluctant to oppose NCLB's noble-sounding goals and share concerns about persistent disparities in student achievement. But the AYP formulas and the "Leave no child behind" rhetoric of the federal law are transparent attempts to set up schools to fail. By shining the spotlight on test-score gaps, NCLB effectively invokes concerns about historic inequities, and provides a platform for official posturing about the soft bigotry of low expectations. But the real measure of such concern is what supporters of NCLB propose to do about this inequality, not only in schools, but in society as a whole. Here the record leaves little room for doubt: inequality is as American as processed apple pie.

Take, for example, income inequality among some of the same groups NCLB says must reach 100 percent test-score equality within twelve years. Education research has established a strong link between student performance on standardized tests and family income. While income inequality in a community is no excuse for school failure, certainly any serious federal plan to close academic achievement gaps needs to concern itself with contributing factors, like the resources that families and schools have to work with.

But a look at the data on income inequality—especially through the prism of AYP—reveals the hypocrisy at the heart of the NCLB legislation. In 1991, the median household income for black families was about 58 percent of white income. Hispanic income was about 70 percent. If we applied the AYP system to this key measure of how our economy works, income gaps for blacks would have had to narrow by 3.5 percent each year to pull even within twelve years—the same time frame schools have been given to equalize test scores. Hispanics, starting with a smaller gap, would have had to close the gap by 2.5 percent a year.

But if you compare this to how the economy actually performed between 1991 and 2002, a period of supposedly unprecedented economic growth, you'll find the U.S. economy did not come anywhere near to making "adequate yearly progress" toward the goal of income equality. At the end of twelve years, the gap between black and white income had narrowed only 3.7 percent; for Hispanics the gap was a pitiful .4 percent less than it was in 1991.[2]

If we lived in an alternate universe where income equality really was a goal of federal economic policy and an NCLB-like system of sanctions put pressure on the titans of industry and commerce to attain such a lofty goal, what might be appropriate remedies for such a dismal performance: "corrective action"? to borrow the language of NCLB sanctions; economic restructuring? reconstitution of our major corporations? How about "state takeover"?

The point, of course, is that there is no indicator of equality—including household income, child poverty rates, health-care coverage, home ownership, or school spending—where federal policy currently mandates equality among all population groups within twelve years under threat of sanctions—except standardized test scores in public schools.

If this sounds unfair and absurd, that's because it is. Imagine a federal law that declared that 100 percent of all citizens must have adequate health care in twelve years or sanctions will be imposed on doctors and hospitals. Or all crime must be eliminated in twelve years or the local police department will face privatization.

Inequality in test scores is one indicator of school performance. But test scores also reflect other inequalities in resources and opportunities that exist in the larger society and in schools themselves. Fifteen percent of white children live in poverty, while about 30 percent of black and Latino children live in poverty. Students in poor schools, on average, have thousands of dollars less spent on their education than those in wealthier schools. About 10 percent of whites don't have health insurance, but 20 percent of blacks and over 30 percent of Latinos have no health insurance. Unemployment rates for blacks and Latinos are nearly double what they are for whites.[3]

Why are there no federal mandates demanding the elimination of these gaps? Don't these inequalities leave children behind?

In October 2003, the Educational Testing Service, the largest producer of standardized tests in the world and no hotbed of educational radicalism, issued a report on the achievement gap that tracked fourteen contributing factors from birth weight and child nutrition to class size and teacher qualifications. The results were "unambiguous." The study found that, "In all fourteen factors, the gaps in student achievement mirror inequalities in those aspects of school, early life, and home circumstances that research has linked to achievement."[4]

Yet, except for standardized test scores, none of these measures of inequality appear in the charts used to label schools and impose penalties. Narrowly focusing in on test-score gaps as the sole indicator of educational inequality is just one more way that standardized tests impose high-stakes consequences on the victims of educational failure rather than on those responsible for it.

Another study by the Economic Policy Institute (EPI) found that, "Before even entering kindergarten, the average cognitive scores of children in the highest SES (socio-economic status) group are 60 percent above the scores of the lowest SES group."[5] Some of these differences are the direct result of highly preventable, but still pervasive, social and economic gaps. For example, in Detroit, African American children under five have sixteen times the chance of being overexposed to lead than whites. Lead poisoning has dramatic and devastating effects on the academic potential of young children and has been effectively reduced in many areas. But, in Detroit, the black/white gap in the risk of lead exposure is twice the level that existed in the 1980s.[6] To allow this kind of inequality to grow, while mandating 100 percent equality in standardized test scores in Detroit public schools not only makes no sense educationally, it is morally inexcusable.

As the EPI study put it, "As a nation, we continue to support the role—even the obligation—of schooling to close these gaps, but at the same time we create or magnify the same gaps with other social policies. Except for continuing support for Head Start (actually a relatively inexpensive program), our public policies do little to address the negative educational effects that income disparities have on young children. The United States should not use one hand to blame the schools for inadequately serving disadvantaged children when its social policies have helped create these disadvantages—especially income disadvantages—with the other hand."[7]

NCLB does not even effectively promote equality in the area of school funding. Originally, the law did include some modest increases in federal funding for Title I schools. But these increases are dwarfed by the impact of sanctions that actually reduce the funds available for schoolwide reform in the affected schools and that divert some Title I funds to State Departments of Education to fund more tests and sanctions.

The funding disparities built into school finance systems are part of the race and class inequalities reflected in achievement gaps but overlooked by NCLB. An annual survey by the Education Trust (a strong supporter of NCLB) notes that, "While the biggest gaps earn the most attention, even small gaps add up to serious inequalities. Take Colorado, for example. Its gap is only $101 per student, one of the smaller gaps in the country. A student in a high-poverty district in Colorado has $101 less spent on him or her than a student in a low-poverty district in Colorado. That might not seem as though it would mean much, but for a classroom of 25 students it means $2,525, which could pay for a classroom library of 250 books. For a standard elementary school of 400, this translates into $40,400, which would come close to paying for a reading specialist or an additional teacher. For a standard high school of

1,500, it is a difference of $151,500, which could pay for three literacy coaches and additional library books."[8]

The gap between the promises NCLB makes and the funding it provides is even larger. Ever since the law passed in 2001, with overwhelming bipartisan support in both Houses of Congress, the media has been filled with complaints by Democrats who voted for NCLB that the Bush Administration has not provided full funding for the law. And it's true that administration budgets have called for billions less in NCLB funding than Congress originally authorized.[9]

But even funding NCLB at the levels that Congressional Democrats have requested would leave it light years away from what it would take to realize the promises NCLB makes, even on its own narrow test-score terms. William Mathis, a superintendent of schools in Vermont and a professor of education finance at the University of Vermont, has tracked studies of the resources required to reach the NCLB mandates. He examined estimates in nearly twenty states that used a wide variety of methods to calculate such costs. These studies show that it would take about a 30 percent annual increase in current school spending for states to come even close to meeting NCLB's mandates. That's about $130 billion a year, or almost ten times what current funding is for Title I programs.[10] To date, the much-touted increase in federal spending accompanying NCLB represents about a 1 percent increase in total U.S. school spending.

Money, by itself, is necessary, if insufficient for school improvement. But to dramatically raise expectations on schools and students without adequately addressing the costs or fixing the inequalities built into our school funding system is neither fair nor reasonable. Educational excellence in low-performing schools and districts can only be built on a foundation of educational equity.

There is no denying that NCLB has brought some long overdue attention to the problem of educational inequality. Those who wrestle daily with the realities of this inequality in our classrooms and our schools welcome this attention. The problem is that what NCLB proposes to do about this inequality is woefully inadequate to the task, and in many ways, is making things worse. It shines the spotlight on problems it has no strategies for solving and it imposes tests and sanctions that will increase inequality in education rather than reduce it.

The more people see how NCLB actually works, the more it becomes clear that NCLB is not a tool for solving a crisis in public education, but a tool for creating one.[11] Public schools need a very different tool kit for the problems we face.

NOTES

1. "More Schools Are Failing NCLB Law's 'Adequate Yearly Progress' Requirements," National Education Association, http://www.nea.org/esea/ayptrends0106.html.

2. All figures from U.S. Census Bureau, adjusted 2002 dollars.

3. See *State of America's Children 2005*, Children's Defense Fund, U.S. Census Bureau & Bureau of Labor Statistics.

4. *Parsing the Achievement Gap*, Educational Testing Service, Oct., 2003.

5. Valerie E. Lee & David T. Burkam. *Inequality at the Starting Gate: Social Background Differences in Achievement as Children Begin School*, Washington, DC: Economic Policy Institute, 2002.

6. "Getting the Lead Out," Erik Ness, *Rethinking Schools*, Winter, 2003.

7. Valerie E. Lee and David T. Burkam. Economic Policy Institute, 2002.

8. *The Funding Gap 2005*, Low-Income and Minority Students Shortchanged by Most States: A Special Report by the Education Trust, 2005.

9. William Mathis. *The Federal No Child Left Behind Act: What Will it Cost States*, Spectrum, Journal of State Government, Spring, 2004.

10. William Mathis. *No Child Left Behind: Costs and Benefits*, Kappan, May, 2003.

11. See *The Accountability Trap: How "No Child Left Behind" creates crises in public schools*, by Danny Rose, Online Journal Aug., 2003.

■ PART IV ■

CITY ISSUES:
BEYOND THE SCHOOL'S
WALLS

INTRODUCTION

Gloria Ladson-Billings

At least a decade ago I was in conversation with a colleague who described what sounded like an exciting project where a researcher gave video cameras to city kids and asked them to film their lives. When the students returned their tapes, the researcher noticed that none of them included segments about school. Apparently, the students filmed their families, their friends, their neighborhood, and many aspects of their communities, but the moment they arrived at the school door, the camera went black. Initially the researcher assumed that the students were unable to film in the school because of rules forbidding it. However, when the researcher asked why there was no school footage a student responded, "You said make a movie of my life. School ain't my life!" This student's response aptly summarizes the way many students think about school and its relationship to their lives. School is a place where they are compelled to spend a considerable portion of their time but, increasingly, students have come to think of school as alien to, and outside of, their "real" lives.

The average youngster spends most of her day outside of school. For approximately 180 days—5–6 hours a day—students are under the supervision of the school. But for another 185 days, and for 18 hours a day during the school year, students' influences are other individuals, groups, and institutions. Thus, any attempt for schools to be more effective with students is linked to improving the relationships between students' in-school and out-of-school lives. When we think of city kids we realize that their out-of-school lives are more likely to be fraught with greater challenges and risks than their suburban counterparts.

The worn-out bromide, "they're from single-parent homes," does not begin to explain the social, economic, and political consequences of life in the city for poor children. The challenge of childhood and adolescence in a postmodern world is that having two parents is no guarantee of a successful adult life. One of the advantages that middle-class and affluent youngsters have over low-income and poor children, particularly low-income and poor *city* children, is the opportunity to be surrounded with caring adults. The life of today's overscheduled child is filled with adults. Once outside of school, many middle-class children have soccer coaches, dance teachers, tutors, language teachers, karate instructors, music and art teachers, and a host of other extracurricular activities that keep them in contact with adults, even in the context of peer groups.

The lack of additional adults in the lives of low-income and city children is symptomatic of larger social concerns that characterize their out-of-school lives. We live in a society in which crime is declining, yet incarceration rates are skyrocketing. Far too many children in cities have firsthand experience with the justice system. According to the American Psychological Association, 80 percent of the 2 million people incarcerated in the United States are parents, and we know that their children are at high risk for second-generation incarceration.

We also know, according to the Children's Defense Fund, that life outside of school often is precarious for city kids. Every twenty seconds a child is arrested. Every twenty-two seconds a baby is born to an unmarried mother. Every thirty-five seconds a baby is born to a mother who is not a high school graduate. Every thirty-six seconds a baby is born into poverty. Every forty-seven seconds a baby is born without health insurance. Every minute a baby is born to a teen mother. Every two minutes a baby is born at low birth weight. Every four minutes a child is arrested for drug abuse. Every eight minutes a child is arrested for violent crimes.

Those statistics reflect a composite of life for too many kids in our society. However, there are a few separate yet interrelated concerns that affect the quality of kids' out-of-school lives: jobs, crime, and health. Urban kids live in communities where almost all of the jobs that offer a living wage have evaporated. Sociologist William Julius Wilson (1997) details the decline of employment in urban communities and the impact of the loss of those jobs on urban families. Jean Anyon (2005) describes how moving jobs (that low- to moderate-income people can qualify for) to the suburbs virtually guarantees that people will struggle to keep those jobs—if they can even get them. The distance to and from work requires reliable transportation and the absence of full benefits requires a workforce that either has access to health insurance (a spouse or partner with a job with decent benefits) or an exceptionally healthy worker.

Without jobs—available opportunities to earn a living—people often turn to crime as a way to survive. Underground economies have existed in cities for centuries. However, the explosion of drugs, organized gangs, and handguns have made these economies more dangerous and more threatening to the civic and social fabric of the community. I do not want to be accused of romanticizing the past, but I argue that crime in the 1950s and early 1960s was seen as less sinister and brutal than that of the twenty-first century. The urban community of the 1950s had neighborhood stores and other small businesses—corner stores, barbers, beauticians, restaurants, diners, florists, dry cleaners, Laundromats, gas stations, mechanics, drugstores, and other services. In addition, people regularly supplemented low-paying jobs (or their lack of jobs) with what we called a "side hustle." My father was one such person. In addition to a grueling forty-hour-a-week hard-labor job, he often did side jobs. His weekends were spent painting other people's houses and selling products for a mail-order company.

Others in my family were more "entrepreneurial" in that they worked in the city's lucrative policy racket. For those who do not understand policy, it is a form of illegal gambling that mimics today's state lotteries. Typically, organized crime ran the policy (or more commonly called, "numbers") business. Individuals paid local numbers' runners a few cents—10, 25, and sometimes 50—to play a three-digit number. The payoff for "hitting" the number is six hundred to one. Other side hustles include selling "hot" clothes (probably the result of some robbery) and food from the back of one's car. These "businesses" were prevalent in my community. Yet I never remember anyone being shot or killed in the pursuit of their side hustles. Like most people, those with a hustle were attempting to pay their bills and take care of their families.

In addition to the loss of jobs and the escalation of crime, urban families are faced with fewer health-care options. Fewer physicians and

hospitals are willing to accept Medicare and other government pay-
ments for reimbursement. Increasingly the poor find themselves using
the emergency room as their primary care physician. Fewer low-
income and poor families have the advantage of ongoing, preventative
health care such as regular physicals, dental checkups, and prenatal and
infant care. Richard Rothstein (2004) argues that the big problem that
schools ought to concern themselves with is health care, not reading or
math methods. Indeed, if students are not healthy enough to take advantage of what schools have to offer, what difference does the reading
method or math approach matter?

One of my favorite approaches to integrating what is happening
outside of school into the curriculum was implemented by Paul
Skilton-Sylvester (1994) in his third-grade Philadelphia classroom.
Skilton-Sylvester was disturbed by his principal's decision to "pay" students with "school dollars" for being good citizens. Skilton-Sylvester
pointed out that we are not paid to be citizens; we are paid for our work.
In the students' neighborhood, close to sixty thousand jobs had evaporated in less than ten years. Most of his students were affected by that
loss of jobs. Skilton-Sylvester used this economic reality to set up a
classroom economy that had some of the same sad realities. His students were paid to work the jobs in the classroom economy but sometimes those jobs "moved" to the suburbs. Other times people did not
have the skills and experience to compete for a job they wanted.

In addition to creating the classroom economy, Skilton-Sylvester
(1994) took the students into the community to meet the local business
people—barbers, beauticians, shop owners, and the owner of the bar-
beque joint—to learn how they developed those businesses and how
hard it was to maintain them. The lessons that students learned in this
third-grade classroom were that obstacles to employment are often beyond one's educational level or willingness to work. Sometimes work is
just not there.

But the lessons beyond the school's walls are not all negative. There
are community resources that exist even in the midst of the loss of jobs,
the rising crime, the lack of health care, and other challenges (e.g. adequate housing, drugs, HIV/AIDS, obesity, and so on). Specifically, there
continue to be cultural institutions and practices that are central to stu-

dents' well-being and development. These institutions include youth-generated music and art forms (hip-hop, spoken word), churches and other religious organizations, and sports and recreation.

Despite the recent backlash against hip-hop culture and the high-profile artists who use negative messages against women, other races, and homosexuals—while glamorizing violence, drugs, and money—there is a core of hip-hop artists whose music and messages are important elements of the youth culture urban students are crafting. By understanding the power of words over guns and other forms of violence, students are developing a form of self-expression that is energetic, sometimes raw, and brutally honest about what it means to grow up in urban communities.

In Los Angeles, after the insurrection that occurred in the wake of the verdict in the Rodney King case, a youth movement emerged that moved away from fighting and toward dancing. In the film *Rize* (LaChappelle, 2005) we see the dance forms Clowning and Krumping as radical, energetic, and extreme styles that young people have developed as an alternative to fighting and physical confrontations. The dances are rooted in cultural forms found in Africa, the Indies, and Latin America. However, the youth place their own specific signature on this work as they strive to express themselves.

Sports, too, play an important role in urban communities, and provide many youth unique venues for success and accomplishment. It's important to note that the blacktop, the gym, and the playing field are sites of energy and investment; it is in these places that young people develop a keen sense of justice, ethical action, compromise, and resolution.

Finally, we cannot minimize the role that churches and other religious organizations play in the life of urban children, youth, and their families. Because of its independent status, the African American church continues to be one of the only full-service institutions located in urban communities. The churches do not rely on city, county, state, or federal budgets that may or may not allow a community service to continue. The churches become places that meet physical needs with little or no red tape. People are invited to eat because they are hungry. They are given clothes because they say they need them. Increasingly,

African American churches are offering ministries and services that reflect the reality of life in urban communities. Ministries serving single parents, recovering alcohol and drug addicts, senior citizens, and struggling readers are regular features of today's urban church. Children get to sing or dance or act regardless of prior experiences or training. High school students get assistance with college admissions testing, college applications, and scholarship applications. Many of the churches provide job training and financial counseling. A few urban churches maintain credit unions that were a vestige of the 1950s when African Americans could not receive credit at mainstream institutions.

Beyond the school walls, the city remains a vibrant and dynamic space. In spite of very deliberate efforts to remove and discourage its low-income and poor residents through either gentrification (as in Harlem, parts of Chicago, and post-Katrina New Orleans) or neglect (as in Philadelphia and Detroit), the city remains the port of entry for people who are struggling to grab hold of a better life for themselves and their children. It is that vibrancy and dynamism for which educators committed to social justice must fight.

REFERENCES

Anyon, J. (2005). *Radical possibilities: Public policy, urban education and a new social movement.* New York: Routledge.

LaChapelle, D. (2005). *Rize.* Los Angeles, David LaChapelle Studios.

Rothstein, R. (2004). *Class and schools: Using social, economic, and educational reform to close the black-white achievement gap.* Washington, DC: Economic Policy Institute.

Skilton-Sylvester, P. (1994). Elementary school curricula and urban transformation. *Harvard Educational Review 64,* 309–31.

Wilson, W.J. (1997). *When work disappears: The world of the new urban poor.* New York: Vintage Books.

25

EDUCATION IN OUR DYING CITIES

Grace Lee Boggs

A longtime political activist and revolutionary thinker, Grace Lee Boggs was a leading figure in the Black Freedom Movement in the 1960s. With her husband, James Boggs, she wrote the seminal work, Revolution and Evolution in the Twentieth Century, *and she has authored several other books and articles, including a memoir,* Living for Change. *She is founder of the Boggs Center and visionary leader of Detroit Summer, an annual gathering of youth activists engaged in community building. At ninety-two, she remains a prolific writer and speaker. The following piece was adapted from a talk she gave to young activists.*

In the last three years of his life Dr. Martin Luther King Jr., seeking a way to overcome the despair and powerlessness that exploded into the streets during unprecedented urban rebellions, said that what our young people needed "in our dying cities" was "direct action programs," programs to change themselves and, at the same time, programs that would revitalize their environments.

"This generation," he said, "is engaged in a cold war with the earlier generation. It is not the familiar and normal hostility of the young groping for independence. It has a new quality of bitter antagonism and confused anger which suggest basic values are being contested."

"The source of this alienation," he continued, "is that our society has made material growth and technological advance an end in itself, robbing people of participation, so that human beings become smaller while their works become bigger."

The way to overcome this alienation, he said, is by changing our priorities. Instead of pursuing economic productivity, we need to expand our uniquely human powers, especially our capacity for *agape*, which is the love that is ready to go to any length to restore community.

This love, King explained, is not some sentimental weakness but rather the key that unlocks the doors that lead to reality. We can learn its practical meaning from the young people who joined the civil rights movement, putting middle-class values of wealth and career in second place, taking off their Brooks Brothers attire and putting on overalls to work in the isolated rural South because they felt the need for more direct ways of learning that would strengthen both society and themselves.

That is why we founded Detroit Summer fifteen years ago to engage young people in rebuilding, redefining, and respiriting the city from the ground up.

Just imagine how much safer and livelier and more peaceful our neighborhoods would be almost overnight—if we reorganized education along the lines of Detroit Summer; if instead of trying to keep our children isolated in classrooms for twelve years and more, we engaged them in community-building activities right now with the same audacity with which the civil rights movement engaged them in desegregation activities forty years ago: planting community gardens, recycling waste, organizing neighborhood arts and health festivals, rehabbing houses, painting public murals. By giving our children and young people a better reason to learn than just the individualistic one of getting a job or making more money, by encouraging them to exercise their soul power, we would also deepen and strengthen their intellectual engagement. Learning would come from practice, which has always been the best and most powerful way to learn.

Instead of trying to bully young people to remain in classrooms isolated from their communities and structured to prepare them to become cogs in the existing decaying economic system, we need to recognize that huge numbers of young people are dropping out of city schools, voting with their feet against an educational system that sorts, tracks, tests, and rejects or certifies them like products of a factory created for the age of industrialization. They are crying out for

another kind of education, another way of being that gives them opportunities to exercise their creative energies because it values them as
human beings.

There once was a time when these kids could drop out of school in
the ninth grade and get a job in a factory making enough money to get
married and raise a family if they chose to, and in any case to become a
stable member of the community. One of the root causes for the urban
rebellions of the late 1960s was the realization by young people that this
future had been closed off to them by hi-tech. Since then the export of
jobs overseas by transnational corporations has made young people
more painfully conscious of their expendability.

A new approach is urgently needed in all our educational institutions. Instead of viewing the purpose of education as giving students
the means for upward mobility and success and/or to become the technological elites that will enable the United States to compete in the
world market, we need to recognize that the aptitutdes and attitudes of
people with BAs, BSs, MBAs, and PhDs bear a lot of responsibility for
our planetary and social problems. Formal education bears a large part
of the responsibility for our present crisis because it produces morally
sterile technicians who have more know-how than know-why. At a time
when we desperately need to heal the earth and build durable economies
and healthy communities, our schools and universities are stuck in the
processes and practices used to industrialize the earth in the nineteenth
and twentieth centuries.

What we urgently need are school boards, school superintendents,
college presidents, teachers, and parents with the imagination and courage
to introduce innovative curriculums and structures that create a much
more intimate connection between intellectual development and practical activity. We need to root students and faculty in their communities
and natural habitats, and engage them in the kind of real problem solving in their localities that nurtures a love of place and provides practice
in creating the sustainable economies, equality, and community that are
the responsibilities of citizenship.

We need to create a vision and develop strategies to transform our
children from angry rebels into positive change agents. To do this we
need to go beyond the issue of power or who controls our schools and

begin grappling with fundamental questions about the purpose of education and how children learn. The time has come to go beyond the top-down factory model of education, which was created at the beginning of the twentieth century to supply industry with a disciplined workforce, and begin creating a new model, which empowers young people to make a difference.

Children need to be given a sense of the unique capacity of human beings to shape and create reality in accordance with conscious purposes and plans. This means that our schools need to be transformed to provide children with ongoing opportunities to exercise their resourcefulness to solve real problems. Like all human beings, children and young people need to be of use. They cannot just be treated as objects and taught subjects. Their cognitive juices will flow more forcefully if and when their hearts, heads, and hands are engaged in improving their daily lives and their surroundings.

However, instead of rethinking the purposes and methods of education in a postindustrial society, school boards and administrators have come up with all sorts of palliatives. Magnet schools, charter schools, and vouchers have been created, skimming off the students most likely to succeed in the existing system, thus turning the teachers in the remaining schools into wardens. Every couple of years, school superintendents have been replaced with new more military-minded ones. Privatization has been tried in some cities. In other cities like Detroit, elected school boards have been replaced with state-appointed ones. With the advent of the Bush administration, testing has become more frequent and more punitive, forcing teachers to teach to a sterile and often meaningless test, suppressing the creativity of committed teachers. At the same time, restive and resistant students have been made more restive and resistant by increasingly harsh disciplinary measures—"zero tolerance" suspensions or expulsions that are aimed at cowing students into obedience and conformity, keeping out those who are disruptive or who are feared to drag down the school's test averages. The result is a climate of growing unrest in our schools. We are not going to solve this crisis with more money, more computers, new buildings, or new CEOs. To achieve the miracle that is now needed to transform our schools into places of learning we need to tap into the creative energies of our children and our teachers. In this connection we have much to learn from the struggles in Alabama and Mississippi in the early 1960s.

In the spring of 1963 the Southern Christian Leadership Conference led by Dr. King launched a "fill the jails" campaign to desegregate downtown department stores and schools in Birmingham. But few local blacks were coming forward. Black adults were afraid of losing their jobs, local black preachers were reluctant to accept the leadership of an outsider, and city police commissioner Bull Conner had everyone intimidated. Facing a major defeat, King was persuaded by his aide, James Bevel, to allow any child old enough to belong to a church to march. So on May 2, before the eyes of the whole nation, thousands of school children, many of them first-graders, joined the movement and were beaten, fire-hosed, attacked by police dogs, and herded off to jail in paddy wagons and school buses. The result was what has been called "The Children's Miracle." Inspired and shamed into action, thousands of adults rushed to join the movement. All over the country rallies were called to express outrage against Bull Connor's brutality. Locally the power structure was forced to desegregate lunch counters and dressing rooms in downtown stores, hire blacks to work downtown, and begin desegregating the schools. Nationally the Kennedy administration, which had been trying not to alienate white "Dixiecrat" voters, was forced to begin drafting civil rights legislation as the only way to forestall more Birminghams. The next year as part of Mississippi Freedom Summer, activists created Freedom Schools because the existing school system (like ours today) had been organized to produce subjects, not citizens. To bring about a "mental revolution," reading, writing, and speaking skills were taught through the discussion of black history, the power structure, and the need to build a movement to struggle for positive change. In 1963 and 1964 the creative energies of children and young people were tapped to win the battle for desegregation and voting rights, and today they need to be tapped to rebuild our communities and our dying cities and to create a vibrant society and a democratic citizenry.

Schools and colleges dedicated to this new kind of education would look and act differently from today's educational institutions. For example, much more learning would take place *outside* school walls, while *inside* an integral part of the educational process would be the design and operation of the building—classes would audit resource flows of food, energy, water, materials, waste, and investments. Recognizing that education is about learning to be helpful and responsible citizens and that children don't learn only from books, segregation in schools based upon abilities would be ended. And more.

To resolve our deepening school crisis and to rebuild our dying cities we need this paradigm shift in our approach to education, a shift that Martin Luther King, Jr. anticipated. Let's make it happen.

26

UNNATURAL DISASTERS: RACE AND POVERTY

Michael Eric Dyson

An engaged scholar and public intellectual, Michael Eric Dyson is a widely read social and cultural critic whose writing spans the worlds of literature and the arts, history and politics, theology and popular culture. A frequent commentator on television and radio and University Professor at Georgetown University, he has been called "the hip-hop intellectual." In this piece, taken from his book on Hurricane Katrina, Come Hell or High Water, *Dyson reminds us that for many of the poor in New Orleans—as in other American cities—the water had been rising long before the storm.*

The barrage of images in newspapers and on television tested the nation's collective sense of reality. There were men and women wading chest-deep in water—when they weren't floating or drowning in the toxic whirlpool the streets of New Orleans had become. When the waters subsided, there were dead bodies strewn on curbsides and wrapped in blankets by fellow sufferers, who provided the perished their only dignity. There were unseemly collages of people silently dying from hunger and thirst—and of folk writhing in pain, or quickly collapsing under the weight of missed medicine for diabetes, high blood pressure, or heart trouble. Photo snaps and film shots captured legions of men and women huddling in groups or hugging corners, crying in wild-eyed desperation for help, for any help, from somebody, anybody, who would listen to their unanswered pleas. The filth and squalor of their confinement—defecating where they stood or sat, or, more likely, dropped, bathed in a brutal wash of dredge and sickening pollutants that choked the air with ungodly stench—grieved the camera lenses that recorded their plight.

Men, women, and children tore through deserted streets lined with empty stores, hunting for food and water and clothing for their bodies. They were hurried along by the steadily diminishing prospect of rescue by the government, by *their* government, whose only visible representatives were the police who came after them for looting. There were wailing infants clasping crying mothers who mouthed prayers for someone to please just save their babies. There were folk stuffed in attics pleading for the cavalry to come. Many colors were present in this multicultural stew of suffering, but the dominant color was black. From the sight of it, this was the third world—a misnomer, to be sure, since people of color are two-thirds of the world's population. The suffering on screen created cognitive dissonance; it suggested that this must be somewhere in India, or the outskirts of Biafra. This surely couldn't be the United States of America—and how cruelly that term seemed to mock those poor citizens who felt disunited and disconnected and just plain dissed by their government. This couldn't be the richest and most powerful nation on the globe, leaving behind some of its poorest citizens to fend for themselves.

And yet it was. It was bad enough to witness the government's failure to respond to desperate cries of help scrawled on the tattered roofs of flooded homes. But Hurricane Katrina's violent winds and killing waters swept into the mainstream a stark realization: the poor had been abandoned by society and its institutions, and sometimes by their well-off brothers and sisters, long before the storm. We are immediately confronted with another unsavory truth: it is the exposure of the extremes, not their existence, that stumps our national sense of decency. We can abide the ugly presence of poverty so long as it doesn't interrupt the natural flow of things, doesn't rudely impinge on our daily lives or awareness. As long as poverty is a latent reality, a solemn social fact suppressed from prominence on our moral compass, we can find our bearings without fretting too much about its awkward persistence.

It's not as if it was news to most folk that poverty exists in the United States. Still, there was no shortage of eureka moments glistening with discovery and surprise in the aftermath of Katrina. Poverty's grinding malevolence is fed in part by social choices and public-policy decisions that directly impact how many people are poor and how long they remain that way. To acknowledge that is to own up to our role in the misery of the poor—be it the politicians we vote for who cut programs aimed at helping the economically vulnerable; the narrative of bootstrap individualism we invoke to deflect the relevance of the considerable benefits we've received while bitterly complaining of the few breaks the poor might get; the religious myths we circulate that bring shame on the poor by chiding them for lacking the appropriate hunger to be prosperous; and the resentment of the alleged pathology of poor blacks—fueled more by stereotypes than by empirical support—that gives us license to dismiss or demonize them.

Our being surprised, and disgusted, by the poverty that Katrina revealed is a way of remaining deliberately naive about the poor while dodging the responsibility that knowledge of their lives would entail. We remain blissfully ignorant of their circumstances to avoid the brutal indictment of our consciences. When a disaster like Katrina strikes—a *natural* disaster not directly caused by human failure—it frees us to be aware of, and angered by, the catastrophe. After all, it doesn't directly implicate us; it was an act of God. Even when human hands get involved, our fingerprints are nowhere to be found. We're not responsible for the poor and black being left behind; the local, state, or federal government is at fault.

We are thus able to decry the circumstances of the poor while assuring ourselves that we had nothing to do with their plight. We can even take special delight in lambasting the source of their suffering—a source that is safely external to us. We are fine as long as we place time limits on the origins of the poor's plight—the moments we all spied on television after the storm, but not the numbing years during which we all looked the other way. Thus we fail to confront our complicity in their long-term suffering. By being outraged, we appear compassionate. This permits us to continue to ignore the true roots of their condition, roots that branch into our worlds and are nourished on our political and religious beliefs.

There are 37 million people in poverty in our nation, 1.1 million of whom fell below the poverty line in 2004.[1] Some of the poorest folk in the nation, people in the Delta, have been largely ignored, rendered invisible, officially forgotten. FEMA left them dangling precipitously on rooftops and in attics because of bureaucratic bumbling. Homeland Security failed miserably in mobilizing resources to rescue Katrina survivors without food, water, or shelter. President Bush lighted on New Orleans only after Mayor Ray Nagin's profanity-laced radio-show diatribe blasting the federal government for its lethal inertia. Because the government took its time getting into New Orleans, Katrina took many lives. Hundreds of folk, especially the elderly, died while waiting for help. But the government and society had been failing to pay attention to the poor since long before one of the worst natural disasters in the nation's history swallowed the poor and spit them back up. The world saw just how much we hadn't seen; it witnessed our negligence up close in frightfully full color.

The hardest-hit regions in the Gulf states had already been drowning in extreme poverty: Mississippi is the poorest state in the nation, with Louisiana just behind it.[2] More than 90,000 people in each of the areas stormed by Katrina in Louisiana, Mississippi, and Alabama made less than $10,000 a year. Black folk in these areas were strapped by incomes that were 40 percent less than those earned by whites. Before the storm, New Orleans, with a 67.9 percent black population, had more than 103,000 poor people. That means the Crescent City had a poverty rate of 23 percent, 76 percent higher than the national average of 13.1 percent.[3] New Orleans's poverty rate ranked it seventh out of 290 large U.S. counties.[4]

Although black folk make up 31.5 percent of Louisiana's population, their offspring account for 69 percent of the children in poverty. Though the national average for elders with disabilities is 39.6 percent, New Orleans hovers near 57 percent. The New Orleans median household income is $31,369, far beneath the national median of $44,684.[5] A full 9 percent of households in New Orleans didn't own or have access to a vehicle.[6] That means that nearly one in four citizens in New Orleans, and one in seven in the greater New Orleans metropolitan area, had no access to a car.[7]

In fact, New Orleans ranks fourth out of 297 metropolitan areas in the country in the proportion of households lacking access to cars.[8] The top three metropolitan spots are in the greater New York area, which has the most extensive public transportation system in the country. New Orleans ranks ninth among 140 big cities for the same category, a far higher ranking than cities with similar demographic profiles such as Detroit and Memphis.[9] Black households nationwide generally have far less access to cars than white households, a trend mirrored in New Orleans, where only 5 percent of non-Latino whites were without car access, while 27 percent of blacks in New Orleans were without cars.[10] Nationwide, 19 percent of blacks lack access to cars.[11]

And children and elderly folk are even more likely to live in households without access to cars. Children and the elderly made up 38 percent of the population in New Orleans, but they accounted for 48 percent of the households without access to cars in the city.[12] The poor and the near-poor made up the vast majority of those without car access in New Orleans, accounting for nearly 80 percent of the city's carless population.[13] These facts make it painfully clear just why so many folk could not evacuate before Katrina struck. They weren't shiftless, stupid, or stubborn, as some have suggested (FEMA's Michael Brown blamed the poor for staying behind and drowning while discounting or ignoring the many obstacles to their successful exodus). They simply couldn't muster the resources to escape destruction, and, for many, death.

The most glaring feature of their circumstance suggests that Katrina's survivors lived in concentrated poverty—they lived in poor neighborhoods, attended poor schools, and had poorly paying jobs that reflected and reinforced a distressing pattern of rigid segregation.[14] Nearly 50,000 poor folk in New Orleans lived in areas where the poverty rate approached 40 percent. In fact, among the nation's fifty largest cities with poor black families jammed into extremely poor neighborhoods, New Orleans ranked second. Those households living in concentrated poverty often earn barely more than $20,000 a year. In neighborhoods with concentrated poverty, only one in twelve adults has a college degree, most children are reared in single-parent families, and four in ten working-age adults, many of whom are disabled, have no jobs.[15] Nearly every major American city has several neighborhoods that are desperately poor and severely segregated. Cities like Cleveland, New York, Atlanta, and Los Angeles have economically distressed neighborhoods where more than 30 percent of their population's poor blacks live.[16]

Concentrated poverty is the product of decades of public policies and political measures that isolate black households in neighborhoods plagued by severe segregation and economic hardship. For instance, the federal government's decision to concentrate public housing in segregated inner-city neighborhoods fueled metropolitan expansion. It also cut the poor off from decent housing and educational and economic opportunities by keeping affordable housing for poor minorities out of surrounding suburbs. The effects of concentrated poverty have been amply documented: reduced private-sector investment and local job opportunities; higher prices for the poor in inner-city businesses; increased levels of crime; negative consequences on the mental and physical health of the poor; and the spatial dislocation of the poor spurred by the "black track" of middle-class households to the suburbs.[17]

In the antebellum and post–Civil War south, New Orleans brought together slaves, former slaves, free blacks, Creoles of color, and Cajuns and other whites in an ethnically diverse mélange that reflected the city's Spanish, French, and African roots and influences. Despite the bustling ethnic and racial interactions—driven in part by the unique "backyard" patterns, where blacks and whites lived near each other, a practice that had its roots in slavery—the city endured increasing segregation as suburbanization made New Orleans blacker in the latter half of the twentieth century.[18] In the case of New Orleans, patterns of extreme exodus from urban centers to suburban communities followed a national trend. As the city got blacker, it got poorer. In 1960, New Orleans was 37 percent black; in 1970, it was 43 percent black; by 1980, it was 55 percent black. In 1990 the city was 62 percent black, and by 2000 it was more than 67 percent black. As whites fled New Orleans, they turned to Jefferson Parish, which is 69.8 percent white and only 22.9 percent black; to St. Bernard Parish, which is 88.29 percent white with a paltry 7.62 percent black population; and to St. Tammany Parish, which is 87.02 percent white and 9.90 percent black. The black middle class sought refuge in Gentilly and New Orleans East, intensifying the suffering of a largely black and poor inner city.[19]

Perhaps most damaging for the young, concentrated poverty stifles the academic success of black children. A child's socioeconomic status, along with other influential factors like teacher/pupil ratio, teacher quality, curriculum materials, expenditures per student, and the age of the school building, greatly affects her or his academic success. Wealthier parents are able to send their children to better public schools and higher-quality private schools, which, in turn, clear the path for admission to prestigious colleges and universities.[20] New Orleans has a 40 percent illiteracy rate; over 50 percent of black ninth-graders won't graduate in four years. Louisiana expends an average of $4,724 per student and has the third-lowest rank for teacher salaries in the nation.[21] The black dropout rates are high and nearly 50,000 students cut class every day.

When they are done with school, many young black males end up at Angola Prison, a correctional facility located on a former plantation where inmates still perform manual farm labor, and where 90 percent of them eventually die.[22] New Orleans's employment picture is equally gloomy, since industry long ago deserted the city, leaving in its place a service economy that caters to tourists and that thrives on low-paying, transient, and unstable jobs.[23]

If President Bush is serious about what he said in his first speech on national television in Katrina's aftermath, that the "deep, persistent poverty" of the Gulf Coast "has roots in a history of racial discrimination, which has cut off generations from the opportunity of America," and that we must "rise above the legacy of inequality," then he must foster public policy and legislation that help the poor to escape their plight.[24] But can a self-proclaimed antigovernment president develop policy that actually improves people's lives? Bush would have to change his mind about slashing $35 billion from Medicaid, food stamps, and other social programs that help the poor combat such a vile legacy. The federal government also owes the black poor better schools. Bush's No Child Left Behind Act of 2001 promised to bolster the nation's crumbling educational infrastructure, but conservative politics have only exacerbated the problems: underperforming schools, low reading levels, and wide racial and class disparities. The schools that need money the most—those whose students are up against challenges like outdated curriculum materials and poor teacher/pupil ratios—have their funding cut when their test scores don't measure up. Oddly enough, Bush has also failed to sufficiently fund his own mandate, reinforcing class and educational inequality.

Bush also owes it to the poor to use the bully pulpit of the presidency to address the health crisis in black America. When Katrina swept waves of mostly poor and black folk into global view, it also graphically uncovered their poor health. More than 83,000 citizens, or 18.8 percent of the population in New Orleans, lacked health insurance (the national average is 15.5 percent); the numbers for black women doubled those for white women.[25] Nationally, there are nearly 40 million folk without health insurance, many of them black and poor. They resort to the emergency ward for health maintenance. Their survival is compromised because serious diseases are spotted later than need be. If President Bush is the compassionate conservative he says he is, then he must help fix a health-care system that favors the wealthy and the solidly employed.

Concentrated poverty does more than undermine academic success and good health; since there is a strong relationship between education and employment, and quality of life, it keeps the poor from better-paying jobs that might interrupt a vicious cycle of poverty. In New Orleans, severe underemployment and unemployment, and unstable employment, gang up on the black poor. This circumstance is made worse by the densely populated communities and housing in which they live, the sheer social misery of much of postindustrial urban Southern life, and their dreadful infant-mortality and homicide rates—the disenfranchised turn more readily and violently on each other rather than striking against the inequality that puts them at each other's throats.

The Lower Ninth Ward is a perfectly bleak example of the concentrated poverty the city's poor black residents confront. The Lower Ninth Ward, also known as the Lower 9, is symptomatic of the geographical isolation on which concentrated poverty feeds. The Lower 9 "crouches behind a pile of dirt, separated by a big bend in America's biggest river and a thick canal and eons of tradition from the 'high-class people' up on the high ground over in the French Quarter."[26] The Lower Ninth was one of the last neighborhoods in the city to be developed. To its west lies the Industrial Canal; to the north are the Southern Railway railroad and Florida Avenue Canal; to the east lies the parish line; and the river traces its southern border.[27] The Lower 9 grew so slowly because it was isolated from the rest of the city and because it lacked adequate drainage systems.[28] The Lower 9 evolved from a cypress swamp to a series of plantations that extended from the river to the lake. Poor black folk in search of affordable housing—and Irish, German, and Italian immigrant workers, too—fled to the area although risking disease and natural disaster.

The Lower 9's growth was so delayed that by 1950 half of it remained undeveloped. The dry docks of the Industrial Canal were the center of development at the time, while some activity trickled out to residential areas in the neighborhood's northern section. By the end of the decade, the second bridge between the city and the Lower 9, the Claiborne Avenue Bridge, was built across Industrial Canal at Claiborne Avenue.[29] During this time, retail development along St. Claude Avenue took off and corner stores became popular. By 1965, industrial and commercial enterprise thrived on the strip that ran along the Industrial Canal between Claiborne and Florida Avenues.[30]

In September of 1965, Hurricane Betsy visited its deadly fury on New Orleans, killing eighty-one people and covering 80 percent of the Lower 9 in water. The storm's surge rose to ten feet, overwhelming the eight-foot levee. As with Katrina, survivors waded through waist-deep water holding babies to escape Betsy's aftermath. Other victims awaited rescue from their rooftops. Critics maintain that Betsy's carnage fueled the decline of the Lower 9, especially since many residents didn't receive adequate loans or other financial aid to help rebuild the neighborhood. Many longtime residents fled, and several commercial and industrial businesses soon followed.

The area received assistance in the late sixties and early seventies from a federal program that targeted blighted neighborhoods to spark metropolitan development and revitalization—leading to the Lower

Ninth Ward Neighborhood Council, Total Community Action's Lower Ninth Ward Head Start Program, the Lower Ninth Ward Housing Development Corporation, and the Lower Ninth Ward Health Clinic. The Lower 9 has many small businesses, barber and beauty shops, corner grocery stores called "superettes," eating spots, gasoline stations, day care centers, churches, and laundromats called "washeterias."[31] Despite its rich cultural and racial pedigree—the Lower 9 is home to famed entertainer Fats Domino and features during Carnival some of the most exciting "second-line" parades, characterized by churning rhythms and kinetic, high-stepping funk grooves—the area has continued to struggle with persistent and concentrated poverty.[32]

Before Katrina, the Lower 9 was peopled with poor blacks who were the maids, bellhops, and busboys who looked after tourists on pleasure hunts and thrill quests in New Orleans. They are now the clerks, cops, and carpenters who are helping to revive and rebuild the city, along with the sculptors, painters, and musicians who are staples of the local scene.[33] The vast majority of the Lower 9's 20,000 residents were black, and more than a third of them, 36 percent, lived beneath the poverty line, nearly double the statewide poverty rate.[34] The Lower 9's residents were often victims of the complicated racial dynamics in New Orleans, where police brutality and retail and business profiling dogged them from outside their neighborhood, and where bigotry against poorer, often darker, blacks echoed within many African American communities. The faces of the Lower 9's residents—though forgotten by their government and overlooked by their fellow citizens—looked out from their watery wasteland and for a moment focused the eyes of the world on their desperate plight.

But it was not merely that we forgot to see or know the poor that forged the searing image of our national neglect and American amnesia. And neither was it the fact that Katrina exposed, to our horror and amazement, the bitter outlines of concentrated poverty that we have reason to be ashamed. It is not all about what we saw—which, after all, may be a perverse narcissism that makes *their* plight ultimately about *our* failure and what *we* must learn at their great expense. It is also about what *they*, the poor, saw in us, or didn't see there, especially the government that didn't find or feed them until it was late—too late for thousands of them. It is their surprise, not ours, that should most concern and inform us. Perhaps it is their anger, too, that is inspiring, since the outrage of the black survivors proved their tenacious loyalty to a country that hasn't often earned it.

As Michael Ignatieff argues, the poor blacks struggling to survive Katrina's backlash saw more clearly than most others "what the contract of American citizenship entails."[35] For Ignatieff, a contract of citizenship "defines the duties of care that public officials owe to the people of a democratic society." Ignatieff says that the "Constitution defines some parts of this contract, and statutes define other parts, but much of it is a tacit understanding that citizens have about what to expect from their government." Ignatieff contends that the contract's "basic term is protection: helping citizens to protect their families and possessions from forces beyond their control."[36] According to Ignatieff, when a woman at the convention center proclaimed "We are American," it was "she—not the governor, not the mayor, not the president—[who] understood that the catastrophe was a test of the bonds of citizenship and that the government had failed the test." Ignatieff explores the racial backdrop to the government's disregard of the poor while clarifying the demand of the poor that we honor a contract by which we claim to abide:

It may be astonishing that American citizens should have had to remind their fellow Americans of this, but let us not pretend we do not know the reason. They were black, and for all that poor blacks have experienced and endured in this country, they had good reason to be surprised that they were treated not as citizens but as garbage. . . . Let us not be sentimental. The poor and dispossessed of New Orleans cannot afford to be sentimental. They know they live in an unjust and unfair society. . . . So it is not—as some commentators claimed—that the catastrophe laid bare the deep inequalities of American society. These inequalities may have been news to some, but they were not news to the displaced people in the convention center and elsewhere. What was bitter news to them was that their claims of citizenship mattered so little to the institutions charged with their protection.[37]

In his lucid explanation of the compelling bonds of citizenship, Ignatieff outlines detriments to the social contract that make us all less than what we ought to be. Ignatieff calls attention to the role of race in coloring perceptions on either side of the cultural and political divide about how we should have met our moral and civic obligations to the poor. The deeper we dig into the story of Katrina, the more we must accept culpability for the fact that the black citizens of the Big Easy—a tag given New Orleans by black musicians who easily found work in a city that looms large in the collective American imagination as the home of jazz, jambalaya, and Mardi Gras—were treated by the rest of us as garbage.

NOTES

1. Jacques Amalric, "Crises in New Orleans Is History Repeating Itself," WatchingAmerica.com, Sept. 8, 2005, http://www.watchingamerica.com/liberation000040.html.
2. "Who Are Katrina's Victims?" Center for American Progress, Sept. 6, 2005, p. 1. www.americanprogress.org.
3. Ibid.
4. Alan Berube and Bruce Katz, "Katrina's Window: Confronting Concentrated Poverty Across America," Brookings Institution, Oct. 2005, http://www.brookings.edu/metro/pubs/20051012_concentratedpoverty.htm.
5. "Who Are Katrina's Victims?" pp. 1–2.
6. Ibid., p. 2.
7. Alan Berube and Steven Raphael, "Access to Cars in New Orleans," Brookings Institution, Sept. 15, 2005, http://www.brookings.edu/metro/20050915_katrina carstables.pdf.
8. Ibid.
9. Ibid.
10. Ibid.
11. Ibid.
12. Ibid.
13. Ibid.
14. Berube and Katz, "Katrina's Window."
15. Ibid.
16. Ibid.
17. Ibid. I first used the term "black track" to describe a pattern of black out-migration that mimics patterns of earlier out-migration of white middle-class

families to suburban communities. See Michael Eric Dyson, *Reflecting Black: African-American Cultural Criticism* (Minneapolis: University of Minnesota Press, 1993), p. 188.

18. As historian Lawrence N. Powell argues: "Because habitable land was so scarce, the population of New Orleans had to squeeze together, cheek-by-jowl— upper-class gents next door to or one street over from raw-boned stevedores, Irish next to German, black next to white, in a salt-and-pepper pattern that still baffles visitors to the city. New Orleans never had ethnically and racially pure enclaves until modern suburbanization began slotting the population into seg-regated subdivisions." Lawrence N. Powell, "New Orleans: An American Pom-peii?" Sept. 2005, p. 21. Paper in author's possession.

19. Anthony Fontenot, "How to Rebuild New Orleans" (compiled by Aaron Kin-ney and Page Rockwell), Salon.com, Sept. 30, 2005, http://www.salon.com/news/feature/2005/09/30/rebuild_reaction.

20. "The Racial Wealth Gap Has Become a Huge Chasm that Severely Limits Black Access to Higher Education," *The Journal of Blacks in Higher Education*, 2005, pp. 23–25.

21. Jordan Flaherty, "Notes from Inside New Orleans," *New Orleans Independent Media Center*, Sept. 2, 2005, http://neworleans.indymedia.org/news/2005/4043.php.

22. Ibid.

23. Ibid.

24. "Bush: 'We Will Do What It Takes'" (transcript of Bush speech from Jackson Square in the French Quarter of New Orleans), CNN.com, Sept. 17, 2005, http://www.cnn.com/2005/POLITICS/09/15/bush.transcript/index.html.

25. "Who Are Katrina's Victims?" p. 2.

26. Manuel Roig-Franzia, "Once More, a Neighborhood Sees the Worst," *Washington Post*, Sept. 8, 2005, p. A18.

27. "Lower Ninth Ward Neighborhood Snapshot," Greater New Orleans Com-munity Data Center, Oct. 10, 2002, http://www.gnocdc.org/orleans/8/22/snapshot.html.

28. Ibid.

29. Ibid.

30. Ibid.

31. Ibid.; Roig-Franzia, "Once More," p. A18.

32. Roig-Franzia, "Once More," p. A18; Ceci Connolly, "9th Ward: History, Yes, but a Future?; Race and Class Frame Debate on Rebuilding New Orleans Dis-trict," *Washington Post*, Oct. 3, 2005, p. A01.

33. Connolly, "9th Ward."

34. Ibid.; Roig-Franzia, "Once More."

35. Michael Ignatieff, "The Broken Contract," *New York Times Magazine*, Sept. 25, 2005, p. 15.

36. Ibid.

37. Ibid.

27

AND WHAT WILL BECOME OF CHILDREN LIKE MIGUEL FERNANDEZ?: EDUCATION, IMMIGRATION, AND THE FUTURE OF LATINOS IN THE UNITED STATES

Pedro A. Noguera

Pedro A. Noguera, professor at the Steinhardt School of Education at New York University and Director of the Metropolitan Center for Urban Education, has served as an advisor to urban school districts throughout the United States. A prolific writer, his books include City Schools and the American Dream *and* Unfinished Business: Closing the Racial Achievement Gap in Our Schools. *In the following piece he focuses on the plight of Latino immigrant students and our collective failure to embrace the strengths and dreams of youth.*

It is a common cliché to say that the youth are our future, but if this is the case for Latinos in the United States then we have good reason to be worried. Latinos have the highest dropout rates and the lowest college attendance rates (Garcia, 2001). On most measures of academic performance we are overrepresented in the negative categories (i.e., enrollment in special-education and remedial programs, and the number of students who are suspended or expelled, etc.) and we are underrepresented in the positive categories (honors and advanced-placement courses, gifted and talented programs) (Meier & Stewart, 1991). In higher education, we are not at the bottom of the achievement hierarchy, but since the advent of high-stakes testing in several states across the country, more and more Latino students are leaving high school without diplomas, and are unable to matriculate to college (Haney, 2003).

Miguel Fernandez is one such student. Miguel is from the South

Bronx, a community once described by a presidential candidate as a "hell hole," and by yet another as the poorest census tract in the United States (Kozol, 1995). Despite these negative characterizations of his community, for Miguel the South Bronx is home. He doesn't think much about the fact that his neighborhood has some of the highest rates for asthma, teen pregnancy, or juvenile homicide in the nation, or for that matter, the highest unemployment rates in the city (Gonzalez, 2004). The litter on the streets, the deteriorated and dilapidated buildings, or the long walk he must take to the subway to get to and from school doesn't bother him, either. For Miguel, the South Bronx is where his *abuelita*, his *familia*, his many, many *primos* all live, as does his *novia* Sonja, and Wilson, his best friend. In fact, Miguel has a sense of pride about being from the Bronx, and he'll be the first to tell you that it is home to Jennifer Lopez, the world famous New York Yankees, and a long list of notable Latinos.

Although I was born in Manhattan and raised in Brooklyn, I have a connection to the South Bronx, too. Unlike Miguel my thoughts of the South Bronx aren't so pleasant. When I think of the South Bronx, the image that comes most quickly to my mind is one of violence and danger. I remember when the South Bronx was burning in the 1970s as a result of fires set by arsonists working for absentee landlords who would rather burn down beat-up old buildings to collect insurance than improve them for the people who lived there (Wallace & Wallace, 1998; Wunsch, 2001). My grandmother lived in the Mitchell Houses on Willis Avenue and 138th Street for over twenty years. The projects are still there, but they are no longer regarded as such a rough or dangerous place to live as they once were. The South Bronx is in the midst of a revival now (Jonnes, 1986; Wunsch, 2001) and gentrification has brought with it a change in residents. Of course, as property values rise and old buildings are torn down, those who cannot afford to pay market rate rents—people like Miguel's family—will be pushed out.

When I visited my grandmother in the South Bronx as a boy we were not allowed to go outside to play on the swings or monkey bars. My father told us that dangerous hoodlums controlled the play areas, and perverts lurked in the stairways and alleys. My cousin, who also lived in a "safer" section of the Bronx, served as a proof that my father's dire warnings were no joke. He was murdered at the age of fourteen; stabbed to death because he made the mistake of refusing to give up his hard-earned leather jacket to a couple of young thieves. Today, there is a community center in the eastern Bronx named after him off of Gun-hill Road, but that too has become a victim of gentrification and has since been torn down.

Times have changed since the bad old days in the 1960s and 1970s, and the gentrification that prompted the makeover of Manhattan in the 1990s has finally hit even this neighborhood. Many of the worst projects and many run-down tenements have been torn down and replaced by single-family homes. The changes are striking and despite the obvious improvement, they are somewhat disturbing. For someone like me who has been away from the South Bronx for many years, it's easy to get a strange and eerie feeling when walking through the neighborhood. As you observe all of the new construction and the new homes that have been built, you get a clear sense that the neighborhood is being improved for people who do not live there yet, and while there are many sites from the past that are familiar, there is also a lot that is new and strange and that seems out of place. The elevated train still runs along Jerome Avenue, and many of the bodegas and White Castles I once frequented are still on Fordham Road. But things look different to me. The neighborhood is still home to some of the poorest people in New York City (Wunsch, 2001; Jonnes, 2002), and still has a reputation for crime, violence, drug dealing and gangs. But the Bronx, like the rest of New York City, is changing as property values rise and the middle class moves back to reclaim once blighted areas.

This kind of change means that for Miguel, his family, and thousands of other recent immigrants, the South Bronx may be a temporary home. Interestingly, Miguel is not unaware of the changes being brought about by gentrification and what they may mean in the long term for his family, but he doesn't feel threatened by them, either. He and his family regard the South Bronx as a temporary stop on their journey to progress; a place that served its purpose when they first moved in, but not a place to become attached to. His family didn't pick the South Bronx out of a catalogue when they arrived from the Dominican Republic. They moved there because housing was cheap and his mother's cousin was able to help them find a place to live not far from her. They are well aware of the problems in the neighborhood so for them, the greatest sign of upward mobility would be to leave the South Bronx for good.

When she arrived, Miguel's mother was unmarried and raising six children on her own. She knew she would need family support to get by in this strange new country, so she moved to the South Bronx without a second thought, despite the warnings about danger that she received from others. Like most immigrants, she came full of hopes and dreams, with high expectations, and a firm belief that life in America would be better. Better because that's what everyone had told her about America since she was a child, and better because it would allow her and her children to escape the unhappiness and hardships they knew in the Dominican Republic. She didn't dwell on the fact that when she left she was leaving behind a whole network of extended *familia* and community. All she thought about was that she was trading it in for the possibility of eventual prosperity in the United States of America. For her, the South Bronx was merely a starting point on the way to that better life. Eventually she hoped that she and her children would find a home with a yard in the suburbs of New Jersey or Long Island. But for now, they like thousands of immigrants before (Tobier, 1998) them would find a way to make it in America by starting in the South Bronx. With faith and determination they could view the hardships they encountered as temporary obstacles; bumps in the road that one day they could look back upon just like their hard lives in the Dominican Republic, as another part of what they had overcome.

This is the Faustian bargain that many immigrants embrace. They give up a world they know for one that is completely foreign based on the belief that they can find a way to make the new country work for them (Portes & Rumbaut, 2001). They are overwhelmingly risk takers, brave enough to settle in a strange land where they do not speak the language or know the customs, because they hold on to the tenuous belief that with hard work, good fortune will eventually come their way. Latino immigrants and their children are people of the future. They are a people whose gaze is so firmly affixed on the promise of a better life that it becomes possible for them to endure a host of hardships and inconveniences that might set others back completely. They are a people who manage to hang on to their optimism even in miserable ghettoes like the South Bronx.

Miguel was only eleven when his family arrived from the Dominican Republic. When he first arrived he spoke no English and he often felt afraid and intimidated at school. On the playground other Latino kids, who barely spoke English themselves, teased him because he spoke only Spanish. For years, he felt intimidated when riding the subway with bigger kids from other parts of the city. They were mean and aggressive. They pushed to get a seat, they used foul language, and they knew how to scare a person with little more than a stare. Those days of being scared are over now, and Miguel isn't afraid or intimidated anymore. He's not a big kid, but he knows how to carry himself and he knows how to stare back and give the look that lets others know he's not a punk. Because he's no longer afraid, Miguel is now at ease in the South Bronx. The many obstacles he has confronted and overcome have made him stronger and have not dampened his optimism about the future in the slightest.

Miguel attends Walton High School, a school that gained notoriety during the 2003–2004 academic year because of severe overcrowding. I worked with the school during that academic year and was amazed to learn that it had an enrollment of 4,200 even though it was built to accommodate no more than 2,000.[1] The school was in the news on more than one occasion that year because of rising concerns about school violence. In response, Mayor Michael Bloomberg placed Walton on his list of unsafe schools and promised to do whatever it would take to make it safe again, even if it took placing a policeman in every classroom. As a result of the mayor's posturing, students at Walton were required to wait in long lines each morning, sometimes in subzero

---

[1] During the 2003–2004 academic year, I worked as a consultant to Region I, one of the ten school districts that comprise the New York City public schools. I was asked to assist Walton High School, which was being broken down from one large, comprehensive high school into several smaller autonomous learning communities. I spent much of the year assisting administrators of the school as they carried out this task.

temperatures, to pass through metal detectors before entering the school building. Once inside, I was often struck by the irony that while the officials were fastidious in their security screening, they paid little attention to whether or not students were actually attending class.

Despite less than ideal conditions at his school, Miguel is a diligent and dedicated student. He appreciates the importance of getting a good education to achieve his dreams so he studies hard and strives to do his best. However, as the eldest of six children, Miguel also works thirty hours a week at a local fast-food restaurant to help support his family. He works after school, sometimes till 10:00 P.M., and every weekend for eight to ten hours a day, but he never complains. He knows that his mother needs the money to pay the bills and he likes the fact that he's able to buy clothes he likes to wear with what's left over.

Miguel is well liked by his teachers. They appreciate his positive attitude, honesty, hard work, and the respect he shows to them. These traits, along with the excellent grades he earns, have distinguished him from his peers. On more than one occasion he has been singled out by the principal as a positive example; a person other students should strive to emulate. He receives ample helpings of praise and encouragement from his teachers who tell him with great confidence that if he keeps up the good work his future will be bright.

However, his guidance counselor knows better. After his second attempt, Miguel was still not able to pass the English portion of the New York State Regents exam. Though he's lived in this country eight years and attended schools in New York City, his command of English remains weak, and without a Regents diploma, Miguel will not be able to attend a public college. To complicate things even further, Miguel is also an undocumented immigrant. Though his counselor has told him that there is legislation pending in the U.S. Congress that would allow undocumented immigrants to receive financial aid to attend public universities, there is no guarantee that the Dream Act will ever be approved. Particularly given the recent defeat of the Comprehensive Immigration Reform Act that was supported by President Bush, the prospects seem increasingly unlikely that undocumented immigrants like Miguel will receive any support at all from the Federal government.

Understandably, the combination of his testing troubles and the legal complications he faces have caused Miguel to reevaluate his goals. Instead of college, Miguel plans to stay on at the fast-food restaurant. His manager has praised him for his reliability and work ethic, and promised that he would recommend him for an assistant manager's position in six months if he hangs on. This would mean he would be entitled to health benefits and a salary close to $30,000 a year. For Miguel, the possibility of a stable job and a position of authority is a reward so alluring that he decides it makes far more sense to hang in there rather than working to pass the Regents exam at night school.

In my work with schools,[2] I have met many students like Miguel. Though not all are as studious, as focused, or as disciplined, there's no shortage of promise and potential among the students I meet. This is especially true for those who have recently migrated from the Caribbean and Latin America. In cities like New York, Boston, Oakland, Los Angeles, and Newark, the Latino students I meet, especially those who are recent immigrants, are often ambitious and respectful toward adults. They are also full of hope about the future. Like their parents, they have the drive, the work ethic, and the persistence to take advantage of opportunities that come their way, and unlike so many urban youth, they have the will to find a way to improve the circumstances they find themselves in.

Of course, it is risky to generalize or to overstate the importance of will and work ethic. As the experiences of young people like Miguel show us, drive and optimism can sometimes take you only so far. When you live in a community like the South Bronx, sometimes circumstances beyond your control—the school you attend, the neighborhood you live in, whether or not any jobs are available—are far more powerful in determining how far you'll go or where you'll end up. Attitude and drive certainly count, too, and the research literature suggests that many immigrant students are willing to work hard and make sacrifices, particularly when compared to U.S.-born youth (Suarez-Orozco & Suarez-Orozco, 2001).

[2] As a researcher and the Director of the Metro Center at NYU, I work with many schools throughout the United States. For a description of my research see *City Schools and the American Dream* (NY: Teachers College Press, 2003).

As part of a study on high schools in Boston (Noguera, 2004), I conducted an interview with a Honduran honors student from English High School in Boston. During the course of our conversation I asked her about the source of her motivation to succeed in school. With a sense of clear resolve and a wisdom that seemed extraordinary for a person her age, she informed me: "If I don't do well in school my mother told me she will send me back to Honduras to wash clothes. That's what she did there, and I know for sure that I don't want to do that. You can hardly live there on the money you make from washing clothes. That's why we had to leave Honduras. People are barely surviving over there. So I try to do my best in school. If can get into college and become a nurse or something I'm going to be able to help my family and myself. I definitely don't want to end up washing no clothes."

Of course, not all of the Latino students I meet are so full of drive, determination, or clarity about their goals. Some are angry and sullen, less optimistic about the future, less focused about the purpose of their education and less inclined to believe in the elusive American Dream. These are usually the second and third generation Latino students. The ones whose ties to home—Mexico, El Salvador, the Dominican Republic—are more remote. Unlike their immigrant counterparts, these are children of the present. Children who are so consumed with surviving, with getting by, with learning how to make it from day to day, that they make no plans for the future, and often have trouble contemplating life past eighteen. They are also the ones who speak broken Spanish, if they speak it at all, and who identify as Latino, Chicano, Hispanic, or simply claim ties to the clique in their hood.

The research literature on the socialization of Latino students has identified this disturbing trend, one that results in the transformation of hopeful Latino immigrant youth into angry and frustrated Hispanic Americans (Portes & Rumbaut, 2001; Zentella, 2002). In a reversal of past patterns, assimilation no longer serves as the pathway into mainstream American culture and middle-class status for many Latinos as it once did for European immigrants. Instead, the evidence suggests that the socialization associated with acculturation and assimilation is sometimes harmful to academic achievement and performance for Latino students (Suarez-Orozco & Suarez-Orozco, 2001).[3] Interestingly, the research also suggests a similar pattern with respect to health and well-being. It turns out that recent Latino immigrants are less likely to smoke, contract heart disease, diabetes, or cancer, or to have out-of-wedlock births (Hayes-Bautista, 2002).

Berkeley anthropologist John Ogbu tried to explain the difference between Latinos, which he categorized as "castelike," nonvoluntary minorities, and earlier European immigrants who were drawn to the United States voluntarily. According to Ogbu, because the nonvoluntary minorities were incorporated through coercion, conquest, colonization, or slavery (Ogbu, 1987), they were more likely to develop oppositional attitudes toward assimilation, and by extension, toward school. Though Ogbu's theory has been widely embraced by scholars of immigration (Noguera, 2004), try as he might, his framework never really worked for Latinos. There is simply too much diversity among Latinos; while some might be categorized as nonvoluntary immigrants (e.g., Chicanos, Puerto Ricans, and possibly Panamanians), others (especially those from Central and South America) clearly came to the United States voluntarily; at least if fleeing war, repression, or hunger can be considered a voluntary move.

Once they arrive in the United States, new forces take over in shaping social identities, and Ogbu paid little attention to how variations in social context influence patterns of social adaptation. A Mexican arriving in L.A., or a Dominican arriving in Washington Heights in New York, can function in a monolithic culture for quite some time. However, for Latinos who settle in a community that is more diverse, new forms of affiliation may emerge and the significance attached to national identities may melt away, particularly among the youth. For a young person like Miguel, identifying as a Dominican becomes less important when your friends are not just from the Dominican Republic but also from Mexico, Puerto Rico, and Central America. Hybrid identities forged through cultural fusion happen naturally. Perceptions of self invariably become even more complicated when you look black, at

---

[3] In much of the sociological literature on immigration it has been held that assimilation would lead to social mobility for immigrants. Second- and third-generation immigrants have generally fared better than new arrivals. For Latinos, available research suggests the opposite may be true. See *Ethnicity and Assimilation* by Robert Jibou.

least by U.S. definitions, speak English with an Ebonics accent, and when the music you listen to is a mix of hip-hop, merengue, reggaeton, house, and rock. Even as the steady arrival of new Latino immigrants gradually begins to change the face and the character of American culture, our presence here also transforms who we are, and most importantly, who we are becoming.

The patterns evident in education mirror other disturbing trends for Latinos in the United States. Latinos in the United States constitute the youngest, fastest growing, yet poorest subgroup of American society (Smith, 2002). We stand out from other groups because in several states, we are both more likely to be employed and more likely to be poor (Clark, 1998). This is because more often than not, Latinos are trapped in the lowest paying jobs. We are the laborers, the busboys, maids, nannies, gardeners, mechanics, and waiters. We specialize in doing the dirty work, the work U.S.-born Americans reject. We remove the asbestos from buildings, we handle the toxic waste, and we take care of the sick and the aged. In cities across America we wait patiently on street corners for contractors seeking cheap labor, and we take the subways and busses early in the morning to arrive on time to watch the children of those who earn salaries exponentially greater than our own (Hondagneu-Sotelo, 2001).

We are the backbone of the U.S. economy, and we are despised because of it. Instead of gratitude and appreciation for all we do, we are subjected to resentment and scorn, and increasingly overt hostility and violence. We are accused of taking American jobs, of making neighborhoods unsafe, of deteriorating the quality of life in affluent areas, and of spreading communicable diseases (Cornelius, 2002). Though American society is historically a nation of immigrants, and though increasingly the U.S. economy is dependent upon the labor of Latino immigrants in particular, we are treated as a burden, as unwanted parasites, as problems that must be tolerated, or if possible, removed.

Education should serve as our ladder out of poverty. Just as it has for other groups in the past, education should be the source of opportunity and the pathway to a better life. Unfortunately, more often than not, the schools that serve Latinos are not unlike Miguel's Walton High School. Such schools have failed to serve as the vehicle through which our collective dreams and aspirations can be fulfilled. Too many Latino students attend schools that are overcrowded, underfunded, and woefully inadequate in terms of the quality of education they provide (Garcia, 2001). More often than not, Latino students are trapped in the worst schools, and more than other ethnic groups, Latinos are likely to attend schools that are segregated on the basis of race and class (Orfield & Eaton, 1996). For all of these reasons, Latinos have thus far had limited success in using education as a vehicle to fulfill collective dreams and aspirations.

Of course, our hardships are relative. Compared to those we leave behind in our countries of origin, many of us are far better off. That is why we are able to send money home, to support those who are still struggling and barely surviving. And that is why so many more continue to come. The United States is the land of opportunity, and though there are always sacrifices and costs associated with leaving, for those who risk the journey, there are also often rewards. Our home countries know this, too, and increasingly, the governments of Latin America regard us—Latino immigrants in the United States—as a prized resource. The remittances we send home are a stable source of foreign exchange, worth more than oil exported from Mexico, the bananas shipped out of Central America, or the tourists who visit Puerto Rico and the Dominican Republic (Suarez-Orozco & Qin-Hilliard, 2004).

Immigration is a complicated issue, one that does not lend itself to simplistic, dichotomous analysis. In 1996, I participated in a debate over Proposition 187, the first of several wedge-issue measures, used by conservatives in California to mobilize their base (e.g., white voters), against a vulnerable scapegoat, namely us. I was asked to debate an economist from UC Davis about the merits and fairness of the proposed law, which if passed would deny undocumented immigrants, or aliens, as they preferred to describe us, access to public services like health care and education. In response to his assertion that the law was not racist but merely a rational response to the fact that immigrants were displacing Americans in the labor market and taking unfair advantage of public services, I pointed out that even if the law was approved by the voters it would not succeed in curtailing illegal immigration. I suggested that the reason why so many immigrants were making the dangerous trip across the border was not in pursuit of education, health care, or other social services but because of the tremendous imbalance in wealth between the United States and Latin America. Certainly it was not the attraction of California's public schools, widely regarded as some of the most inequitable in the nation (Oakes, 2002). Rather, immigration is driven by the need to escape poverty and suffering, by the hope that success will make it possible to send money home, and by the often unrealistic belief that by leaving it will be possible to obtain a small piece of the American Dream that has been so creatively marketed to the rest of the world.

Speaking in front of liberal and idealistic undergraduates at UC Berkeley, it was easy to win the debate against a conservative economist, but I knew even then that we would lose the larger battle. Not only was Proposition 187 approved by over two-thirds of California voters, it set the stage for a string of other grassroots initiatives aimed at rolling back gains in civil rights that had been made in previous years. The end to race-based affirmative-action policies in higher education, the end to bilingual education under the so-called English-only initiative, the get-tough three strikes law, and the juvenile crime initiative, which lowered the age at which adolescents could be prosecuted as adults, all had harmful effects on the status and well-being of Latinos in California.[4] In yet another public debate, this time against Ward Connerly, the African American member of the University of California Board of Regents who has spearheaded the effort to eliminate affirmative action in higher education, I pointed out that if we had to rely on a referendum to bring an end to slavery, forced servitude might still be around. As noted legal philosopher John Rawls has pointed out, democracy in the form of majority rule can be the worst form of tyranny (Rawls, 1987). Ironically, but perhaps not surprisingly, this series of race-based initiatives were adopted at just the time that California was becoming a nonwhite majority state (Clark, 1998), and while the new laws have not deterred the

---

[4] For an analysis of these propositions and their impact on Latinos in California, see *Covering Immigration* by Leo Chavez.

growth of the Latino population in California or throughout the nation, they have made the path to progress much more difficult.

I saw the effects of crushed dreams and vanquished aspirations vividly during a recent visit to New Bedford, an old industrial town on the southeastern coast of Massachusetts. I was asked to assist the city in a planning effort designed to reduce the number of juvenile homicides. Over the last year, there had been a startling rise in the number of adolescents who had been murdered in the city—startling because none of the community leaders could understand why. They had a hunch that maybe the high unemployment in New Bedford might be a factor (the official estimate was 25 percent at the time of my visit in May 2004), or similarly that the high school dropout rate, which officially was listed at 12 percent, but unofficially was presumed to be closer to 50 percent, might also have something to do with the problem. But these were factors and not causes, and with no way to link these factors to a strategy that might aid the city in preventing more violence, there was no reason to believe that the carnage would be abated on its own.

I was asked to conduct a workshop on youth violence prevention with community leaders to help them to gain a better understanding of how various factors were linked to this social phenomenon, and hopefully to begin to devise a strategy for prevention. With all of the key stakeholders from the city present, including school district officials, members of the city council, churches, nonprofits, the police and probation departments, an interesting discussion unfolded about the lack of opportunity for youth in New Bedford. Though no concrete solutions emerged from the meeting, we did leave with an agreement to do two things: first, to include young people in the process of formulating solutions to the problem; and second, to keep this group of stakeholders meeting and planning together until there were clear signs that progress was being made.

All of us, myself included, left the meeting hopeful that we had started a process that would have a meaningful impact on this pressing problem. Later that evening, I was asked to speak at a community cultural celebration in a large high school auditorium. I generally don't like being asked to give lectures between performances by local hip-hop artists and Cape Verdean folk dancers, but I obliged with the understanding that I would keep my remarks very short. I knew before I spoke that the juvenile homicides were a big issue for the community because earlier in the day I had passed by homes where large banners were hung carrying pictures of young people who had recently been killed. Many of the banners and posters carried a simple message, imploring all who would take time to read to STOP THE VIOLENCE. Aware of how salient the issue was, I tried to speak directly to the problem of youth violence the community was grappling with, but to do so with a sense of hope about what might be done to address the problem. After my remarks, I was surprised to learn that the MC wanted to take questions from the floor rather than returning immediately to the entertainment. I was even more surprised to see a young Latino male raise his hand immediately without any prodding from the MC or myself.

Speaking loudly and with no apparent apprehension, the young man declared: "Maybe if there was something for young people to do in New Bedford we wouldn't be killing each other. It's boring like hell here. No jobs, no colleges, no places to hang out. I think people are killing each other because they're bored to death." It was an interesting thesis, one that hadn't been considered by the group of community leaders earlier in the day, and a comment that left me at a loss for a response. Having teenagers of my own who often complain of boredom, I responded by saying that boredom generally emanates from within, and that the only remedy for boredom was imagination. I encouraged him not to sit back and wait for someone to offer him a job but to be creative and think of ways that he might create opportunities on his own. Even as I made my suggestion I knew that, if pressed, I might not be able to come up with any creative examples for self-employment, but I still felt that the young man needed a sense of empowerment instead of seeing himself as a helpless victim.

As it turned out, I didn't have to offer any concrete suggestions. The next hand up was that of a middle-aged Mexican immigrant. Though he struggled with English, he readily shared his own story with the audience, directing his remarks to the young man who had spoken first. He explained that he had moved to New Bedford from Mexico five years ago. When he arrived he knew no one, so he took a job cleaning fish and earning minimum wage. After two years of dirty, backbreaking work, he said he was able to save enough to open a restaurant. He said he now owns two Mexican restaurants in New Bedford and employees twenty people. He then said that the only thing keeping him from doing more to help the community were the young hoodlums who have robbed him several times, and most recently forced one of his employees to be hospitalized as a result of a beating during a holdup. Sounding not unlike a conservative Republican, the man challenged the young people present not to be afraid of hard work, but to get off their butts, and to stop waiting for someone to give them something.

Again, I was taken aback by the direction our conversation had taken. Stumbling to figure out what I might say in response to the immigrant's challenge, I was bailed out by a young Latina who was so eager to speak that she jumped out of her seat and demanded the microphone. Speaking with passion and defiance, she blurted out, "I'm sick of hearing people in New Bedford put young people down. I ain't going to clean no fish for minimum wage and I shouldn't have to. I went to school right here at this high school (the meeting actually took place at New Bedford High School), and I had plans to go to college after graduation. But I got into problems with the law, and now I have a criminal record. A lot of businesses won't hire you if you have a record. I'm willing to work hard, but I need to get a chance."

Her remarks and the passion with which they were delivered prompted several people in the audience to applaud, and now it was up to me to make sense of the exchange. How would I acknowledge the truths inherent in both perspectives: the hopefulness of the new immigrant, the frustration and resignation of the second generation? Given the late hour and the bad setup for an extended conversation, I punted. I encouraged the young woman and the young man who'd spoken earlier to get together with the restaurateur after the meeting to find out about a job and to learn how he managed to do what he had accomplished.

Reflecting on my visit to New Bedford I was compelled to recognize that the clash in perspectives symbolized a larger division among Latinos: the newly arrived, full of hope and expectation, and the fully settled, who understand the reality of dead-end jobs and racial discrimination. Both perspectives are rooted in "truth" and an understanding of reality, but neither perspective provides a clear way for Latinos as a group to move forward. Can hard work alone help students like Miguel, whose educational opportunities are limited by the kind of school he attends, and whose chances for mobility through employment are constrained by the labor market in his community? Will anger and resentment for those who object to their second-class status help? How do we harness the energy and drive of the newcomers but at the same time refuse to accept a permanent place on the lower rungs of American society?

These are the big questions that face Latinos in America, but who is providing the answers? We are at a moment of incredible possibility. Latinos are being courted by both major parties as swing voters with the ability to decide state and even national elections. Media moguls, baseball-team owners, and fast-food restaurants now recognize Latinos as an important consumer market. However, the fact that political and economic elites recognize that Latinos can vote and spend money does not mean that the status of Latinos will be fundamentally altered anytime soon. If Latinos are to move from the lower tiers of society and not become a permanent underclass, and if our communities, schools, and social institutions are to provide the support and nurturing that our children so desperately need, we will need a new direction and a new strategy. Until that time, we will remain like Miguel: industrious and hopeful, but trapped in circumstances that stifle our ambitions and dreams. We can and we must do more, and those who have more, our small but growing middle class, have an even greater responsibility to act.

REFERENCES

Chavez, L. (2001). *Covering immigration*. Berkeley: University of California Press.

Clark, W. (1998). *The California cauldron*. New York: Guilford Press.

Cornelius, W. (2002). Ambivalent reception: Mass public responses to the new Latino immigration to the United States. In M. Suarez-Orozco & M.M. Paez (Eds.) *Latinos: Remaking America*, Berkeley: University of California Press.

Garcia, E. (2001). *Hispanic education in the United States*. New York: Roman and Littlefield.

Gonzalez, E.D. (2004). *The Bronx*. New York: Columbia University Press.

Haney, W. (September 23, 2003). Attrition of students from New York schools. Invited testimony at public hearing before the New York Senate Committee on Education.

Hayes-Bautista, D. (2002). The Latino health research agenda for the twenty-first century. In M. Suarez-Orozco & M.M. Paez (Eds.) *Latinos: Remaking America.* Berkeley: University of California Press.

Hondagneu-Stoleto, P. (2001). *Domestica: Immigrant workers cleaning and caring in the shadows of affluence.* Berkeley: University of California Press.

Jiobu, R. (1988). *Ethnicity and assimilation.* Albany, NY: State University Press.

Jonnes, J. (1986). *We're still here: The rise, fall, and resurrection of the South Bronx* (1st ed.). Boston: Atlantic Monthly Press.

Jonnes, J., & Jonnes, J. (2002). *South Bronx rising: The rise, fall, and resurrection of an American city* (2nd ed.). New York: Fordham University Press.

Kozol, J. (1995). *Amazing grace: The lives of children and the conscience of a nation* (1st ed.). New York: Crown.

Meier, K. Stewart, J. (1991). *The politics of Hispanic education.* Albany, NY: State University Press.

Noguera, P.A. (2003). *City schools and the American dream.* New York: Teachers College Press.

Noguera, P.A. (April 2004). Social capital and the education of immigrant students: Categories and generalizations. *Sociology of Education,* 77(2).

Noguera, P.A. (May 2004). Transforming high schools. *Education Leadership, 61* (8).

Oakes, J. (2002). Adequate and equitable access to education's basic tools in a standards based educational system. *Teachers College Record,* special issue.

Ogbu, J. (1987). Variability in minority student performance: A problem in search of an explanation. *Anthropology and Education Quarterly, 18*(4), 312–34.

Orfield, G. & Eaton, S. (1996). *Dismantling desegregation.* New York: The New Press.

Portes, A. & Rumbaut, R. (2001). *Legacies: The story of the immigrant second generation.* Berkeley: University of California Press.

Rawls, J. (1987). The basic liberties and their priority. S.M. McMurrin (Ed.) *Liberty, equality, and law: Selected Tanner lectures on moral philosophy,* Salt Lake City: University of Utah Press.

Rooney, J. (1995). *Organizing the South Bronx.* Albany: State University of New York Press.

Smith, R. (2002). Gender, ethnicity, and race in school and work outcomes of second-generation Mexican Americans. In. M. Suarez-Orozco & M.M.

Paez (Eds.) *Latinos: Remaking America*, Berkeley: University of California Press.

Suarez-Orozco, M., & Suarez-Orozco, C. (2001). *Children of immigration*. Cambridge: Harvard University Press.

Suarez-Orozco, M., & Qin-Hilliard, D. (2004). *Globalization, culture and education in the new millennium*. Berkeley: University of California Press.

Sugrue, T.J. (1996). *The origins of the urban crisis: Race and inequality in postwar Detroit*. Princeton, NJ: Princeton University Press.

Tobier, E. (1998). The Bronx in the twentieth century: Dynamics of population and economic change. *Bronx County Historical Society Journal, 35*(2) 69–102.

Wallace, D., & Wallace, R. (1998). *A plague on your house: How New York was burned down and national public health crumbled*. New York: Verso.

Wunsch, J.L. (2001). From burning to building: The revival of the South Bronx 1970–1999. *Bronx County Historical Society Journal, 38*(1) 4–22.

Zentella, A.C. (2002). Latinos @ languages and identities. In M. Suarez-Orozco & M.M. Paez. (Eds.) *Latinos: Remaking America*. Berkeley: University of California Press.

28

EDUCATION AND THE NEW URBAN WORKFORCE IN A GLOBAL CITY

Pauline Lipman

Many U.S. cities are increasingly becoming what University of Illinois at Chicago professor Pauline Lipman calls "dual cities," characterized by "disinvestment and reinvestment, poverty and wealth, marginality and centrality." In her book High Stakes Education: Inequality, Globalization, and Urban School Reform, *Lipman uses Chicago as a case study to examine the relationship between neoliberal education reforms and processes of gentrification and economic restructuring that exacerbate inequities in urban centers.*

Deindustrialization, white flight, fiscal crises of the state, and racial segregation and abandonment have left inner cities and urban schools underfunded and in decay (see Anyon, 1997; Bettis, 1994; Kozol, 1992; Rury & Mirel, 1997). However, processes of economic restructuring and globalization have also led to *selective* reinvestment and reinvigoration of urban areas. Global cities, in particular, embody the contradictions of disinvestment and reinvestment, poverty and wealth, marginality and centrality, that characterize globalization (Castells, 1989, 1998; Sassen, 1994, 1998). They are defined by gentrified neighborhoods and redeveloped downtowns for upscale living, tourism, and leisure alongside deteriorated low-income neighborhoods. These disparities also embody conflicts over representation and the cultural control of urban space. Chicago exemplifies these contradictions and contrasting conditions.

CHICAGO, A GLOBAL CITY?

In 1989, Mayor Richard M. Daley told *Crain's Chicago Business*: "This city is changing. You're not going to bring factories back. . . . I think you have to look at the financial markets—banking, service industry, the development of O'Hare field, tourism, trade. This is going to be an international city" (Phillips-Fein, 1998, p. 28). In 2002, the Daley administration released its Chicago Central Area Plan for downtown development, announcing, "This plan is driven by a vision of Chicago as a global city" (Central Area Plan, 2002). In fact, Chicago has been on a global city track for the last two decades. By 1983, Chicago's downtown was headquarters to twenty-six Fortune 500 companies. In international banking, Chicago's LaSalle Street was surpassed only by Wall Street, and Chicago's Board of Trade and Mercantile Exchange led the nation in futures and commodities trading (Rast, 1999). Daley has continued to promote the agenda of Chicago's business, financial, and real estate interests.

The Daley administration's development policies have fed a boom in upscale housing, restaurants, and other "lifestyle" amenities designed to attract the highly paid technical, professional, and managerial workers essential to a global city economy (Betancur & Gills, 2000; Longworth & Burns, 1999). Whether Chicago qualifies as a global city or not, financial elites and city political leaders are clearly promoting the global city agenda to justify corporate and real estate development policy (Sanjek, 1998).

The dominant narrative about global cities highlights high-income knowledge workers, luxury living, downtown skyscrapers, tourism, and corporate culture. This narrative writes out the legions of low-paid workers, the working-class neighborhoods where they live, and the cultural diversity they bring to the city (Sassen, 1994). Because global cities are command centers for global networks of production and capital mobility, they concentrate high-paid professionals, such as informational technology specialists, lawyers, advertising professionals, and stock analysts, who are primarily white and male. However, the high volume of this work also requires thousands of low-paid workers to enter data, clean corporate offices, staff messenger services, and perform other essential but low-paid work. These workers are primarily immigrants, women, and people of color. Although the high-income knowledge workers and professionals are not a ruling class, they are a culturally hegemonic class that "shapes civil society" by appropriating urban space through real estate acquisition and a culture of consumption (Castells, 1989). This stratum crystallizes in a lifestyle that is markedly distinct from that of low-paid workers but is made possible through their low-paid personal services as dog walkers, nannies, gardeners, house cleaners, personal shoppers, preparers of gourmet takeout foods, and customized clothing makers. They are also the low-paid employees who work in leisure and retail outlets as restaurant workers, sales clerks, and cashiers. Many of these service jobs demand certain dispositions and perceived characteristics (compliance and a "pleasant manner") that are part of the cultural process of racial differentiation—the inclusion of some immigrant groups and the exclusion of African Americans and some Latinos/as. As Abu-Lughod (1999) points out, becoming a global city has only widened the gap between the haves and have-nots in Chicago and increased economic disparities between whites, on the one hand, and African Americans and Latinos/as on the other, as demonstrated by the 2000 census. These disparities are also linked to the restructuring of Chicago's labor force.

ECONOMIC RESTRUCTURING, THE NEW LABOR FORCE, AND INEQUALITY

Feagin and Smith (1987) note, "The unfolding of capital restructuring creates profoundly destabilizing conditions of everyday life in the cities most immediately affected" (p. 24). This observation aptly describes Chicago. The city exemplifies the deepening inequalities and social disruption precipitated by the restructuring of the economy from manufacturing to information and service work. From 1967 to 1990, Chicago manufacturing jobs shrank from 546,500 (nearly 41 percent of all local jobs) to 216,190 (18 percent of total jobs) while nonmanufacturing jobs went from 797,867 (59 percent) in 1967 to 983,580 (82 percent) in 1990 (Betancur & Gills, 2000, p. 27). From 1970 to 1992 the larger Chicago metropolitan region lost almost a half-million manufacturing jobs primarily as a result of competition and relocation for cheaper labor. For dislocated manufacturing workers, primarily African Americans and Latinos/as, the alternative is often a low-wage service job, if they can find work at all.

According to Illinois Employment Security Agency data for 1998, 76 percent of the jobs with the most growth in Illinois paid less than a livable wage, calculated at $33,739 a year for a family of four, and 51 percent of these jobs paid below half a livable wage (National Priorities Project, 1998). When we compare average weekly wages for all workers and exclude "supervisory workers," manufacturing workers earn $562 compared with $400 for service and $248 for retail workers (Phillips-Fein, 1998, p. 30). According to the Midwest Center for Labor Research, in 1999, Chicago manufacturing jobs paying an average of $37,000 a year had been replaced with service jobs paying $26,000 (Longworth & Burns, 1999). Since unionized workers are more likely to have health insurance and pension plans, the shift to primarily nonunion service work has compounded wage losses with fewer benefits and less security.

EDUCATION POLICIES AND THE NEW URBAN WORKFORCE

Education reform has been a consistent priority for Chicago's corporate and financial elite. This is clear from a brief overview of the Commercial Club of Chicago's (CCC) economic development proposals since the mid-1980s. The CCC is an extraordinarily active organization of the city's business and financial elite whose influence extends to direct involvement in Chicago-area policy, including education. In its 1984 long-term strategic plan, *Make No Little Plans: Jobs for Metropolitan Chicago* (1984), the CCC called for making Chicago a leading financial services center, noting that although Chicago would have an abundance of workers, these workers needed constant upgrading of skills. In a 1990 update (*Jobs for Metropolitan Chicago*), the CCC asserted, "The failures of Chicago's public schools in previous years have left us with hundreds of thousands of people untrained and ill equipped to fill the jobs of the new economy" (p. 4). The report went on to say that although good progress had been made since the 1988 school reform, education should be at the top of the city's agenda. Again in *Chicago Metropolis 2020*, published in 1998, the CCC identified lack of education and skills training as the first of three key impediments to the Chicago area's becoming a "global metropolis."

STRATIFIED SCHOOLING FOR STRATIFIED JOBS

What kind of training is the CCC talking about? Although there is a perception that the new economy demands significantly upgraded skills for everyone (Murnane & Levy, 1996; National Center on Education & the Economy, 1990), in fact, many of the new low-wage service jobs require basic literacies, the ability to follow directions, and accommodating disposition toward work (Castells, 1996). Although a majority of rapid-growth occupations are projected to require education or training beyond high school, there is expected to be only a modest change in educational levels for all new jobs created in 1992–2005 (Castells, 1996). This is confirmed by a Bureau of Labor Statistics' prediction that between 1992 and 2005 there would be overall 6.2 million new professional workers and 6.5 million new low-wage service workers (Castells, 1996, p. 225; also Apple, 1996). In Chicago, a CCC report defined the need for "ever-more-skilled employees" required by the new economy as people "who can, at the minimum, read instruction manuals, do basic math and communicate well" (Johnson, 1998, p. 6). The report also noted that "minorities" in low-performing schools will become a greater part of the workforce and will need these new basic competencies. These competencies are corroborated by Rosenbaum and Binder's (1997) interviews with fifty-one urban and suburban Chicago employers, the majority of whom said they needed employees with "eighth-grade math skills and better than eighth-grade reading and writing skills."

Carlson (1996) summarizes this trend: "The 'basic skills' restructuring of urban schools around standardized testing and a skill-based curriculum has been a response to the changing character of work in postindustrial America, and it has participated in the construction of a new postindustrial working class . . . of clerical, data processing, janitorial, and service industry jobs" (pp. 282–83). Further, in the era of Fordist assembly line production, manufacturing workers needed very specific skills (e.g., welding), but through rapid technological advances, specific tasks are increasingly accomplished by computers and robotics, and these jobs are constantly being redefined. The new low-wage service and post-Fordist manufacturing jobs, as well as the large number of jobs filled by part-time and temporary labor, require the flexibility to adapt to changing job requirements. Basic reading and math literacy is essential to this learning. The overwhelming majority of Chicago high school students, largely students of color, are enrolled in neighborhood high schools organized around these competencies.

Another tier of high schools, education-to-career academies (ETCs), are linked to skill-specific manufacturing and service work, for example, automotive technology, hospitality management, mechanical design, cosmetology, and secretarial science. The ETCs are coordinated with local businesses and vocational programs at community colleges. Some ETC programs prepare students for entry-level jobs, and others, such as some health services, require further training or education. The goal of ETCs is to prepare students with "a solid background of vocational training in their field" (Personal communication, CPS official, April 12, 2000) or to prepare them to attend a postsecondary vocational program. But in an economy of simultaneously higher skilled and downgraded labor, many of the jobs ETCs target may not include the benefits or security of unionized industrial jobs of the past. For example, whereas clerical work today demands new skills, it is often part-time and temporary. Other ETC courses, such as hospitality management, have a nonacademic curriculum core, and entry-level jobs are likely to be low wage. At the same time, college prep magnets and International Baccalaureate programs (IBs) prepare the top tier of students for four-year colleges and universities and orient them toward technical and professional knowledge work. (The goal is not to prepare these students specifically for Chicago jobs, but to keep their middle-class parents in the city.) At the opposite end, the more than 40 percent of students who do not graduate may have little opportunity at all in the formal economy.

Tracking, differentiated curricula, and magnet schools are not new (Oakes, 1985). However, differentiated schooling has new significance in an economy in which knowledge is far more decisive than in the past. In the informational economy, one's education is a key determinant of whether one will be a high-paid knowledge worker or part of the downgraded sector of labor. The differentiation of schools and academic programs results in differential access to specific courses of study with significant implications for students' preparation for college, such as the rigor and level of high school math and science classes taken by students at the college prep magnets versus general high schools. Because of the dualization of the economy, education is becoming an increasingly important determinant of which stratum of the labor force one will enter. Ozga (2000) argues that the closer linkage of education and the economy "has produced the attempted redesign of education systems along less inclusive, more selective lines, with the purpose of reproducing and mirroring the differentiated flexible workforces of the future" (p. 24). Although I am not suggesting a simple correspondence between schooling and the workforce, there is a striking relationship between evolving educational differentiation in Chicago Public Schools (CPS) and the stratification of labor.

PRODUCING DIFFERENTIATED IDENTITIES

Equally important, the discourses of different schools and programs apprentice students to particular ways of being, behaving, and thinking. In this sense, a *discourse* "is composed of talking, listening, reading, writing, interacting, believing, valuing . . . so as to display or to recognize a particular social identity" (Gee et al., 1996, p. 10):

> Immersion inside the practices—learning *inside* the procedures, rather than overtly *about* [emphases original] them—ensures that a learner takes on the perspectives, adopts a world view, accepts a set of core values, and masters an identity without a great deal of critical and reflective awareness about these matters, or indeed about the Discourse itself. (p. 13)

Students construct identities from many social–cultural resources, but disparate school experiences provide them with disparate resources on which to draw.

Scripted direct instruction programs, IBs, ETCs, military academies, college prep magnet high schools, and so on, constitute social practices that "teach" students particular identities. In the "new capital-ism [which] requires a core of relatively well-paid knowledge leaders and workers supplemented by a bevy of people 'servicing' them for the least possible price" (p. 47), this has profound implications. The open and relaxed environment of Northside Prep, where students lounge in spacious hallways and participate in Wednesday afternoon colloquia, teaches students social roles and expectations quite different from those the military discipline at Chicago Military Academy teaches. I want to emphasize that this is not necessarily purposeful; nor is it determined. Teachers and administrators I have talked with who champion Direct Instruction, military schools, and ETCs are generally dedicated to im-proving the academic performance and future of their students, but they see few alternatives. It is the ideological effect of differentiated learning that is the point here.

Differentiated programs, curricula, and pedagogies also have a sym-bolic function. The prestigious IB program with its stringent admission requirements and diploma "recognized worldwide" has a cachet quite different from that of the Military Academy's enforced subordination to authority. The ideological force of racially coded "basic skills," scripted instruction, probation, and military schools is publicly to define African American and Latino/a youth as requiring special forms of discipline and regimentation. Despite Daley's claim that military schools simply offer students "another option," the schools were established with much public fanfare in low-income African American communities—not white or middle-class communities. The media coverage of the schools' boot-camp discipline commends them for putting under control "dan-gerous" and "unruly" youth (Johnson, 2002) and turning around "at-risk" students by exposing them to "order and discipline" (Quintanilla, 2001). Media accounts are filled with stories of failing and undisciplined youth who do not speak "proper English" and are members of "dysfunc-tional" homes who have been transformed through the military acade-mies into young men and women who work hard in school, help out at home, respect adults, and even learn to speak "correctly." The schools are exemplars of a new "truth"—if schooling is going to work for many urban youth of color, it will need to be highly regimented and be sepa-rate and distinct from college-prep schools like Northside.

CPS policies also frame schooling in a language business understands—regulation, accountability, and quality assurance (see Mickelson, Ray, & Smith 1994). The steps for education reform outlined by a consortium of top business organizations in 1996 (*Common Agenda for Improving American Education*) read as a blueprint for Chicago: "First, helping educators and policymakers set tough academic standards . . . ; second, assessing student and school-system performance against those standards; and third, using that information to improve schools and create accountability, including rewards for success and consequences for failure" (quoted in Sheldon & Riddle, 1998, p. 164). High-stakes tests define education as a commodity that can be quantified, regulated, and designed much as any other commodity. Symbolically, as well as practically, a tough retention policy, standardized tests, and discipline and control of both students and schools certify for Chicago business that CPS graduates will have the specific literacies and dispositions it demands. The retention policy, for example, stamps a seal of approval on students who pass to the next grade, confirming that they meet "industry" standards.

This symbolism is highly racialized. In addition to basic mathematical and print literacy, employers are particularly concerned with future workers' attitudes and "work ethic" (Ray & Mickelson, 1993), their reliability, trustworthiness, ability to take directions, and, in the case of in-person service workers, pleasant manner (Gee et al., 1996). Eighty percent of the business leaders sampled by the Commission on the Skills of the American Workforce said they were seeking a stronger work ethic, appropriate social behavior, and a good attitude in their new workers (Ray & Mickelson, 1993). Moberg (1997) argues that Chicago is at a disadvantage in attracting new firms because there is a widespread perception that Chicago's workforce is "ill-educated, untrained, and difficult to manage," and that this perception "especially affects the hiring of black men" (p. 79). Interestingly, the description of ETCs, including "job-readiness" and "employability skills," addresses this "problem," as does CPS's overall focus on discipline and individual responsibility.

Public perception and the actual production of a disciplined workforce are constructed through a set of policies and a rhetoric that emphasize hard work and personal responsibility, individual achievement, regulation, and control. This is the pedagogy of scripted instruction, basic skills, test preparation, and discipline through which students are trained to follow directions and learn according to a strict protocol. Programs and policies that discipline, regulate, and control also teach students their "place" in a race and class hierarchy (Bartlett & Lutz, 1998). They are a powerful selection mechanism, bringing in line those who comply and pushing those who do not outside the bounds of formal work and legitimated social intercourse. But parental support for military academies, ETCs, and emphasis on test scores is also rooted in a realistic assessment of the limited opportunities available to low-income students of color. In the absence of good high schools, resources to attend college, or prospects for a good job, as well as the threat of gangs in high schools, military academies (like military service itself) and ETCs are viable choices in a world of limited options. And parents are well aware that test scores are a potent selection mechanism, particularly for students who do not possess the social networks and dominant cultural capital that are the hidden advantages of middle-class white students. This good sense speaks to the urgency to create equitable alternatives to restrictive and militarized "choices."

SCHOOL POLICY, GLOBAL CITY DEVELOPMENT, AND THE CULTURAL POLITICS OF RACE

School improvement is also central to Chicago's image as a global city. In its 1998 report, the Commercial Club praised the mayor's school reforms and identified education as one of three top priorities to realize its vision of a multicentered region of "knowledge, expertise, and economic opportunity" (Johnson, 1998, p. 3). State-of-the-art schools are key to attracting high-paid, high-skilled workers. New York City, for example, has an established upper tier of elite public as well as private schools. A series of articles in the *Chicago Tribune* on Chicago's bid to become a global city noted that key business spokespeople consistently identify the need to "fix" the schools, "both to provide a pool of good workers and to persuade middle-class and upper-class families to settle in the city" (Longworth & Burns, 1999, p. A14). CPS leaders have been quite explicit about this. Gery Chico, head of the CPS Board of Trustees, said in a CPS press release announcing three new magnet high schools, "Students who are ready for a challenging academic program will be able to find it at a school in their area" (Three More Schools, 1999). And a 1998 *Chicago Tribune* article on the "hottest" real estate markets in the city noted that "Chicago's improving public school system is making young families less leery of rearing their children in the city" (Pitt, 1998). CPS's open appeal to middle-class families is seen as legitimate, in part because it is taken for granted that middle-class children are essential to a good school system. As in the argument for mixed-income housing, the assumption is that there cannot be good working-class schools (or good working-class neighborhoods).

CONCLUSION

As a whole, the CPS policy agenda and the discourses that surround it are part of a politics of race and class that serves global city development and economic restructuring and has a life of its own rooted in Chicago's racialized history. Magnet high schools, IB programs, and publicity about rising test scores are complemented by policies that emphasize regulation and centralized control, primarily of students of color. School policies that discipline African American and Latino/a youth not only certify the production of a disciplined workforce, they signify that city leaders are "taking back" the city as a space of middle-class rationality and whiteness from African Americans and Latinos/as whose neighborhoods, "place-making practices" (Haymes, 1995), and identities are a threat to "stability." The white supremacist myth of African Americans as dangerous in the city is realized in the imagery of education policies and programs that discipline and regulate these youth. As does the vocabulary of the "urban frontier" that rationalizes gentrification and displacement as the taming of urban neighborhoods (Smith, 1996), racially coded "basic skills," scripted instruction, probation and reconstitution of schools, and military high schools legitimate the segregation and/or dispersal of low-income communities of color. These policies (the "flip side" of elite high schools) instill order and help make the city "safe" for new upscale enclaves, much as "the new urban pioneers seek to scrub the city clean of its working-class geography and history . . . its class and race contours rubbed smooth" (pp. 26–27). The discourse of control and authority may also be a preemptive response to an urban context simmering with potentially explosive contradictions of wealth and poverty, development and abandonment, and blatant economic and social power alongside disempowerment.

REFERENCES

Abu-Lughod, J.L. (1999). *New York, Chicago, Los Angeles: America's global cities.* Minneapolis: Univeristy of Minnesota Press.

Anyon, J. (1997). *Ghetto schooling.* New York: Teachers College Press.

Apple, M.W. (1996). *Cultural politics and education.* New York: Teachers College Press.

Barlett, L., & Lutz, C. (1998). Disciplining social difference: Some cultural politics of military training in public high schools. *The Urban Review, 30,* 119–36.

Betancur, J.J., & Gills, D.C. (2000). The restructuring of urban relations. In J.J. Betancur & D.C. Gills (Eds.), *The collaborative city: Opportunities and struggles for Blacks and Latinos in U.S. cities* (pp. 17–40). New York: Garland.

Bettis, P. J. (1994). Deindustrialization and urban schools: Some theoretical considerations. *Urban Review, 26,* 75–94.

Carlson, D. (1996). Education as a political issue: What's missing in the public conversation about education? In J.L. Kincheloe & S.R. Steinberg (Eds.), *Thirteen questions: Reframing education's conversation* (2nd ed., pp. 281–91). New York: Peter Lang.

Castells, M. (1989). *The informational city.* London: Blackwell.

Castells, M. (1996). *The rise of the network society.* London: Blackwell.

Castells, M. (1998). *End of the millennium.* London: Blackwell.

Central Area Plan to help guide downtown growth. (July 2, 2002). City of Chicago, Department of Planning and Development. Retrieved September 5, 2002 from http://www.ci.chi.il.us/PlanAndDev . . . PressReleases/centralareaplan.html.

Commercial Club of Chicago. (1984). *Make no little plans: Jobs for metropolitan Chicago.* Chicago: Author.

Commercial Club of Chicago. (August 1990). *Jobs for metropolitan Chicago—an update.* Chicago: Author.

Feagin, J.R., & Smith, M.P., eds. (1987). Cities and the new international division of labor: An overview. In *The capitalist city: Global restructuring and community politics* (pp. 3–34). Oxford, England: Basil Blackwell.

Gee, J.P., Hull, G., & Lankshear, C. (1996). *The new work order: Behind the language of the new capitalism.* Boulder, CO: Westview Press.

Haymes, S.N. (1995). *Race, culture and the city.* Albany: State University of New York Press.

Johnson, D. (January 21, 2002). High school at attention. *Newsweek.* Retrieved January 25, 2002 from http://www.msnbc.com/news/686928.asp?cp1=1.

Johnson, E. (November 1998). *Chicago metropolis 2020: Preparing metropolitan Chicago for the 21st century: Executive summary.* Chicago: Commercial Club of Chicago.

Kozol, J. (1992). *Savage inequalities.* New York: Perennial.

Longworth, R.C., & Burns, G. (February 7, 1999). Progress, trouble on economic front. *Chicago Tribune*, pp. A1, 14–15.

Mickelson, R.A., Ray, C., & Smith, S. (1994). The growth machine and the politics of urban educational reform: The case of Charlotte, North Carolina. In N.P. Stromquist (Ed.), *Education in urban areas: Cross-national dimensions.* Westport, CT: Praeger.

Moberg, D. (1997). Chicago: To be or not to be a global city. *World Policy Journal*, *14*, 71–86.

Murnane, R.J., & Levy, F. (1996). *Teaching the new basic skills.* New York: The Free Press.

National Center on Education and the Economy. (1990). *America's choice: High skills or low wages.* Rochester, NY: Author.

National Priorities Project. (1998). *Working hard, earning less: The story of job growth In Illinois.* Grassroots Factbook (Vol. I, Series 2). Northhampton, MA: Author.

Oakes, J. (1985). *Keeping track: How schools structure inequality.* New Haven, CT: Yale University Press.

Ozga, J. (2000). *Policy research in educational settings.* Buckingham, England: Open University Press.

Phillips-Fein, K. (September–October, 1998). The still-industrial city: Why cities shouldn't just let manufacturing go. *The American Prospect*, *9*(40), 28–37.

Pitt, L. (August 31, 1998). Hot houses. *Chicago Sun Times*, p. N8.

Quintanilla, R. (March 13, 2001). It's more than a school, it's the drill. *Chicago Tribune*, Sec. 1, pp. 1, 10.

Rast, J. (1999). *Remaking Chicago: The political origins of urban industrial change.* Dekalb: Northern Illinois University Press.

Ray, C.A., & Mickelson, R.A. (1993). Restructuring students for restructured work: The economy, school reform, and non-college-bound youths. *Sociology of Education*, *66*, 1–20.

Rosenbaum, J.E., & Binder, A. (1997). Do employers really need more educated youth? *Sociology of Education, 70,* 68–75.

Rury, J.R., & Mirel, J.E. (1997). The political economy of urban education. In M.W. Apple (Ed.), *Review of Research In Education, 22,* pp. 49–110. Washington, DC: American Educational Research Association.

Sanjek, R. (1998). *The future of us all: Race and neighborhood politics in New York City.* Ithaca, NY: Cornell University Press.

Sassen, S. (1994). *Cities in a world economy.* Thousand Oaks, CA: Pine Forge Press.

Sassen, S. (1998). *Globalization and its discontents.* New York: The New Press.

Sheldon, K.M., & Riddle, B.J. (1998). Standards, accountability, and school reform: Perils and pitfalls. *Teachers College Record, 100,* 164–80.

Smith, N. (1996). *The new urban frontier: Gentrification and the revanchist city.* New York: Routledge.

Three More Schools approved for the International Baccalaureate program (January 28, 1999). [Press release]. Retrieved February 12, 1999 from http://www.cps.k12.il.us/AboutCPS/Press Releases/January_28.

29

BROOKLYN

Suheir Hammad

ZaatarDiva *is the latest collection of poetry from Suheir Hammad, a Palestin-ian-American artist, poet, and activist from Brooklyn who has performed in venues across the country and was an original cast member of Russell Sim-mons'* Def Poetry Jam *on Broadway. This piece from* ZataarDiva *is Ham-mad's loving tribute to the borough she calls home.*

————————

sometimes we pose you loud like
a cheap trophy posturing look at me
from the planet of illest mcs and brickest cheese

sometimes quietly we know the streets
is watching our actions recorded
we secret you from those who patrol
our thoughts and study our styles

we leave you in
order to see your beauty from a distance
back home in instants we drop baggage
and settle into our selves

your children travel far and wherever
we are we hear *bk represent*
always the loud-assest

we say if you can make it here
you got nothing to fear

true every hood fashion fly shit
but they come to your streets to make it legit

you got as many stories as streets
as each of us shaped by
your concrete and green

you became the safe jerusalem
for us not chosen
yet did not shelter yusef
hawkins running from hate

if we tell the truth here
we got nothing to fear

you molded heroes
and sent them out on record tours

brooklyn i could write you
forever on every corner
on the backs of handball players
with the exhaust of your buildings
for your exhausted masses i could
write you forever for the absences
and abundances of the childhoods
you gifted us

listen to the way you gallop from my mouth
make folks smile just to hear me talk
cause they trace my cadence
back to you

we always return
like love and heartbreak are one coin two sides

you are your daughters' currency in foreign cities
we always come home
and you always make room
like expandable apartments
filled with immigrants and their labors

you always make room
for our sins and our saviors

you always make room for prodigal daughters
who sometimes talk out loud to our selves
just to hear your stories come out our mouths

30

LITTLE HOUSE IN THE 'HOOD

Patricia J. Williams

Patricia Williams is a professor of law at Columbia University and author of The Alchemy of Race and Rights, *an autobiographical meditation on the law, race, gender, and justice. She was awarded a MacArthur "Genius Grant" in 2000, and writes the "Diary of a Mad Law Professor" column for* The Nation *magazine. The following essay on gentrification in Harlem is from the June 19, 2000 issue.*

———————

I was wandering around Harlem recently, late on a warm Sunday afternoon: I saw Dominican families chatting on stoops. I saw African American families walking home from church. I saw a Cuban Chinese deli and popped in to buy a refreshing something-or-other that resembled a mango egg cream. I saw a busload of Japanese tourists. And I saw lots of young white families unloading weekend gear from Jeep Cherokees lacquered with Bridgehampton beach stickers, their tanned and tousled children wearing sweatshirts with the names of the world's most expensive private schools emblazoned upon them. It was a pleasant stroll, the sort of thing that makes me glad to be living in New York. Indeed, at this particular moment, Harlem may be the most racially, ethnically and class-integrated neighborhood in the world. This is good news. The question, of course, is whether it will stay that way.

As with all of Manhattan, Harlem's real-estate prices have suddenly gone through the roof. Burned-out shells of brownstones go for half a million, while pristine specimens are listed in Sotheby's International. Like most, I am glad for the increased desirability of a Harlem zip code.

But I wonder if there are not a few cautionary reminders one might bring to bear.

The most obvious concern, as one reads breathless newspaper accounts of square footage, is a certain otherworldliness in tone. "Urban pioneers" is the term most often used to describe the largely white families who are moving into this historically black area. No matter that Harlem has always had a substantial black middle class, a stable working class, and eminently respectable social systems; the popular imagery is that of brave, white settlers in their SUVs (doors locked, windows up) traveling in cautious cavalcades to homestead the wild, heathen emptiness.

By all accounts, Harlem is "in transition." If one pokes at that terminology just a little bit—transition from what to what?—one uncovers rather broad assumptions that Harlem is progressing from a state of "blight;" that it is being "redeemed" with new faces, new stores, new investment; and that its ultimate destiny is to be "reclaimed" by those who have made the rest of Manhattan so trendy that an average apartment now costs well over $700,000.

I guess I hope for a number of things. First, I hope that gentrification stops short of Trumpification. As invisible as it has been to many, Harlem's class diversity has always contributed to its vibrant social, cultural and political life.

Second, I hope the new movement to Harlem signals a reversal of the abandonment of inner cities. I hope it signals an era of racial diversity, true tolerance for propinquity and not merely the corollary of white flight—the strategic displacement of black and brown populations. I do not mean to impugn the neighborliness of any of the new residents of Harlem. I am more concerned about the larger institutional manipulations that have contributed to the stark consequences both of white flight and, now, white reflux.

When Northern whites grew afraid of the migrations of blacks from the South from the thirties through the seventies, it was the National Association of Realtors that calculatedly fanned that fear into a panic, realtors going door to door warning that the property values were falling, falling: sell now while you can. In city after city, the story was the same: whites, terrified that the end of civilization was nigh, sold low. Blacks, believing they were purchasing the dream of integration, bought high. The realtors made a killing. The newly segregated neighborhoods went into quick decline as services of all sorts were summarily withdrawn—schools, snow removal, grocery stores, bus lines, police. Banks wouldn't finance home repairs, assessments plummeted, crimes went uninvestigated and thus flourished. Insurers, if they insured at all, charged sky-high rates supposedly based on greater risk, then failed to pay for actual losses.

Today a new breed of real estate speculator has fanned the buzz that is changing Harlem so rapidly. Thanks to complicated incentive programs and community empowerment zoning, banks, too, have begun funneling money back into communities that they had historically redlined. But the degree to which these new financial policies improve the lot of Harlem's low-, moderate- and middle-income populations—or simply drive them out—remains to be seen.

In recent months the City of New York has sold many of its Harlem properties to developers whose interests do not always overlap with those of longtime residents. Consider the tension: I have friends struggling to find immediate financing for the house they have lived in for thirty years. I, on the other hand, received a form letter offering Columbia University faculty very favorable loan terms for housing in Harlem.

In this rush to go upscale, I hope that policy experts and institutional investors do not diminish—with such terms as "blighted"—the role of long-term stable populations, whose insistent struggles have produced the lion's share of the recent turnaround. In using the word "stable" one is often understood to mean church-going, college-educated, middle-class residents with steady incomes. But by "stable" I also mean to include working-class and poor families, people with extended families, with several adults in and out of work, homes where a grandparent or aunt helps make ends meet by looking after their own and the neighbors' children. These are the populations who suffered most from the lack of local grocery stores, for example, and who pressed for the new Fairway market in Harlem—a store so magnificent that Wall streeters travel the length of the city to stock up on guavas and fresh rabbit filets. These are the families who suffered simultaneously from high crime rates and suspect profiling and whose protests made policing tactics a national issue. These are Manhattan's messengers, hospital workers, fast-food servers, secretaries, janitors, nannies, and security guards whose tenacious political passion about issues such as education, health care and garbage removal have made them models of community engagement.

For all these good things, greater credit—both literally and figuratively—is most assuredly their due.

31

RACE WAR: POLICING, INCARCERATION, AND THE CONTAINMENT OF BLACK YOUTH

Bakari Kitwana

In too many U.S. cities, the relationship between struggling schools in poor neighborhoods and growing numbers of incarcerated black and Latino youth is clear. In the following chapter, excerpted from the book The Hip-Hop Generation: Young Blacks and the Crisis in African American Culture, *journalist, lecturer, and co-founder of the National Hip-Hop Political Convention, Bakari Kitwana focuses on the criminalization of black youth at the turn of the century and its impact on the African American community.*

There's a war going on outside
No man is safe from
You can run but you can't hide forever.
—Mobb Deep, "Survival of the Fit"

On April 20, 1995, U.S. Attorney James Burns and Cook County's Illinois State Attorney Jack O'Malley held a press conference to announce the indictments of twenty-three members of the Traveling Vice Lords for federal drug conspiracy charges. An additional eight members of the Chicago street gang, including several juveniles, were indicted on separate state narcotics or weapons charges. Authorities alleged that the gang ran a crack cocaine and heroin market that netted anywhere from $5,000 to $30,000 a day. The gang operated what prosecutors described as one of the city's most lucrative open-air drug markets in the 2700 block of West Flourney Street in Chicago's East Garfield Park neighborhood. "We have taken down one of the major street gang, drug-dealing factions in the city," Burns said.

The three-and-a-half-year sting operation, dubbed Operation Flourney, which led to the arrests, began in July of 1991 and joined Chicago police forces with the ATF and the FBI. However, this herculean effort culminated with the seizure of only four and one-half pounds of powder cocaine at the apartment of the alleged gang leader, Andrew "Bay-Bay" Patterson, and less than $2,000 from two other defendants. Only several gold chains, a watch, and beepers were seized from the remaining defendants. Despite the limited physical evidence, the criminal charges were based on prosecutors' claims that the gang made as much as $24,000 a day from selling crack cocaine in 1994. Further, prosecutors alleged that in 1995, when members started dealing heroin, too, they doubled their daily cash intake.

One year later, nineteen of those indicted for conspiracy were tried simultaneously. Most of the defendants were hip-hop generationers, ranging from twenty-one to forty-one years old. The case had the largest number of defendants for a single trial in the history of the Northern District of Illinois Court. In June 1996, after a trial that lasted five months, fifteen of the defendants were convicted of federal drug conspiracy charges. The remaining four defendants were acquitted. Two of those four were returned to state custody to finish serving sentences on weapons and drug charges. Due to federal sentencing guidelines and mandatory minimum sentencing laws, none of those convicted were sentenced to less than seventeen and one-half years. Three received life sentences.

Operation Flourney offers a glimpse into young blacks' involvement in the criminal justice system and the type of criminal charges and state and federal laws that have landed a disproportionate number of young blacks behind bars during the past two decades. The lengthy mandatory minimum prison sentences for drug crimes, coupled with the general drug prohibition hysteria focused on urban (read: black and Latino) communities that has come to dominate law enforcement at local, state, and federal levels, are characteristic of the 1980s and 1990s. The end result has been the prison crisis, a crisis that has profoundly influenced our generation.

The war on drugs is the focal point for this crisis. In our lifetime, the population incarcerated in U.S. state and federal prisons and local jails has climbed from fewer than 200,000 in 1965 to nearly 2 million today. According to the Bureau of Justice, approximately 50 percent of federal and state prisoners are African American, a startling imbalance. Consider the statistics. According to a 1997 survey by the Substance Abuse and Mental Health Services Administration, blacks make up only 13 percent of monthly illegal drug users, whereas whites constitute 74 percent of monthly illegal drug users. Yet, in 1995, the National Criminal Justice Commission reported that 74 percent of those sentenced to prison for drug possession were black. At the state level, which houses the bulk of America's prisoners, the Justice Department found that the number of blacks incarcerated for drug offenses increased 707 percent during the decade between 1985 and 1995 (compared to a 306 percent increase for whites). By 1996, drug offenders made up 23 percent of the state inmate population and 60 percent of the federal incarcerated population.

These statistics reveal that race is clearly a factor. Approximately 1 million black men are currently under some form of correctional supervision. And the hip-hop generation is suffering the greatest casualties; approximately one-third of all black males age 20–29 are incarcerated, or on probation, or on parole. In the past two decades, few issues have altered black life as much as the incarceration of young blacks.

MANDATORY MINIMUMS

For their drug crimes, the fifteen former residents of the 2700 block of South Flourney received sentences determined under federal sentencing guidelines and mandatory minimum sentencing laws, which went into effect in the 1980s, some established under the 1980s provisions tacked onto the 1970 Racketeering Influenced Corrupt Organization Act (RICO) and the 1970 Continuing Criminal Enterprise Act (CCE). As noted above, none were sentenced to anything less than seventeen and one-half years. The youngest defendant, twenty-one-year-old Andrew L. "Maine" Patterson, who prosecutors said was an enforcer for the gang, was sentenced to twenty-five years and ten months. He would have received life imprisonment under mandatory minimum sentencing laws, but Judge Robert Gettleman said that police failed in their responsibility under Illinois' Juvenile Court Act (which gives police authority to take into custody without a warrant any minor they have reasonable cause to believe is living in an "injurious environment") to turn him over to juvenile authorities when they discovered he was involved in dealing illegal drugs in 1991. At that time, Andrew was only fifteen, but law enforcers claimed that turning him over to juvenile authorities would have compromised the investigation. Federal sentencing guidelines allowed Gettleman to lower the sentence. The harshest sentences were meted out to Bay-Bay Patterson, Robert Patterson, and Tyrone Williams, each of whom received life imprisonment, required by mandatory minimum sentencing laws.

The origin of mandatory minimum sentences (commonly referred to as mandatory minimums) in the United States can be traced back to the 1951 Boggs Act, which imposed mandatory minimum sentences for drug crimes, and the 1956 Boggs Act enhancements, which increased sentences established in the 1951 law. In 1970, Congress threw out the mandatory minimum sentences established in the 1950s because small-time dealers and addicts were receiving sentences meant for big-time dealers, a problem that present-day opponents of mandatory minimums insist we are now repeating. Nevertheless, by the early 1970s some state legislatures began to establish minimum sentencing laws of their own, the most notable of which are New York State's 1973 Rockefeller drug laws. New York's law requires that anyone convicted of selling more than two ounces of cocaine, heroin, or other controlled substances—or possessing more than four ounces—be sentenced to a minimum of fifteen years in prison. Other states subsequently passed their own mandatory minimum sentencing drug laws. But it was a series of federal laws passed by Congress in the mid-eighties that brought into existence the current federal mandatory minimum sentencing for drug crimes.

In 1984, the Comprehensive Crime Control Act was passed. This law established five-year mandatory minimums for using or carrying a gun during drug or violent crimes, in addition to the sentence for the initial crime. Further, a fifteen-year mandatory minimum sentence was created for possession of a gun by a person with three previous state or federal convictions for burglary or robbery. Also established in 1984 was the Sentencing Reform Act, which phased out the seventy-five-year-old federal parole system. At the same time, the U.S. Sentencing Commission was established to create guidelines that would make sentences for the same crime uniform. It also determined how long one could be locked up for a specific crime. This commission is responsible for what are popularly referred to as the federal sentencing guidelines, a small range of sentences for each category of offense. The sentencing judge selects from this range at the time of sentencing. The guidelines, which went into effect in November 1987, limit judges' discretion and give prosecutors so great a role in the sentencing process that many point to this as one of the major changes in the criminal justice system in the last two decades.

In 1986, under the Anti-Drug Abuse Act, Congress established new federal mandatory minimums for offenses related to the most frequently used illegal drugs. Five-year mandatory minimums were created for distributing and importing specific quantities of illegal drugs. Heavily focused on crack cocaine, the bill established a 100-to-1 sentencing ratio between crack and powder cocaine and enacted a death penalty for drug "kingpins."

More mandatory minimums for drug offenses were added with the passage of the 1988 Omnibus Anti-Drug Abuse Act, particularly for crack cocaine possession and conspiracy convictions. Additionally, Congress extended the net for who could be tried for conspiracy, regardless of how central or peripheral the offender. A five-year mandatory minimum was established for simple possession of more than five grams of crack cocaine, whereas possession of the same amount of other drugs, including powder cocaine, remained misdemeanors with mandatory minimums of fifteen days for the second offense. Also under the law, the ten-year mandatory minimum for engaging in a continuing criminal enterprise—a concept originally introduced in 1970—was doubled to twenty years.

More than a decade and hundreds of thousands of convictions later, including those of many hip-hop generationers, the Supreme Court ruled in a 6–3 decision in June 1999 that a prosecutor trying a defendant on continuing criminal enterprise violations must convince the jury that the accused both committed each of the individual violations and committed them in a continuing series. But between 1988 and June 1999, prosecutors only had to convince jurors that defendants had broken the law three times or that they had committed one or two violations in a series but not necessarily the third.

Finally, in 1994, California enacted an even more stringent sentencing law—what has come to be known as "three strikes and you're out." It requires mandatory life imprisonment for a third felony conviction. Since then, at least twenty states have passed similar measures. In addition, 1994 saw the passage of the federal crime bill, which required states to mandate that offenders serve a minimum of 85 percent of their sentences (dubbed "Truth in Sentencing") in order for states to qualify for federal funding for prisons.

Collectively, these laws enacted between 1984 and 1994, along with state mandatory minimums for drug crimes, more than anything else, helped to give the United States the world's largest inmate population and the world's second-highest per capita incarceration rate. This wave of mandatory minimum laws was part of a legislative and judicial process that became more and more antiyouth in the 1980s and 1990s, and it has wreaked havoc on the hip-hop generation. Although the crack cocaine explosion of the 1980s had created a surge of violent crime in such cities as New York City, Chicago, Los Angeles, St. Louis, and Washington, D.C., which contributed to the climate that allowed for the passage of these laws, crime rates had begun to decrease across the country by 1992. Despite these declines, imprisonment has continued to soar, with drug offenders making up one out of every four U.S. prisoners.

IMPACT ON THE COMMUNITY

Nearly 50 percent of America's prison population is black, with hip-hop generationers making up a significant proportion of that population. What will be the long-term effects of this warehousing of such a disproportionate number of young blacks in the criminal justice system? For starters, consider the following.

1. *Prison Culture's Influence on Black Youth Culture.* One of the best indicators of the degree to which prison culture has been infused into black youth culture can be seen in the transformation of black street gangs from the mid-1970s into the 1980s and 1990s. In the 1970s, arrest and imprisonment of gang members led to organized structures within prisons. Prison gangs inevitably became connected to their street gang counterparts. In fact, many gang members report that they first joined gangs while in prison. (Most cite protection as their motivation.) This phenomenon has also affected what experts call gang migration and the evolution of homegrown gangs that in the 1980s and 1990s began to be reported in hundreds of American cities. As the line between street gangs and prison gangs blur, so do the distinctions between prison culture, street culture, and black youth culture.

The blurring can be observed in the evolution of hip-hop music. As hip-hop culture became more commercialized in the late 1980s and early 1990s, primarily through the success enjoyed by rap music, aspects of prison culture became more apparent in rap music and black youth culture, from the use of language and styles of dress to extensive commentary on crime and prison life. With so many blacks entering and exiting prison this influence is inescapable.

2. *Black Families in Transition.* The immensely destructive impact that slavery had on the black family intensified in an age of high imprisonment rates, where hundreds of thousands of young black men and women with lengthy prison sentences are separated from their families. This arrangement affects relationships between children and their parents, relatives, and friends. Often inmates end up hundreds of miles away from their families, making visitation difficult if not impossible. They lament, even for years after their incarceration has ended, time lost from their children and families that can never be regained. Some mothers struggle to keep incarcerated fathers involved in the lives of their children. Those who opt not to often breed longtime resentment. Families are further stressed by having to rely on a single income, and the inability of incarcerated fathers to provide for their children does immeasurable psychological damage in a culture where ideals of manhood are connected to a man's ability to provide for his family.

3. *Increased Rift Between Young Black Men and Women.* Not to be overlooked

is imprisonment's impact on already fragile relationships between young men and women. Interpersonal relationships between men and women are put to the test as partners who aren't incarcerated struggle to fulfill physical, emotional, and financial needs in an incarcerated partner's absence and still maintain the relationship.

4. *Rising Rates of AIDS Among Young Blacks*. According to the most recent statistics available from the Centers for Disease Control, by 1999 AIDS was the leading cause of death for black men and women between the ages of twenty-five and forty-four. The CDC also estimates that at least half of all newly reported HIV infections in the United States occur among those under twenty-five and that most of these young people were infected through sexual activity. Although high rates of AIDS among young blacks have been widely discussed, researchers have been reluctant to add high incarceration rates of young blacks to the list of primary contributors. However, given the number of young blacks in American prisons, such a factor must be considered; it is highly likely that black men who have sex with other men in prison and then have sex with their wives and girlfriends when they return home may be contributing to increases in HIV and AIDS rates among black women. In *Lockdown America: Police and Prisons in the Age of Crisis* (Verso, 1999), Christian Parenti details the ways that sex—both forced and consensual—is part of prison life, with transsexual, straight, and gay men forced into submissive sexual roles by stronger men, as well as the degree to which rape is condoned by the prison administration: "A conservative estimate is that roughly 200,000 male inmates in America are raped every year, and many are raped daily. The group Stop Prisoner Rape estimates the real figure to be closer to 290,000, noting that most investigations into the scope of sexual terror in prisons and jails do not count inmates who have sex after pairing off for protection, and usually ignore the much higher rates of rape at juvenile facilities."

5. *Mental Health*. America's prisons are environments where the most basic notions of civilization are routinely abandoned, where women are separated from men, where the strong rule the weak, where gangs abound, and where survival skills are critical. "The experience of being incarcerated is a negative one," says Judy Stanley, director of Accreditation for the National Commission on Correctional Health Care and a clinician

with twenty-plus years experience in mental health in corrections. "When individuals aren't solid emotionally, they are going to be damaged by that. Very rarely do individuals come out of prison changed for the better. In most cases there is some psychological wounding."

6. *Criminalized Image of Young Blacks.* In a society that has long associated blacks with criminal behavior, high imprisonment rates reinforce this association in the collective public mind. "Given their high incarceration rates, they must commit the most crimes," the thinking goes. In the 1980s and 1990s, this association intensified, particularly as it was advanced in the media, and helped to justify the high incarceration rates. According to a 2001 joint study by Berkeley Media Studies and the Justice Policy Institute titled "Off Balance: Youth, Race, and Crime in the News," as homicides decreased 32.9 percent between 1990 and 1998, homicide coverage on network news increased 473 percent. The study also found that blacks were too often portrayed as perpetrators and disproportionately as victims, whereas Latinos were nearly invisible in the news media except in crime reports. "People rely on the news media for accurate information," Lori Dorfman, one of the authors of the study, told the Associated Press (April 10, 2001). "When it comes to crime, youth, and people of color, they're getting confusion rather than clarity—part of the story, not the whole story." Unfortunately, young blacks in popular culture also often link criminality with blackness. Between pop culture and news media reports, misconceptions continue to define "reality" for an uncritical public. What will the future hold when racial disparities like pay gaps, difficulty in obtaining mortgages, SAT scores, and the like become explainable via incarceration?

7. *Decline of Black Political Power.* As many as one-third of all black men spend time in the criminal justice system. Upon reentering society, many discover that, among other things, imprisonment has robbed them of their voting rights. Only four states (New Hampshire, Maine, Massachusetts, and Vermont) allow inmates to vote. In fourteen states, a felony conviction equals lifetime disenfranchisement. Most of these states have a process by which voting rights can be restored upon release, but it often involves long waiting periods and is a costly procedure, especially for those who have been out of work for years while serving their sentences. According to a 1999 joint study by Human Rights

Watch and the Sentencing Project, 1.4 million or 13 percent of black men are ineligible to vote because of felony convictions.

Although participation in the mainstream political process by eligible voters is at an all-time low, young blacks are increasingly testing their potential political power. Groups like A Movement for CHANGE, AGENDA, and Rock the Vote's Hip-Hop Coalition conduct voter registration drives targeted at young blacks. However, high rates of incarceration have haunted these groups' efforts as they seek to organize young black voters into a viable force in American politics.

8. *Reawakened Black Political and Spiritual Consciousness.* At the very least, imprisoned young blacks become more familiar with both political and spiritual ideas while inside America's prisons. Most end up more politicized in prison than they were before entering. The political consciousness that prison life nurtures is educating a whole generation about social inequalities and is adding fuel to a potential powder keg created by continued racial oppression.

At the same time, given the mental and physical strain demanded by prison's survival-at-all-costs culture, most also seek some type of spiritual/religious belief, either mainstream or alternative, such as Islam or Five Percenters, as a means of rationalizing their existence. (These groups, like gangs, provide protection, hence the prison system's tendency to classify some groups of Five Percenters as gangs.) Often in this context, the spiritual and political are connected. As inmates ponder the political implications of the mostly poor, black, and Latino prison population, religious organizations that help make sense of the black condition serve a dual purpose. That young people's involvement in the black church and other religious groups remained on the decline during much of the 1990s as prison rates increased suggests that prison conversions are confined to prison. Whether they return to religious institutions later in life and what impact this may have on this generation and the black community overall remains to be seen.

Finally, social engineers who endorsed imprisonment as a solution to nonviolent drug crimes neglected to consider what would happen when those terms of imprisonment ended. Within ten to twenty years, many of these 1 million prisoners will reenter society. Some will be in middle age, many will be dysfunctional, and most will be trying to recapture lost years. Some will try to rekindle old relationships. Many will be even more obsolete as workers in America's mainstream economy than they were when imprisoned. What jobs will exist for them? How will they provide for their families? Where will they find housing? How will society accommodate them? Will psychiatrists be deployed to help these individuals and communities, traumatized by race war, heal? If history is any indication, the onus will fall on existing and already stretched thin black community institutions. Are we preparing those communities for the task?

Long before phrases like "ethnic cleansing" became popularized by the news media, the idea of race war had been prevalent in American culture. Hostilities between American blacks and whites, rooted in European imperialism and chattel slavery, have only been tempered by the civil rights era. In the late 1960s and early 1970s, some political activists described the relationship of whites to blacks in America as one of colonizer to colonized. At that time, some activists referred to those imprisoned as prisoners of war. The idea of America maintaining prisoners of war still persists in activist circles; activists protesting America's sentencing laws and the state of its prisons often use this terminology. The high black imprisonment rates and the ways those convictions have been secured in the 1980s and 1990s (from legislation to law enforcement and prosecution) reveal the degree to which the war on drugs has terrorized black communities. Even if the intention of the drug war were not racist, it has taken on overtones of a race war that has pitted the white majority against the black minority, especially the black poor. In the final analysis, the war on drugs has materialized into a wave of racial attacks on black communities and long-term detentions unmatched in the modern era. Those in the eye of the hurricane are young and black. The Patterson family are but fourteen casualties in a war that has claimed hundreds of thousands of hip-hop generationers. Unfortunately, such a fate has become business as usual for young blacks at the turn of the century.

32

REMEMBRANCE: KEEPING KIDS AT THE CENTER OF EDUCATIONAL POLICY

Wayne Au

Wayne Au, an editor at Rethinking Schools *magazine and an Assistant Professor of Secondary Education at California State University, Fullerton, writes extensively on social justice education and critical educational theory. In this piece, adapted from articles he wrote for* Rethinking Schools, *Au uses the stories of two former students to argue that federal education policy too often loses sight of those it should be benefiting: students.*

———————

Rummaging through a desk drawer the other day I came across an old Polaroid picture that was given to me by two former students. The handwritten caption on it read, "Unsuspected picture to Wayne. Remember us. Beto n' Vangie." The shot is of Beto, clad in a white T-shirt, backward black baseball cap, and sagging jeans, and Vangie with teased-up bangs sporting a black and silver L.A. Kings jacket. They are hugging each other in front of the dorms at The Evergreen State College in Olympia, Washington. Their note strikes an especially emotional chord because of the seriousness of their demand: remember us. Their words are a constant reminder to me that students should always be our focus, that they deserve to be at the center of both our educational practice and policy.

I remember Beto vividly. At the time the unsuspected photograph was taken, he was a high school student attending the Upward Bound program at Evergreen, and I was working in the program as a tutor/counselor. A working-class, urban kid who would be the first generation in his family to attend college, Beto was one of those kids who walked a perilously fine line: always on the fringes of gang and drug activities, but also culturally centered within the Northwest Native community.

The contradictions Beto faced pushed and pulled him between street and school life, beckoned him away from his cultural traditions and then called him back again. One day, beautifully dressed in multi-colored regalia, he might fancy dance his way around the local pow-wow. The next day he might ram his fist through a dorm window, angry at one of his homeboys. And the next he might sit down and talk with me about his plans to finish high school and go on to college. Even if he periodically drove me crazy with his hardheadedness, I loved Beto.

I also remember another student, Shannon, a smart young woman from a working-class white family who I taught years later at a public high school for "dropouts" in Seattle. In particular I hold on to an image of Shannon in the midst of Washington State's standardized testing, wringing her hands over the English section, brow creased and back hunched over her multiple-choice exam, visibly frustrated, sad, and angry. Tests like this one took an emotional and psychological toll on our students, making Shannon and most of her peers feel inadequate, insecure, and not very smart.

Before the hour was up, Shannon craned her neck toward me and mournfully confessed, "Mr. Au, I'm sorry. But I just can't do it." The look of disappointment on Shannon's face killed me. Even though I had stressed again and again that tests like this did *not* measure her worth or intelligence, Shannon could not avoid the matrix of judgment brought down upon her by the state exams. Further still, I was her teacher, an adult who cared for her and provided emotional, political, and academic support, and our school had become a source of strength and pride to her and many others. I could tell by the look in her eyes that, in Shannon's mind, to fail the tests was also to fail me and the school.

It immediately struck me that this was not the Shannon I knew and loved. The Shannon I knew was a fighter, someone who made a conscious, hard choice to return to school and try to make a future for herself, sometimes against incredible odds. Like Beto, she sometimes struggled with the lure of drugs and street life while also exhibiting flashes of intellectual ferocity and a real hunger to understand why the world was so messed up—standardized tests and the whole system of education included. On this day, however, the tests were working to literally suck the fight out of this powerful young woman.

Ultimately, city kids like Shannon and Beto are the canaries in the coal mines of our schools. Their educational experiences measure the overall health of our school system and the levels of toxicity in our educational policies. If our high schools weren't so alienating, with their bloated educational bureaucracies and reliance on oppressive test-and-punish policies, the Shannons of the world might not drop out of school in the first place. Likewise, if graduation and college entrance rates for working-class students and students of color weren't so low, the Betos of the world might not need programs like Upward Bound.

Ironically, the central claim of much federal education policy is to increase social and educational equality, to serve kids like Beto and Shannon. Upward Bound, for instance, started under the Economic Opportunity Act of 1964 as part of President Lyndon Johnson's "War on Poverty" to assist low-income, first-generation college students in getting through high school and into college. Over the years, Upward Bound has served hundreds of thousands of students. The federal funding of public education is similar in intent to Upward Bound in that its stated purpose is to ameliorate socioeconomic inequality. In 1965 Congress passed the Elementary and Secondary Education Act (ESEA), and under ESEA's formulas, schools with higher percentages of poor children receive higher percentages of federal monies.

In recent years, however, it has become clear that policymakers in the United States have forgotten students like Beto and Shannon and not kept them at the center of their policies. Every year, for instance, the federal government makes decisions regarding which programs deserve funding and which programs deserve elimination. These budgets, first put forth by the president and then later revised and voted upon by Congress, serve as a set of articulated social and educational priorities, as a remembrance of who and what are deemed important in the eyes of policymakers.

Unfortunately, in both the fiscal year 2006 and 2007 budgets, as well as in preceeding years, Upward Bound—along with a list of other equity-minded programs such as Talent Search, Student Support Services (Upward Bound's middle school and college level counterparts), school dropout prevention, and alcohol abuse reduction programs—has been listed for elimination in the proposed presidential budgets. Fortunately, Congress has voted to keep programs like Upward Bound around, albeit at lower funding levels. However, the fact that the leaders and policymakers in the federal government deign to slash programs that help low-income students and students of color, while simultaneously escalating military expenditures and increasing corporate tax breaks, sends a loud message: students like Beto are not their priority. If they were, then programs like Upward Bound—which on average served over 50,000 students per year between 1993 and 2003—would get increased funding, not continually face threats of deletion.

A similar educational travesty has taken place regarding the federal funding of public education. With the passage of No Child Left Behind in 2001, ESEA monies have been increasingly attached to high-stakes, standardized tests. Significant amounts of research has shown that these types of tests, rather than promoting equality and closing achievement gaps between students of different socioeconomic backgrounds and racial groups, actually increase dropout rates and disproportionately affect poor students and students of color. It has even been found that some schools, such as those in Houston, Texas, have performed what has been termed "educational triage" by pushing low-scoring black and Latino students off their enrollment rosters and out of schools as a means to raise test scores. Things are so bad in some high schools that only 25 percent of black and Latino ninth-graders end up successfully making it through the twelfth grade.

Instead of heeding such research, policymakers continually force hard-working fighters like Shannon to face a battery of tests that only serve to sort students by race and class differences. It is almost as if testing advocates believe that poverty, lack of resources, and narrowed horizons of opportunity can be eliminated through strict programs of measurement and punishment. But if the federal government were really interested in increasing equality through education, it would support education policies that seek to help students achieve, rather than institute policies that further discourage, alienate, and push students out of schools.

In my experience, hardheads like Beto and dropouts like Shannon are the collateral damage of underfunded schools and assessment systems built upon high-stakes tests. My fear is that, without programs like Upward Bound and with the continued implementation of high-stakes educational policies, the Betos and Shannons of the world will lose what few opportunities they have to work towards brighter futures. Instead, they will stand on the edge of a real-life precipice, where everyday experiences both in and out of school may mean the difference between keeping their feet safely on the ground and literally tumbling into harm's way. The reality is that no matter how punitive and wrongheaded our educational policy, and no matter how little money we spend on their futures, these kids will still be there—defiant, ready, demanding to be remembered.

33

PUTTING EDUCATION AT THE CENTER

Jean Anyon

City University of New York professor Jean Anyon is the author of a number of classic articles on the intersections of social class, race, and education. Her book Ghetto Schooling: A Political Economy of Urban Educational Reform *explodes the myths of inferiority and cultural deficit by focusing on institutional neglect of city schools and deep structures of privilege and oppression based on race. The following piece is excerpted from her book,* Radical Possibilities, *and explores the possibility of urban education—and city teachers—becoming the center of a movement for social justice.*

There is no [social] movement.
There needs to be a movement.
—Marion Bolden, District Superintendent,
Newark, NJ Public Schools. June 20, 2004

Why should we put education—and concerned educators—at the center of efforts to build a unified movement for social justice? Other analysts might place progressive labor unions, immigrant rights, activist church groups, or the national living wage campaign at the center. But I believe there are compelling reasons that urban education—and urban educators—ought to be a fulcrum of movement building.

A most important reason is the theoretical location of urban education. Urban schools are at the center of the maelstrom of constant crises that beset low-income neighborhoods. Education is an institution whose basic problems are caused by, and whose basic problems reveal, the other crises in cities: poverty, joblessness and low-wages, and racial and class segregation. Therefore, a focus on urban education can expose the combined effects of public policies, and highlight not only poor schools but the entire nexus of constraints on urban families. A well-informed mobilization centering on education would challenge macroeconomic federal and regional policies and practices as part of an overall plan to improve local educational opportunity.

Moreover, even though education is not guaranteed by the U.S. Constitution, it is often construed as a civil right, and can be located ideologically in the long and powerful tradition of the civil rights struggle (Moses & Cobb, 2001, p. 1; see also http://www.civilrights.org). This legitimacy may lend movement building through education an acceptance that could affect public attitudes toward new policies regarding the need for jobs, decent wages, and affordable housing.

Indeed, educators are in an excellent position to build a constituency for economic and educational change in urban communities. Teachers and principals have continual access to parents and urban youth. If they are respectful, caring, hard-working educators, trusted by students and parents, they have a unique opportunity to engage residents and youth in political conversations and activity.

A final reason to center movement building in education is that there is a rich tradition of liberal/left advocacy to build on. I, like many others, entered teaching "to change the world" (Oakes & Lipton, 2002). There are teachers in every city today who teach a critical, thought-provoking curriculum, and who utilize the classroom to discuss issues their students face. Hundreds of scholarly books and articles have been written offering insight and inspiration to teachers who concern themselves with social justice. In addition, there exist widely read progressive publications like *Rethinking Schools*, proactive organizations like National Coalition of Educational Activists and Educators for Social Responsibility, and professional conferences that enrich critical teaching. There is possibility here, and great promise in the work of these educators. We can take this work further in our appropriation of the institution for radical purposes.

For all these reasons, I believe that those of us in education who have social justice as a goal can play a crucial role in movement building for economic and educational rights of the poor. We can do this in our daily lives, as we "cast down our buckets" where we are. We can commit to the radical possibilities in our everyday work in schools, despite the onslaught of institutional mandates.

STUDENT SELF-ESTEEM AND POLITICIZATION

Social movement theorists argue that fear, despair, and negative valuations of self can be immobilizing, and may keep social actors who have cause to get involved in political contention from participating. Feelings of efficacy, righteous anger, and strength, on the other hand, are more likely to lead one to activism. A first step in movement building in urban schools, then, is to help students appreciate their own value, intelligence, and potential as political actors.

African American and Latino scholars write tellingly about the fears harbored by many students of color that they fit the stereotypes White society has of them—that they are incapable of high academic achievement, not interested in education, and to blame for their lack of advancement (see Hale, 2001; Perry, 2003; Steele, 2003; Suarez-Orozco & Suarez-Orozco, 2002; Valdes, 1996; Valenzuela, 2001). An important mechanism is that this "stereotype threat" can prevent students' full engagement in academic work, as they fear failure and fulfillment of the stereotype (see, in particular, Steele, 2003). This is tragic in and of itself. But I want to point out that blaming oneself, rather than locating causes of failure in the wider structure of opportunities, has another consequence: It can also mitigate against a perceived need to change the system.

Theresa Perry argues that in order to undermine the ideology and practice of victim blaming, educators need to create a *counter narrative* to the story of failure and low intelligence of students of color. She notes that we could learn from successful all-black schools in the antebellum South, where teachers emphasized the relation between education and freedom: "Freedom for literacy, and literacy for freedom" (2003, p. 92). Perry exhorts teachers to counter the damaging dominant social narrative by building an intentional classroom community spirit of education for "racial uplift, citizenship and leadership" (p. 93). In order to demonstrate to students that they are capable and worthy, "teachers must explicitly articulate, regularly ritualize, and pass on in formal public events the belief in minority students as scholars of high achievement and of social value" (pp. 99, 100). A supportive and trusting environment provides "identity security" to students, who are then emotionally more ready to challenge the stereotypical myths (Steele, 2003).

As Lisa Delpit reminds us, however, we must also teach minority students the culture and knowledge held by powerful whites and the middle and upper classes (Delpit, 1997). They need to understand this coded cultural capital and be able to parse it—just like affluent white students are taught to do (Anyon, 1980, 1981).

A healthy education of this sort would urge minority students toward a stance of *entitlement* regarding the responsibility of governments to provide equal opportunities; and this would encourage them to hold the system accountable. Thus, a politically energizing education for African Americans must explicitly recognize and acknowledge with students that they and their families are *not* free—and that social change is necessary. This is one reason a history of both oppression and resistance is so important. Students who are knowledgeable about dominant forms of power and how this power affects them can better move from self-blame to informed efforts at change. Teachers and administrators who would assist students in this development could begin by working with the community of which the students are a vital part.

WORKING WITH THE COMMUNITY

Teachers, administrators, and other professionals in urban public schools are not usually from the neighborhood. Their social class and often their race differentiate them from students, families, and other residents. In this sense, many of those who work to appropriate the educational institution for social justice are outsiders and bicultural brokers. They can contribute important resources and knowledge to that which students and families already possess. In education organizing across urban America, educators are increasingly playing a brokering, bridging role, as they join with parents and communities to combat policies that oppress.

When educators work with community residents as equals and as change agents to organize for better education, movement building is taking place; and as a not inconsequential outcome, schools typically improve and student achievement increases. Research suggests that there are several reasons for this raised student achievement, including community pressure for more resources and district accountability, increased parental engagement, and improved staff development and pedagogy (Gold, Simon, & Brown, 2002; Henderson & Berla, 1994; Henderson & Mapp, 2002).

I would like to highlight two other causes of the increased achievement. First, education organizing has been shown to lower the rate at which students move from one school to another (mobility), sometimes by as much as 50 percent. Studies show that in schools where educators work closely with the community as partners in change, parents and students often report that they do not want to leave the school because of their involvement in and satisfaction with the activities (Hohn, 2003; Whalen, 2002).

Another reason for increased achievement in schools where parents and educators work together as change agents may be an increase in trust and respect between the parties. Tony Bryk and Barbara Schneider have demonstrated convincingly that trusting relationships in daily interactions in low-income urban schools are correlated with raised achievement over time (2002, pp. 98–99, 120).

Community and parent organizers regularly utilize several strategies that teachers and administrators might incorporate to work for change and build personal relationships and mutual trust. Teachers can involve parents and other residents in one-on-one conversations designed to identify their concerns, can hold meetings in parents' homes where groups of residents address these concerns, and can engage parents, other community members, and educators in "neighborhood walks"— during which participants tour the area around the school and reach a common understanding and vision of what changes are needed (Gold, Simon, & Brown, 2002, p. 22).

School principals who work with the Industrial Areas Foundation say that "an angry parent is an opportunity"—an opening to organize the community for increased accountability of officials and politicians

(IAF Principal Claudia Santamaria, Cambridge, MA Conference, February 20, 2004). A major strategy utilized by the IAF that educators could apply is what organizers call "accountability sessions"—meetings to which district and elected officials or candidates for office are invited and asked to give their opinions on important issues. Candidates are asked to respond to yes/no questions, without speeches. Local media are invited and report on the official and candidate responses, thus providing a public record to which the officials can later be held accountable (Gold & Simon, 2004, p. 2).

Some education organizers also work with parent groups and teachers to monitor district and state programs and policies by carrying out research that identifies discrepancies between stated goals of district, city, or state policies and programs, and the actual experience of students and teachers. These can also be useful as the basis for calling officials to account (for examples, see the Institute for Democracy, Education, and Access at http://www.idea.gseis.ucla.edu/, the National Center for Schools and Communities at http://www.ncscatfordham .org/pages/home.cfm, and the Institute for Education and Social Policy at http://steinhardt.nyu.edu.iesp).

ACQUIRING COMMUNITY ORGANIZING SKILLS

The foregoing strategies provide an introduction to working with parents and communities as partners for change. This section provides suggestions for organizing parents in extended issue campaigns.

Chicago-based Cross City Campaign for Urban School Reform (Cahill, 1999) and the Institute for Education and Social Policy in New York (Zimmer & Mediratta, 2004) have prepared advice (based on many years of organizing experience) that is useful for educators interested in carrying out issue campaigns with community members.

A short summary follows:

1. Choose issues from the bottom up. Issues to pursue should come from parents, students, and other residents. Knock on doors in two-people teams (for example, one parent and one teacher or principal) to identify issues important to the community; and recruit people for home

meetings to discuss the issues they feel are important and what to do about them. Visit area congregations to discuss local problems, and develop relationships with members and clergy. Systematic personal contact and the building of personal relationships are key to successful engagement of residents. Keep parents in forefront.

2. Begin to build a community constituency for long-range reform through immediate, specific, and winnable issues. Frame broad demands like "better schools" more specifically to attract particular constituencies: bilingual programs for Latino parents, and after-school job training and placement for parents and high school students. Building a base among parents and community members will provide a force and legitimacy to the demands you will make. Because you also want to develop working relationships with other educators, it may be best to start with a neighborhood issue rather than one that directly targets problems in the school.

3. Locate key school and district personnel who can assist you in gathering data to document the problems you want to address. Work with local community-based organizations to see what system information they already have. Collaborate with them in writing and disseminating a report, if possible.

4. Develop a program of needed changes and present this to authorities. Plan demonstrations and other activities that attempt to obtain concessions, promises, and behavioral responses from those in power in the district and city (I would add that one should attempt coalitions of organizing groups across the city, region, and state).

5. Develop a plan for what to do when people in power ignore you, refer you to others, delay you, or try to placate you. Officials may try to discredit you. Or they may attempt to buy off your leaders, or propose a substitute that does not meet your needs. Some of the strategies you could consider when this happens may be cooperative, like setting up meetings; but some may be confrontational—like pickets, demonstrations, political theater, press conferences, etc.

6. Keep the pressure on administrators and officials by demonstrations and actions of various sorts. A "presence in the streets" is necessary to hold their attention and get results. (Zimmer & Mediratta, 2004, p. 3)

I want to emphasize that, whenever possible, link educational issues to community issues regarding jobs, housing, transportation, and investment. Education organizing by itself can improve schools in low-income areas to the point that housing values rise, businesses increasingly invest in the neighborhood, and low-income residents are pushed out by higher rents. This creep of gentrification is occurring on two blocks in Chicago's Logan Square area, in part because of the success of education organizing by the Logan Square Neighborhood Association (LNSA). In response, LSNA has intensified its lobbying at the state level for housing reform (Hohn, 2003; Halsband, 2003). Gentrification resulting from education organizing and improved local schools is a reminder that without other public policy changes (in this case, housing policies to maintain low-income housing or policies providing better-paying jobs), successful school reform in low-income urban neighborhoods can have unfortunate, unintended consequences for residents.

CLASSROOMS AS MOVEMENT-BUILDING SPACES

Middle and high school teachers, in particular, can make a powerful contribution to movement-building by engaging students in civic activism. Both the civil rights movement and successful youth efforts to reduce the voting age from twenty-one to eighteen (legalized in 1971) demonstrate that activism by young people can make a huge impact on American society.

But, you might respond, urban students are not interested in political activity. To that I reply that behavioral resistance to typical methods of teaching does not necessarily transfer to alternative, more appealing methods. Moreover, I believe it is the case that most urban teens *want* an education—a high *quality* education. College readiness is the top priority of urban youth who are involved in organizing. A comprehensive assessment of forty-nine youth groups in eighteen states found that the issues youth most frequently address have to do with education. Most (61 percent) want college preparation from their high school; the next issue is criminal and juvenile justice (49 percent), and then economic justice (18 percent) and immigrant rights (14 percent). Indeed, programs run by organizations in urban communities that promote teenage activism typically attract youth who are alienated from school. Teachers, then, may not find it difficult to interest students in political projects; and they may find that through such activities, students who are dropping out can be brought back in (Mattie Weiss, 2003; also Wheeler, 2003, available at http://www.theinnovationcenter.org).

Numerous benefits accrue to youth who work for increased opportunities in their communities. Studies have documented that civic activism by low-income students of color typically fosters teenagers' positive personal development, and improves their academic engagement and, therefore, achievement (see, for example, Benson & Leffert, 1998; Forum for Youth Investment, 2004; Ginwright & Taj, 2002; Hilley, 2004; Lewis-Charp, 2003; Zeldin & Price, 1995).

There are several other benefits, as well. Organizing urban youth to work with others to improve their schools and neighborhoods gives teenagers *connections*, embedding them in constructive community networks. This connectedness is a worthy alternative to that offered by most street gangs (Hilley, 2004).

In addition, by organizing others to work responsibly for social change, minority youth counter the view that they constitute a social "problem." Teens also are encouraged to understand how the poverty of their families and their peers arises from systemic rather than personal failings. And it provides them with the concrete lesson that they can bring about changes in society, giving them a foundation for pursuing this kind of activity as adults.

A final benefit to working with students on political projects that aim to achieve youth and family rights is that it puts educators and students on the same "team," and increases trust between them, which, as we have seen, has been found to increase academic achievement (Bryk & Schneider, 2002).

An example of teachers organizing students demonstrates several of these positive outcomes. In 1995, youth at Gratz High School in Philadelphia started the first chapter of what became a citywide student union (PSU). The original impetus for organizing was students' complaints about inadequate textbooks and dirty bathrooms. When the students asked administrators why there were no new textbooks, they were told it was their fault because "students tear them up." When students complained about the bathrooms, they were told "students mess them up." Students' first reaction was to agree with school administrators that they were themselves to blame. However, with their adviser's help they were encouraged to ask themselves the following questions: "Why didn't they consider it their school and their property? Why did they deface their school as if they didn't respect it or own it? Why didn't they feel comfortable at school?" After years and years in a failing system, the students were frustrated and self-blaming. Their adviser assisted them as they got to work to advocate for improvements in the school.

Since 1995, many changes have resulted from PSU's activism in Philadelphia high schools, including new student governments, creation of school ombudsmen to stop the harassment and abuse by school security officers, a district-level student platform on planned school reforms, a rally of 2,450 students at City Hall, which helped to defeat planned privatization of Philadelphia high schools, new networks of organized students in multiple city schools, and a statewide campaign to increase school funding to the level of nearby affluent suburbs (American Youth Policy Forum, 2002, p. 103).

As shown in research studying the benefits of youth organizing in Los Angeles, many of the Philadelphia students who became involved as activists and leaders had been on the verge of dropping out, but remained in school when it became clear that they had a voice. A number of teachers reported that these new youth leaders became academic "stars."

CONCLUSION

The consequence of my overall analysis for the ways we conceptualize education policy is fundamental. Governments and corporate elites depend on education to deflect the pain inflicted by the economy. That cover does not work any longer for larger percentages of the population. The discovery by urban students as early as the fifth grade (Anyon, 1997) that education does not "matter" has a chilling effect on motivation; rightly contextualized, however, this realization can ultimately be politically activating.

To be adequate to the task of relevant prescription—as well as political mobilization—education policy cannot remain closeted in schools, classrooms, and educational bureaucracies. It must join the world of communities, families, and students; it must advocate for them and emerge from their urgent realities. Policies for which we press would therefore take on a larger focus: education funding reform would include the companion need for financing of neighborhood jobs and decent wages. Small schools would be created as an important part of the coordinated efforts at neighborhood revitalization for low-income residents. Lawsuits to racially integrate districts will acknowledge housing segregation as fundamental and target legal challenges appropriately.

Policies that set the standards schools must meet would identify the money, materials, teachers, courses, and neighborhood needs that should be fulfilled in order to provide opportunities to learn at high levels. Educational accountability would be conceived as a public undertaking, centrally involving families, communities, and students, in consultation with district and government officials. And college would be understood as a continuation of government's financial responsibility for public education, thus providing a material basis for motivation and effort on the part of K–12 students and educators.

In this new paradigm of educational policy, the political potential of pedagogy and curriculum would be realized. Critical pedagogy would take to the streets, offices, and courtrooms where social justice struggles play out. Curriculum could build toward and from these experiences. Vocational offerings in high school would link to living wage campaigns and employers who support them. And educational research would not be judged by its ostensible scientific objectivity, but at least in part by its ability to spark political consciousness and change—its "catalytic validity" (Lather, 1991).

In this approach to school reform, "policy alignment" does not refer to the fit between education mandates issued by various levels of government and bureaucracy. The fit we seek is between neighborhood, family, and student needs and the potential of education policies to contribute to their fulfillment.

This reorientation of education policy is unabashedly radical, and brings me to a final point. Whether one is born to radicalism or acquires it along the way, the premises on which it rests affirm the deeply rooted connections and disjunctures between democracy and capitalism. A radical frame provides the understanding that, for example, economic exclusion and educational underachievement flow fundamentally from systemic causes, even in the face of what appears to be democratic process and individual failure. And a radical analysis points toward concrete, long-lasting solutions.

In 1967, at the height of the Vietnam War, Martin Luther King Jr. argued that civil rights, poverty, and war are all part of the same problem. He preached that Americans need to fight these as part of the same struggle. But, he said, in order to do that we must "recapture the revolutionary spirit" of freedom and equality, which defines true democracy.

If those of us who are angry about injustice can recapture this revolutionary spirit of democracy, and if we can act on it together, then we may be able to create a force powerful enough to produce economic justice and real, long-term school reform in America's cities.

REFERENCES

American Youth Policy Forum. (May 17, 2002). *Youth action for educational change: A Forum Brief*. Washington, DC.

Anyon, J. (1980). Social class and the hidden curriculum of work. *Journal of Education, 162*(1), 7–92.

Anyon, J. (1981). Social class and school knowledge. *Curriculum Inquiry, 11*(1), 3–42.

Anyon, J. (1997). *Ghetto schooling: A political economy of urban educational reform*. New York: Teachers College Press.

Ayres, W., Hunt, J.A., & Quin, T. (Eds). (1998). *Teaching for social justice: A democracy and education reader*. New York: New Press.

Benson, P., & Leffert, N. (1998). Beyond the 'village' rhetoric: Creating healthy communities for children and adolescents. *Journal of Applied Developmental Sciences, 2*, 138–59.

Bryk, A. S., & Schneider, B. (2002). *Trust in schools: A core resource for improvement*. New York: Russell Sage.

Cahill, M. (1999). *Community organizing for school reformers: Train the trainers manual*. Chicago, IL: Cross City Campaign for Urban School Reform.

Delpit, L. (1997). *Other people's children: Cultural conflict in the classroom*. New York: New Press.

The Forum for Youth Investment. (May 2004). *From youth activities to youth action, 2*(2).

Ginwright, S., & Taj, J. (Winter 2002). From assets to agents of change: Social justice, organizing, and youth development. *New Directions for Youth Development, 96*, 27–46.

Gold, E., & Simon, E. (January 14, 2004). Public accountability. *Education Week.*

Gold, E., Simon, E., & Brown, C. (2002). *Strong neighborhoods and strong schools: The indicators project on education organizing.* Chicago: Cross City Campaign for Urban School Reform.

Hale, J.E. (2001). *Learning while black: Creating educational excellence for African American children.* Baltimore, MD: Johns Hopkins University Press.

Halsband, R. (November/December 2003). Charter schools benefit Community economic development. *Journal of Housing and Community Development* (pp. 34–38).

Henderson, A., & Berla, N. (1994). *A new generation of evidence: The family is critical to student achievement.* Washington, DC: Center for Law and Education.

Henderson, A., & Mapp, K. (2002). *A new wave of evidence: The impact of school, family, and community connections on student achievement.* Austin, TX: National Center for Family and Community Connections with Schools, Southwest Educational Development Laboratory.

Hilley, J. (May 2004). Teens taking action in Tennessee. *Forum Focus 2*(2), 7–8, http://www.forumforyouthinvestment.org.

Hohn, J. (2003). *Chicago neighborhood discovers delicate balance between success of community schools and resident displacement.* Available at http://www.communityschools .org.

Lather, P. (1991). *Getting Smart: Research and pedagogy with/in the postmodern.* New York: Routledge.

Lewis-Charp, H. (2003). *Extending the reach of youth development through civic activism: Outcomes of the youth leadership for development initiative.* San Francisco, CA: Social Policy Research Associates.

Moses, R., & Cobb, C., Jr. (2001). *Radical equations: Civil rights from Mississippi to the Algebra Project.* Boston: Beacon Press.

Oakes, J., & Lipton, M. (2002). *Teaching to change the world.* New York: McGraw-Hill.

Perry, T. (2003). *Young, gifted, and black: Promoting high achievement among African-American students.* New York: Beacon.

Steele, C. (2003). Stereotype threat and African-American student achievement. In T. Perry, C. Steele, & A.G. Hilliard III, *Young, gifted, and black: Promoting high achievement among African-American students* (pp. 109–30). Boston: Beacon Press.

Suarez-Orozco, C., & Suarez-Orozco, M.M. (2002). *Children of immigration.* Boston: Harvard University Press.

Valdes, G. (1996). *Con respeto: Bridging the distances between culturally diverse families and schools: An ethnographic portrait.* New York: Teachers College Press.

Valenzuela, A. (2001). *Subtractive schooling: U.S.-Mexican youth and the politics of caring.* Albany: State University of New York Press.

Weiss, M. (2003). *Youth rising.* Oakland, CA: Applied Research Center.

Whalen, S.P. (April 2002). Report of the evaluation of the Polk Bros. Foundation's full service schools initiative: Executive Summary. Chapin Hall Center for Children at the University of Chicago. Available at http://www.communityschools.org.

Wheeler, W. (2003). *Lessons in leadership: How young people change their communities and themselves.* Tacoma Park, MD: The Innovation Center.

Zeldin, S., & Price, L. (1995). Creating supportive communities for adolescent development: Challenges to scholars. *Journal of Adolescent Research 10,* 6–15.

Zimmer, A., & Mediratta, K. (2004). *Lessons from the field of school reform organizing.* New York: Institute for Education and Social Policy.

AFTERWORD: THE FIRST DAY

Jeff Chang

Jeff Chang has written extensively on race, culture, politics, the arts, and music in publications such as Vibe, The Nation, *and* Mother Jones. *He is the author of* Can't Stop Won't Stop, *which won both the American Book Award and the Asian American Literary Award, and editor of* Total Chaos: The Art & Aesthetics of Hip-Hop. *An organizer of the National Hip-Hop Political Convention and co-founder of the influential independent hip-hop label, SoleSides, he has served as a board member for several organizations working for change through youth and community organizing, media justice, and hip-hop activism.*

———

On the first day, each child is a story to be told, a revelation awaiting the time. Each teacher is a path to take, a road to unfold.

Here's the boy with the swagger, walking tall with his crew behind him. "Love the first day, man," he cracks. "Everybody all friendly and shit." Soon we learn he is the son of the top triggerman for the westside's crumbling drug gang. He was born into the game. Is his bravado inherited or is it a mask? The boy drifts between indecision and the allure of the streets. His real father is in jail for life. But a fallen ex-police captain sees something in him, and the boy is taken far from the corner, receives the gift of a small salvation.

What of the tall silent one with his head down, his hand alighting softly on his precious little brother's shoulder? He is the son of a crack fiend, struggling to keep his head straight, his brother's mind on the books, and food on the table. An ex-assassin who has opened a boxing facility in a bid for redemption tries to take him in. But this mentoring will be in vain; the tall boy, who cares so much for his innocent brother, cannot resist the pull of the corner. His desire for security takes him into the life of the new triggerman.

These are scenes from "The Wire," the HBO television series that captures decaying Baltimore—from the abandoned inner city to the dank detention facilities, from the doomed housing projects to the neglected schools. Series creator David Simon argues that postmodern institutions destroy vitality and will, and the primary effect is that, in his words, "Every minute, human beings are worth less." But even in this era's new math, writer Marina Werner has said, "There are expensive children and there are cheap children."

When *City Kids, City Teachers* was published in 1996, urban schools were beset by the intensifying criminalization of youth, the emergence of high-stakes testing, and voucher threats to public financing. While budget deficits sidelined the latter problem (if perhaps only temporarily), Americans saw the first two issues reach their apotheosis when California voters passed Proposition 21 in March 2000, and President George W. Bush signed the No Child Left Behind Act in January 2002. As schools reach levels of racial segregation not seen since the 1950s, the Supreme Court has moved to deny the value of integration in everything from school assignment policy to university admissions.

It is not hard to understand these shifts as signaling fears of a browning nation. California's Proposition 21—a War on Youth initiative that made it easier to try youths as adults, unseal their juvenile court records, and qualify them for three strikes, a life sentence or a death penalty—passed overwhelmingly despite the fact that juvenile crime was already on its way to record lows. No Child Left Behind flagged racial achievement gaps, but made little attempt to seriously address them, serving mostly to punish schools who served students of color on the wrong side of that gap. Resegregation appears justified by a popular culture that is more diverse and less idea-oriented (while more niche-marketed and commodity-driven) than ever, and by a Supreme Court that believes racial balance is inconsistent with equal protection. At the same time, the nation is mired in an endless war that costs more than four times the annual California state education budget. Little wonder that so many in this book ask: what is a child worth?

The hip-hop generation came of age under the politics of abandonment and the politics of containment, an era of reversal for the expansive national programs of the mid-twentieth century. But the new millennium has delivered no similar reversal of the narrow-minded callousness of the last four decades of public policy. So the lines have been redrawn—color lines, class lines, and city lines. As this sequel to *City Kids, City Teachers* comes into your hands, urban youths and their teachers find themselves on the frontlines of a dangerous new world.

Every day, the drama of reversals plays out in the nation's urban schools. And yet, the drama of redemption plays out as well. Miracles are made by millions of city teachers and city kids every day: together they discover and rediscover the lesson that unleashes a startling chain of ideas, the method that decodes the string of patterns, the key that unlocks a new language, the spark that lights a lifetime. They struggle mightily and selflessly against the odds, and sometimes they may lose. But as often as not they win.

Even as the market and the body politic continue to urge us to retreat from each other into zones of false comfort, urban teachers and urban students continue to remind us of the responsibility and care we owe to each other. Their work must be seen as courageous, because it is. While we work to bring the arrival of a radical social vision that will defend the notion of the public against the privatizing world, place human value over market value, and uphold the desire for nurturing community above isolating individualism, city kids and city teachers continue to hope, plan, work, and stand. For all of the anxieties, fears, conflicts, and setbacks that they know will come, they are believers in the promise of the first day, that swelling hope that can carry us all through to the very last one.

William Ayers is Distinguished Professor of Education and Senior University Scholar at the University of Illinois at Chicago (UIC), and founder of both the Small Schools Workshop and the Center for Youth and Society. He teaches courses in interpretive research; writing narrative, memoir, and the personal essay; urban school change; and teaching and the modern predicament. A graduate of the University of Michigan, the Bank Street College of Education, and Teachers College, Columbia University, he writes about social justice, democracy and education, the cultural contexts of schooling, and teaching as an essentially intellectual, ethical, and political enterprise. His articles have appeared in the *Harvard Educational Review*, the *Journal of Teacher Education, Teachers College Record, Rethinking Schools*, the *Nation*, the *New York Times* and the *Cambridge Journal of Education*. He has written or edited fifteen books including *A Kind and Just Parent: The Children of Juvenile Court, To Teach: The Journey of a Teacher*, which was named Book of the Year in 1993 by Kappa Delta Pi and won the Witten Award for Distinguished Work in Biography and Autobiography in 1995, *Fugitive Days: A Memoir, On the Side of the Child: Summerhill Revisited, Teaching Toward Freedom: Moral Commitment and Ethical Action in the Classroom*, and *Race Course: Against White Supremacy*.

    Gloria Ladson-Billings is the Kellner Family Professor of Urban Education in the Department of Curriculum & Instruction at the University of Wisconsin-Madison and past president of the American Educational Research Association. Her research examines the pedagogical practices of teachers who are successful with African American students. Her work has won numerous scholarly awards, including the H.I. Romnes faculty fellowship, the Spencer Post-doctoral fellowship, and the Palmer O. Johnson Outstanding research award. In 2002, Ladson-Billings was awarded an honorary doctorate from Umea University in Umea, Sweden and in 2003–2004 was a fellow at the Center for Advanced Study in the Behavioral Sciences at Stanford University. She is also the 2004 recipient of the George and Louise Spindler Award for ongoing contributions in educational anthropology, given by the Council on Anthropology & Education of the American Anthropological Association. Ladson-Billings also investigates Critical Race Theory applications to education. The author of the critically acclaimed books, *The Dreamkeepers: Successful Teachers of African American Children* and *Crossing Over to Canaan: The Journey of New Teachers in Diverse Classrooms*, has also written numerous journal articles and book chapters.

Gregory Michie teaches in the Department of Curriculum and Instruction at Illinois State University, where he serves as liaison to a year-long student teaching internship program in Chicago Public Schools. He taught for nine years in Chicago, where he developed a media literacy course for middle school students and an award-winning student video-production program. In 1996 he received the Golden Apple Award for Excellence in Teaching, which is given annually to ten outstanding teachers in the greater Chicago area. For the past several years he has worked as a teacher educator, preparing undergraduates and career-changers for work in urban classrooms. He has published numerous essays and articles in journals such as *Multicultural Perspectives* and *Rethinking Schools*, and is the author of *Holler If You Hear Me: The Education of a Teacher and His Students* (Teachers College Press, 1999), and *See You When We Get There: Teaching for Change in Urban Schools* (Teachers College Press, 2005).

Pedro A. Noguera is a professor in the Steinhardt School of Education and the Director of the Metropolitan Center for Urban Education at New York University. An urban sociologist, Noguera's scholarship and research focus on the ways in which schools are influenced by social and economic conditions in the urban environment. Noguera has held tenured faculty appointments at the Harvard Graduate School of Education and at the University of California, Berkeley. He has published over 150 research articles, monographs, and research reports on topics such as urban school reform, conditions that promote student achievement, youth violence, the potential impact of school choice and vouchers on urban public schools, and race and ethnic relations in American society. His work has appeared in several major research journals and many are available online at inmotionmagazine.com. He is the author of *The Imperatives of Power: Political Change and the Social Basis of Regime Support in Grenada* (Peter Lang Publishers, 1997), *City Schools and the American Dream* (Teachers College Press, 2003), and *Unfinished Business: Closing the Achievement Gap in Our Nation's Schools* (Jossey-Bass, 2006).

PERMISSIONS

INDEX

ALSO AVAILABLE FROM THE NEW PRESS

Beyond the Bake Sale: The Essential Guide to Family-School Partnerships
Anne T. Henderson, Karen L. Mapp, Vivian R. Johnson, Don Davies

A practical, hands-on primer on helping schools and families work better together to improve children's education.

978-1-56584-888-7 (pb)

Black Teachers on Teaching
Michele Foster

An oral history of black teachers that gives "valuable insight into a profession that for African Americans was second only to preaching" (*Booklist*).

978-1-56584-453-7 (pb)

The Case for Make Believe: Saving Play in a Commercialized World
Susan Linn

From the author of *Consuming Kids*, a clarion call for preserving play in our material world—a book every parent will want to read.

978-1-56584-970-9 (hc)

City Kids, City Teachers: Reports from the Front Row
Edited by William Ayers and Patricia Ford

A classic collection exploding the stereotypes of city schools, reissued as a companion to *City Kids, City Schools*.

978-1-56584-051-5 (pb)

Dismantling Desegregation: The Quiet Reversal of Brown v. Board of Education
Gary Orfield and Susan E. Eaton

"Powerful case studies . . . the authors convincingly argue that the ideal of desegregation is disappearing" (*Kirkus Reviews*).

978-1-56584-401-8 (pb)

Everyday Antiracism: Getting Real About Race in School
Edited by Mica Pollock

Leading experts offer concrete and realistic strategies for dealing with race in schools in a groundbreaking book that should become required reading for every teacher in the country.

978-1-59558-054-2 (pb)

Fires in the Bathroom: Advice to Teachers from High School Students
Kathleen Cushman

This groundbreaking book offers original insights into teaching teenagers in today's hard-pressed urban high schools from the point of view of the students themselves. It speaks to both new and established teachers, giving them firsthand information about who their students are and what they need to succeed.

978-1-56584-996-9 (pb)

Fires in the Middle School Bathroom: Advice to Teachers from Middle Schoolers
Kathleen Cushman and Laura Rogers

Following on the heels of the bestselling *Fires in the Bathroom*, which brought the insights of high school students to teachers and parents, Kathleen Cushman now turns her attention to the crucial and challenging middle grades, joining forces with adolescent psychologist Laura Rogers.

978-1-59558-111-2 (hc)

Made in America: Immigrant Students in Our Public Schools
Laurie Olsen

With a new introduction by the author, this timely reissue probes the challenges facing teachers and immigrant students in our public schools.

978-1-59558-349-9 (pb)

The New Press Education Reader: Leading Educators Speak Out
Edited by Ellen Gordon Reeves

The New Press Education Reader brings together the work of progressive writers and educators—among them Lisa Delpit, Herbert Kohl, William Ayers, and Maxine Greene—to discuss the most pressing and challenging issues now facing us, including schools and social justice, equity issues, tracking and testing, combating racism and homophobia, and more.

978-1-59558-110-5 (pb)

Other People's Children: Cultural Conflict in the Classroom
Lisa Delpit

In this anniversary edition of a classic, MacArthur Award–winning author Lisa Delpit develops ideas about ways teachers can be better "cultural transmitters" in the classroom, where prejudice, stereotypes, and cultural assumptions breed ineffective education.

978-1-59558-074-0 (pb)

Race: How Blacks and Whites Think and Feel About the American Obsession
Studs Terkel

Based on interviews with over 100 Americans, this book is a rare and revealing look at how people feel about race in the United States.

978-1-56584-989-1 (pb)

Racism Explained to My Daughter
Tahar Ben Jelloun

The prizewinning book of advice about racism from a bestselling author to his daughter, introduced by Bill Cosby. The paperback version includes responses from William Ayers, Lisa Delpit, and Patricia Williams.

978-1-59558-029-0 (pb)

She Would Not Be Moved: How We Tell the Story of Rosa Parks and the Montgomery Bus Boycott
Herbert Kohl

From a prizewinning educator, a meditation that reveals the misleading way generations of children have been taught the story of Rosa Parks, offering guidance on how to present the Civil Rights movement to young students.

978-1-59558-127-3 (pb)

The Skin That We Speak: Thoughts on Language and Culture in the Classroom
Edited by Lisa Delpit and Joanne Kilgour Dowdy

A collection that gets to the heart of the relationship between language and power in the classroom.

978-1-59558-350-5 (pb)